*The Scholarship of Teaching
and Learning Reconsidered*

Pat Hutchin

Mary Huber

Tony Ciccone

The Scholarship of Teaching and Learning Reconsidered

Institutional Integration and Impact

Pat Hutchings
Mary Taylor Huber
Anthony Ciccone

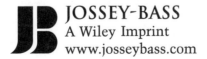

JOSSEY-BASS
A Wiley Imprint
www.josseybass.com

THE CARNEGIE FOUNDATION FOR THE ADVANCEMENT OF TEACHING

Published by Jossey-Bass
A Wiley Imprint
989 Market Street, San Francisco, CA 94103-1741—www.josseybass.com

Jossey-Bass books and products are available through most bookstores. To contact Jossey-Bass directly call our Customer Care Department within the U.S. at 800-956-7739, outside the U.S. at 317-572-3986, or fax 317-572-4002.

Jossey-Bass also publishes its books in a variety of electronic formats. Some content that appears in print may not be available in electronic books.

Library of Congress Cataloging-in-Publication Data

Hutchings, Pat.
The scholarship of teaching and learning reconsidered : institutional integration and impact / Pat Hutchings, Mary Taylor Huber, Anthony Ciccone.
    p. cm. – (The Jossey-Bass higher and adult education series)
    Includes bibliographical references and index.
        ISBN 978-0-470-59908-2 (pbk.)
        ISBN 978-1-118-07552-4 (ebk.)
        ISBN 978-1-118-07553-1 (ebk.)
        ISBN 978-1-118-07555-5 (ebk.)
    1. Education, Higher–Study and teaching–United States.   2. Professional learning communities–United States.   I. Huber, Mary Taylor, 1944–
        II. Ciccone, Anthony.   III. Title.
        LB2331.H88 2011
        378.73–dc23

                                                                            2011015807

Printed in the United States of America
FIRST EDITION
PB Printing   10 9 8 7 6 5 4 3 2

The Jossey-Bass Higher and Adult Education Series

CONTENTS

PREFACE

The world of teaching and learning in higher education has become a lively place. Over the past twenty-five years, a shift in focus from teaching toward learning has energized a reform movement that is engaging large numbers of educators across academic ranks and roles. What was once a sleepy pedagogical backwater is now a buzzing hive of initiatives to improve the learning experience for college students, to increase their rate of completion, and to raise their level of achievement. Problems that were once the province of isolated pedagogical specialists are increasingly the shared concern of all who teach in higher education. And the language of learning, once a foreign tongue to most academics, has become more widely spoken and more deeply understood.

In short, a rather extraordinary development is under way: the emergence in higher education of a *teaching commons*, where "communities of educators committed to pedagogical inquiry and innovation come together to exchange ideas about teaching and learning, and use them to meet the challenges of educating students" (Huber and Hutchings, 2005, p. x).

In *The Advancement of Learning: Building the Teaching Commons*, two of us explored how a growing stream of faculty members had begun to engage with this commons through the scholarship of teaching and learning (Huber and Hutchings, 2005). We documented the history of this approach to teaching and identified its defining features: asking questions about one's students' learning; gathering and analyzing evidence to help answer those questions; trying out and exploring new insights about learning in one's teaching; and making what one has found public, so that it can be reviewed, critiqued, and built on by others. We mapped the contributions to knowledge that this generation of scholars of teaching and learning was making to the commons, the pathways that were bringing faculty into the work, the growth of the campus as a teaching commons, and the development of new networks and genres for knowledge building and exchange. Throughout, our interest was in how regular faculty were producing pedagogical knowledge and using it to improve student learning in their classrooms and fields.

In this book, *The Scholarship of Teaching and Learning Reconsidered,* our focus is on the spread of the teaching commons to core areas of institutional work. We have chosen four sites where the coordination of individual and institutional priorities is progressively more challenging: classroom teaching, professional development, institutional assessment, and the recognition and reward of pedagogical work. Sites like these, where the interests of participants are often "substantially diverse," are particularly important to theorists of the commons, who are interested in "factors affecting institutional design and the patterns of interaction occurring within action arenas" (Hess and Ostrom, 2007, p. 44). For us, these sites are important for an additional reason: they are key to bringing the scholarship of teaching and learning more fully into the mainstream of institutional life. Indeed, it is our view that the scholarship of teaching and learning should no longer be seen as a discrete project or special initiative, but rather as a set of principles and practices that are critical to achieving the institution's goals for student learning and success.

Key to this vision of the work's institutional possibilities is our conviction that the scholarship of teaching and learning provides an approach to educational design and problem solving that has promise far beyond individual classrooms. It's possible for faculty to do this kind of work pretty much on their own, of course, relying on colleagues away from campus for conversation and feedback—and many scholars of teaching and learning do so. But working with others who share a local context is not only more efficient and pleasurable; it can also lead to the kind of collaborative inquiry and shared responsibility for student learning that is important for the design, assessment, and improvement of academic programs. Indeed, it's hard to think of an academic function that couldn't benefit from colleagues looking together for answers to questions like: Who are our students? What do we want them to learn? What opportunities do they need to learn these things? How can we coordinate and evaluate our efforts?

Another advantage of a more collective approach to the scholarship of teaching and learning follows closely from the first. A framework that brings people together through a cycle of inquiry and improvement can give everyone involved—faculty, staff, students—a clearer view of educational issues of common concern, and a stronger voice. The process of asking questions, drawing on literature, and seeking evidence fosters critical and creative engagement. It's a way of involving a wider array of thoughtful people in setting the agenda for institutional work beyond particular classrooms or departments: for example, revisions to general education and honors programs, efforts to better integrate study abroad or service learning into the curriculum, or initiatives to raise levels of student retention and achievement. As the distinguished British educator Lewis Elton has argued, the scholarship of teaching and learning is not just about doing good things better (although that is very important); it's also about doing better things (2000).

A third reason for bringing the scholarship of teaching and learning to bear on institutional agendas is its capacity to broaden and enrich what's known about student learning on campus and to make it accessible for wider use. Many educators nodded their heads in assent when Derek Bok wrote in *Our Under-achieving Colleges* (2006) about how little most institutions actually know about what and how much their students are learning. Bok was calling for more formal education research. But he also recognized that sound local knowledge—the special province of the scholarship of teaching and learning—could be even more important for the practical work that college and university educators do. As we argue in this book, the scholarship of teaching and learning can complement the efforts of institutional research and assessment, helping a campus build systematic knowledge about student learning in forms that can make a real difference to teachers and students in their everyday educational lives.

The reason why the scholarship of teaching and learning can make such a difference is its approach to teaching itself. *Scholarship Reconsidered* (Boyer, 1990) and *Scholarship Assessed* (Glassick, Huber, and Maeroff, 1997), two influential Carnegie Foundation reports, called for teaching to be practiced as serious intellectual work. What "serious intellectual work" means—how it can best be developed, supported, evaluated, recognized, and rewarded—has been the subject of lively debate ever since. But no one doubts that it means, at least, teaching with an informed and critical eye on one's students' learning. Teaching, in this view, takes into account theory, inquiry, and evidence about learning, and, like other intellectual pursuits, is enriched by participation in a wider community of people similarly engaged. It's in the working groups, conferences, and other forums (face-to-face, print, and online) that comprise a campus's own teaching commons that local knowledge about teaching and learning truly becomes "community property" (Shulman, 1993), as people share, critique, and build on insights from their own and others' work.

This view of teaching, the intellectual work it entails, and the communities that these teachers form to grow and thrive are much needed in higher education today. The scholarship of teaching and learning brings important habits of inquiry, analysis, exchange, and knowledge building to the profession's broader, and increasingly complex, challenges in educating students for to-morrow's life and work. And though these challenges are most immediately experienced in the context of teaching particular things to particular students, there is growing recognition that the learning experience for students tran-scends those particulars. How are courses in a program connected to each other? Are there opportunities for students to connect their learning across dif-ferent fields of study? Do students have opportunities for progressively more sophisticated development of widely agreed-upon liberal learning outcomes? There may always be some tension between the questions that engage the in-terests of individual faculty members and the educational priorities officially embraced by the institution. But with good leadership, attentive to the legiti-macy of both, the scholarship of teaching and learning can be a transformative approach to addressing the difficult educational challenges colleges and uni-versities face today.

As we note in this book, there are many arenas that need cultivation, atten-tion, and support if the scholarship of teaching and learning is to reach its full potential. After an overview in Chapter 1, we look in Chapter 2 at the work in its home settings—in the classroom, among small groups of colleagues, and in the conferences and publications where it joins the larger teaching commons. Chapter 3 argues that faculty development programs can play an important role in bringing people together around shared educational agendas, in providing forums for making work public, and in creating networks across the institution, through which promising ideas about good practice can flow. In Chapter 4, we turn our attention to opportunities for building bridges between institutional assessment and the scholarship of teaching and learning, so that instead of occupying separate spheres, each can enrich the other. Chapter 5 looks at the significant, yet still uneven, progress that's been made toward giving the intel-lectual work of teaching a more prominent place in systems of faculty roles and rewards—clearly an area where much remains to be done. Our final chapter explores what it will take to succeed and what success will look like when (not if!) it is achieved.

This book is addressed to campus leaders—presidents, provosts, deans, de-partment chairs, boards of trustees, participants in campus governance, leaders of professional development, and the many faculty and staff who shape the institution's work—and we hope it will answer their questions about the schol-arship of teaching and learning, what it is, why it matters, and how it can help the campus community meet its core educational responsibilities. It is impor-tant to emphasize that making an institutional commitment to the scholarship of teaching and learning does not come without cost. Many faculty engaged in this work do so now out of a sense of curiosity about learning, a commitment to their students, and a new vision of what professionalism in teaching entails. But it cannot simply be an add-on to faculty's already overloaded

PREFACE xiii

plates. Leadership for learning means recognizing that teaching well is a demanding intellectual task; it means budgeting for such work with time, recognition, reward, and support.

These are trying economic times for colleges and universities of all institutional types. We hope the arguments we make in this book will persuade campus leaders that supporting the scholarship of teaching and learning is a good investment, and that our account of the work's impact and promise will help them see where and how it can make its greatest contributions. As the work of many individual scholars suggests, the scholarship of teaching and learning is already improving the learning experience for students in classrooms and courses. It is also beginning to make good on its promise to change the culture of teaching in higher education, enlarging the repertoire of what's possible and desirable to do as a teacher, creating contexts for teaching that are more collaborative and collegial, and making the colleges and universities that support the scholarship of teaching and learning better places to work in and more worthy places to work for.

It is important to recognize that the scholarship of teaching and learning is not only a U.S. phenomenon. As the movement has grown, so too have connections between pedagogically engaged scholars around the world. This wider range of exchange and collaboration is what one would expect with the development of the teaching commons, of course. A growing set of international conferences, disciplinary interest groups, journals, speaking engagements, consultancies, and initiatives have enriched the professional lives of scholars of teaching and learning everywhere, and helped increase the circulation of pedagogical ideas across national boundaries.

But it is also true that the work has different histories in each country (or set of countries—as among the United Kingdom, Canada, Australia, and New Zealand, which had long-standing habits of exchange), and that it unfolds in particular constellations of higher education institutions and policies. Each country's system has unique features, but the U.S. system, with over 4,000 public and private accredited colleges and universities, including doctoral universities, master's universities and colleges, baccalaureate colleges, and a huge community college sector, is still among the largest and most diverse national systems in the world. So this book, while drawing on literature and examples from colleagues and institutions abroad, focuses on the United States because it is concerned primarily with weaving the scholarship of teaching and learning into the institutional fabric of U.S. higher education. Of course we hope our international colleagues will find our analysis useful to their efforts in their own circumstances as well.

We hope too that readers will bear with us on our choice of terminology. Although many participants in the larger movement use "SoTL" as a convenient abbreviation in referring to the scholarship of teaching and learning, we will forego the acronym and use the longer phrase, or, when the antecedent is clear, refer to it simply as "this work."

Finally, a word about the title of this book. *The Scholarship of Teaching and Learning Reconsidered* deliberately echoes the title of *Scholarship Reconsidered*, the 1990 report by Ernest Boyer that launched the term "the scholarship of teaching" into the discourse of higher education in the United States. The two volumes are bookends, if you will, for two decades of effort by The Carnegie Foundation for the Advancement of Teaching to develop the idea, encourage the practice, and build leadership for the work. As we hope this book will show, it's been an extraordinary endeavor, involving two Carnegie Foundation presidents (Boyer and his successor, Lee Shulman, who established the Carnegie Academy for the Scholarship of Teaching and Learning—CASTL), a talented set of colleagues at "project central," hundreds of faculty fellows, campus collaborators, and scholarly societies. The movement has, of course, gone far beyond the Carnegie circle itself—so far, in fact, that no one person or group can speak for all who use the term. This "reconsideration," with an eye on the work's transformation from individual initiative to institutional integration, is our own take on its current state and future prospects. So while *The Scholarship of Teaching and Learning Reconsidered* is a bookend to twenty years of Carnegie Foundation involvement, it is just a milestone on the journey its readers will take—to the next stage, the one after that, and the one after that, again.

ACKNOWLEDGMENTS

We have many colleagues to thank for inspiration, companionship, assistance, and support throughout our engagements with the scholarship of teaching and learning. First, of course, are two Carnegie Foundation presidents. Ernest Boyer introduced the idea in the context of an ambitious agenda for broadening the kinds of scholarship recognized in the academy; Lee Shulman established the Carnegie Academy for the Scholarship of Teaching and Learning (CASTL) and made its work a centerpiece for the Foundation. Russell Edgerton was important to the development of the scholarship of teaching and learning too, first as president of the American Association for Higher Education, which provided important forums for discussion and debate about this new work, and then as education program director at The Pew Charitable Trusts, which provided a generous grant to initiate CASTL. Other important funders for Carnegie's work on the scholarship of teaching and learning have included the Wabash Center of Inquiry in the Liberal Arts and The William and Flora Hewlett Foundation.

The CASTL program engaged a very large number of people over its 12-year history, including some 160 faculty members in the six cohorts of its national fellowship program; leaders on the more than 250 campuses participating in three iterations of its campus program; representatives from some two dozen scholarly and professional societies; and participants in the programs that these fellows, leaders, and representatives organized under the CASTL name. We are grateful to all involved for their energy, commitment, good will, and good work. Their accomplishments, challenges, and opportunities form the core of what we discuss in this book. (Readers interested in the history of the CASTL program will find an overview in Appendix B.)

We owe a special acknowledgment to Barbara Cambridge. Director of the first two iterations of CASTL's campus program while she was based at the American Association for Higher Education, Barbara continued on, with the three of us, as a member of the leadership team for the CASTL Institutional Leadership and Affiliates Program. She joined us in writing the report from our survey of institutional leaders (Appendix A) and is author of the scenarios we used in our concluding colloquium (Appendix C). We have been fortunate indeed to have Barbara as a colleague throughout the history of the CASTL program. We would also like to acknowledge our former Carnegie colleague, Richard Gale, who served as CASTL's second director (between Pat Hutchings and Anthony Ciccone) and was responsible for the initial design of the CASTL Institutional Leadership and Affiliates Program.

The leaders of the 13 groups of campuses and organizations participating in the CASTL Institutional Leadership and Affiliates Program were central to making the whole add up to more than the sum of its parts. These colleagues not only led work in their own institutions but also coordinated collaboration between the other institutions in their groups—and, through their interaction with each other, contributed to the spread of ideas across the program. Individually and collectively these colleagues served as valuable advisors to the Carnegie leadership team, helping to plan the program's colloquia, surveys, and other activities. Our deepest gratitude to the following individuals who served in these roles as our collaborators and friends: Cheryl Albers (Institutional Culture Group); Jaqueline M. Dewar (Affiliates); Donna Duffy (COPPER Group); Áine Hyland (Graduate Education Group); Teresa Johnson (Communities Group); Alan Kalish (Communities Group); Lisa Kornetsky (System Group); Lin Langley (Cross-Cutting Themes Group); Cheryl McConnell (Mentoring Group); Renee Meyers (System Group); Renee Michael (Mentoring Group); Patti Owen-Smith (Cognitive Affective Group); Nancy Randall (Undergraduate Research Group); Jennifer Robinson (Commons Group); Mary Savina (Cross-Cutting Themes Group); David Schodt (Liberal Education Group); and Carmen Werder (Student Voices Group).

This book has benefited from the advice and consent of many good colleagues both within and beyond the CASTL community. Readers will find them acknowledged for assistance with specific points in the text and in notes to the chapters that follow. We would, however, like to thank here our three anonymous reviewers for their sharp eyes, kind words, and smart suggestions. We are fortunate too in having had the opportunity to work with David Brightman, Aneesa Davenport, and their colleagues at Jossey-Bass (Wiley) Publishers. It has been a real pleasure.

We would also like to acknowledge the help of the many good colleagues who have contributed to the writing and production of this book. Stephanie Waldmann at the University of Wisconsin-Milwaukee contributed substantially to the chapter on faculty development, put our reference section in good order, and readied our manuscript for submission to the press. Nisha Patel and Megan Downey of the Carnegie Foundation provided expert technical assistance in the design and administration of our survey of participants in the Institutional Leadership and Affiliates Program (see Appendix A). Lisa Wilson, also of Carnegie, stepped in with timely assistance in copying and mailing our manuscript.

Indeed, we owe a very deep thank you to everyone at The Carnegie Foundation for the Advancement of Teaching who worked with us on CASTL from 1998 through 2009. Carnegie housed a lively intellectual community of scholars throughout these years, where the people engaged in various programs of work—on the scholarship of teaching and learning, on doctoral education, on preparation for the professions, on civic formation for undergraduate students, on developmental education in community colleges—learned from and informed each other's work every day. We thank Gay Clyburn for her continuing efforts to bring Carnegie's work on the scholarship of teaching and learning to a wider audience. And we thank Carnegie's current president, Anthony Bryk, for his interest in CASTL's work and his strong support for the program during its concluding year.

Finally, we would like to thank one another—Pat, Mary, and Tony—for the fun we've had as colleagues over CASTL's long haul, as well as in the rigors of writing this particular book. Don, Ernie, and Kathy have been unfailingly supportive and gracious about our commitments to this work. That's a good thing too, because in all likelihood we'll be continuing our journeys with the scholarship of teaching and learning for many years to come. Projects end but the work goes on.

ABOUT THE AUTHORS

Pat Hutchings was the vice president of The Carnegie Foundation for the Advancement of Teaching from 2001 to 2009, and senior scholar there beginning in 1998, when she assumed the role of inaugural director of the Carnegie Academy for the Scholarship of Teaching and Learning. She has written, spoken, and consulted widely on student outcomes assessment, integrative learning, the investigation and documentation of teaching and learning, the peer collaboration and review of teaching, and the scholarship of teaching and learning. Recent publications include *The Formation of Scholars: Rethinking Doctoral Education for the Twenty-first Century*, with four Carnegie colleagues (2008); *The Advancement of Learning: Building the Teaching Commons*, with Mary Taylor Huber (2005); *Ethics of Inquiry: Issues in the Scholarship of Teaching and Learning* (2002); and *Opening Lines: Approaches to the Scholarship of Teaching and Learning* (2000). Prior to joining Carnegie, she was a senior staff member at the American Association for Higher Education, where she directed the AAHE Assessment Forum (1987–1989) and the AAHE Teaching Initiative (1990–1998). From 1978 to 1987 she was a faculty member and chair of the English department at Alverno College. Her doctorate in English is from the University of Iowa.

Mary Taylor Huber is senior scholar emerita and consulting scholar at The Carnegie Foundation for the Advancement of Teaching. Involved in research at the Carnegie Foundation since 1985, Huber has directed projects on Cultures of

Teaching in Higher Education; led Carnegie's roles in the Integrative Learning Project and the U.S. Professors of the Year Award; and worked closely with the Carnegie Academy for the Scholarship of Teaching and Learning. She speaks, consults, and writes on the scholarship of teaching and learning, on integrative learning, and on faculty roles and rewards. Coauthor of *Scholarship Assessed: Evaluation of the Professoriate* with Charles Glassick and Gene Maeroff (1997), her recent books include *Disciplinary Styles in the Scholarship of Teaching and Learning*, coedited with Sherwyn Morreale (2002); *Balancing Acts: The Scholarship of Teaching and Learning in Academic Careers* (2004); and *The Advancement of Learning: Building the Teaching Commons* with Pat Hutchings (2005). Huber is U.S. editor for *Arts and Humanities in Higher Education* and writes the book review column for *Change* magazine. A cultural anthropologist, she has also written books and essays on colonial institutions and cultures in Papua New Guinea, and she holds a doctorate in anthropology from the University of Pittsburgh.

Anthony (Tony) Ciccone is professor of French and director of the Center for Instructional and Professional Development at the University of Wisconsin-Milwaukee. He was senior scholar and director of the Carnegie Academy for the Scholarship of Teaching and Learning at The Carnegie Foundation for the Advancement of Teaching (2007–2010). Ciccone has authored a book and several articles on Molière, as well as two French-language textbooks. He has presented and consulted on the scholarship of teaching and learning nationally and internationally, provided essays for *Campus Progress* (2002), *Creating a New Kind of University* (2006), and *Arts and Humanities in Higher Education* (2008). Ciccone is past director of the Wisconsin Teaching Scholars program, which received a Hesburgh Certificate of Excellence in 2005. He has received an AMOCO Award for Teaching Excellence and the French Teacher of the Year Award from the Wisconsin Association of Foreign Language Teachers. At UW-Milwaukee, Tony works with faculty and staff to incorporate the principles of the scholarship of teaching and learning into general education reform, assessment, and first-year instruction. Currently, he teaches a freshman seminar, *What's So Funny? Historical and Contemporary Notions of Comedy and Laughter*. He holds a doctorate in French from the University at Buffalo, The State University of New York.

EXECUTIVE SUMMARY

The scholarship of teaching and learning encompasses a broad set of practices that engage teachers in looking closely and critically at student learning in order to improve their own courses and programs, and to share insights with other educators who can evaluate and build on their efforts. Over the last two decades, college and university faculty engaged in such work have accomplished a great deal. Yet, if higher education is to meet growing imperatives around student attainment, in regard to both quantity and quality of learning, the scholarship of teaching and learning must be better integrated into the fabric of campus life. This cannot be achieved by individuals or by small groups acting alone.

Bringing the principles and practices of the scholarship of teaching and learning to bear on critical educational goals requires action and advocacy by campus leaders—committee heads, chairs, deans, professional development leaders, assessment officers, provosts, and presidents—who understand how such work can strengthen intellectual community and institutional performance in their setting. Toward that end, this book examines four areas that we believe to be the growing edge for the scholarship of teaching and learning's impact on higher education: classroom teaching, professional development, institutional assessment, and the recognition and reward of pedagogical work. Our concluding chapter offers the following recommendations, mindful that they are necessarily broad and must be tailored and adapted to each campus's distinctive mission, history, and culture.

1. *Understand, communicate, and promote an integrated vision of the scholarship of teaching and learning.* There are many ways to support the scholarship of teaching and learning, and all of them depend on leadership's own understanding of the character of such work, and why it matters. This understanding must be informed by the views of faculty and staff who have embraced this new form of scholarship, and it must be communicated, in turn, to the broader campus community, a task that requires both vision and translation skills.

2. *Support a wide range of opportunities to cultivate the skills and habits of inquiry into teaching and learning.* If the practices of the scholarship of teaching and learning are to be woven into institutional life and work, they must be cultivated in multiple sites and settings. Leaders can help introduce such practices into the wide range of campus initiatives on teaching and learning that offer opportunities for inquiry-based professional development today.

3. *Connect the scholarship of teaching and learning to larger, shared agendas for student learning and success.* Bringing scholars of teaching and learning together around agendas that invite collaboration and cross-fertilization builds relationships among individuals with common interests in ways that can significantly advance institutional initiatives and goals.

4. *Foster exchange between the campus scholarship of teaching and learning community and those with responsibility for institutional research and assessment.* These two higher education movements can strengthen each other in important ways, building toward an integrated, multilayered system of evidence gathering and use for the ongoing improvement of student learning.

5. *Work purposefully to bring faculty roles and rewards into alignment with a view of teaching as scholarly work.* Many campuses have revised institutional policies and language, but much remains to be done to craft guidelines for evaluation, documentation, and peer review that adequately recognize the scholarship of teaching and learning. Leaders must also push this work forward at the department and program level, where policies are translated into practice.

6. *Take advantage of and engage with the larger, increasingly international teaching commons.* Campus leaders can make a place for the scholarship of teaching and learning *within* the institution by supporting it though words, actions, and funding. But signals from outside the institution matter as well, and there is much to be gained by connecting with the broader scholarship of teaching and learning community and the opportunities it affords.

7. ***Develop a plan and time line for integrating the scholarship of teaching and learning into campus culture, and monitor progress.*** Developed collaboratively with others who have a stake and interest in the work, a good plan provides a shared sense of direction, purpose, and momentum, and reinforces connections to institutional goals and mission.

8. ***Recognize that institutionalization is a long-term process.*** Integrating the scholarship of teaching and learning into the ongoing work and life of the campus will necessarily entail setbacks and slowdowns. Success will require sustained leadership, creativity, and flexibility on the part of everyone involved.

The Scholarship of Teaching and Learning Reconsidered

CHAPTER ONE

Why the Scholarship of Teaching and Learning Matters Today

We believe the time has come to move beyond the tired old "teaching versus research" debate and give the familiar and honorable term "scholarship" a broader, more capacious meaning, one that brings legitimacy to the full scope of academic work.
—Ernest Boyer[1]

In 1990 The Carnegie Foundation for the Advancement of Teaching published Ernest Boyer's short book, *Scholarship Reconsidered: Priorities of the Professoriate*. It was a time of transition for U.S. colleges and universities. The Cold War's end had weakened the conventional rationale for federally funded research; America's diminished economic position had raised questions about higher education's teaching effectiveness; a host of social and environmental crises called out for renewed attention to service. "Challenges on the campus and in society have grown," Boyer stated, "and there is a deepening conviction that the role of higher education, as well as the priorities of the professoriate, must be redefined to reflect new realities" (p. 3).

Scholarship Reconsidered proposed a novel approach for addressing these problems. As Russell Edgerton, then president of the American Association for Higher Education, explained in an endorsement for the book: "The problem is not simply one of 'balance'—of adjusting the weights we attach to teaching, research, and service—but of reclaiming the common ground of scholarship that underlies all these activities."[2] By identifying *the scholarship of teaching*, along with the scholarships of discovery, integration, and application as "four separate, yet overlapping functions" of the professoriate (p. 16), Boyer introduced an intriguing new term into academic discourse, and initiated a lively conversation about what it might mean to undertake college and university teaching as serious intellectual work.

Since 1990 that conversation has traveled far. In concert with a broad shift in focus from teaching to learning among thoughtful educators, the scholarship of teaching has become "the scholarship of teaching *and learning*," and the work has widened too. Today "the serious study that undergirds good teaching" (Boyer, 1990, p. 23) is understood to include not just knowledge of the discipline, but also "the latest ideas about teaching the field" (Hutchings and Shulman, 1999, p. 13). Teaching and learning have both become more public: faculty are reflecting on their teaching in ways that can be shared with a wider community of educators, and, using a variety of evidence-gathering and documentation strategies, they are making their students' learning more visible too. Today's scholars of teaching and learning treat their classrooms and programs as a source of interesting questions about learning; find ways to explore and shed light on these questions; use this evidence in designing and refining new activities, assignments, and assessments; and share what they've found with colleagues who can comment, critique, and build on new insights (Huber and Hutchings, 2005).

By going public with their work, scholars of teaching and learning are also venturing into and helping to create a new space for pedagogical exchange and collaboration that two of us have called the *teaching commons*, a space in which "communities of educators committed to pedagogical inquiry and innovation come together to exchange ideas about teaching and learning and use them to meet the challenges of educating students for personal, professional, and civic life" (Huber and Hutchings, 2005, p. x). Of course, there have always been small communities of scholars in every field who have made pedagogically relevant work available to each other through regular channels of scholarly discourse—conferences, publications, collaborations, and the like. And there have long been networks of specialists in education and the learning sciences. But scholars of teaching and learning—typically faculty who teach their subjects but have not generally considered themselves pedagogical experts—are making distinctive contributions. They are helping through their own work to connect different regions within this commons (bringing literature from their own fields to bear on teaching issues, borrowing from the literature of other fields); they are finding ways to use the ideas they discover through the commons to understand and improve learning in their own classrooms and programs; and they are adding to that commons a new body of knowledge derived from inquiry and innovation in situations of practice.[3]

The number of faculty engaged in this work, though as yet modest, is growing.[4] And these men and women are worth watching because the scholarship of teaching and learning, as practiced today, foreshadows what members of the academic profession will be doing as educators tomorrow. The United States provides *access* to higher education for a wide population. But student *success* lags too far behind. The most urgent matter concerns the large number of students who start but don't complete college.[5] But the broader issue, as Derek Bok argues in *Our Underachieving Colleges*, concerns "unfulfilled promises and unrealized opportunities" (2006, p. 57). Undergraduates, even those who complete degrees, are not learning as much or as well as they should. If students are to be adequately prepared for life, work, and civic participation in the twenty-first century, colleges and universities must pay closer attention to the heart of the educational enterprise. What is it really important for students to know and be able to do? How can higher education institutions and their faculty help students get there? The scholarship of teaching and learning brings powerful new principles and practices to ground deliberations about these questions in sound evidence and help point the way.[6]

This book is about the scholarship of teaching and learning, why it matters today—and what it promises for tomorrow. In this first chapter, we situate the work in the broader context of the turn toward learning in higher education policy and practice, and discuss the challenges this shift poses for institutions and faculty. Because we draw many of our examples and insights from the experience of individuals and institutions participating in the Carnegie Academy for the Scholarship of Teaching and Learning (CASTL, 1998–2009), we will describe that program and its place in the larger movement that is broadening the scope and deepening understanding of this work. We then look briefly at four areas we believe to be the growing edge for the work's impact on higher education. These areas, subjects of the next four chapters, include classroom teaching and learning, professional development, assessment, and the value (and evaluation) of teaching. Our final chapter asks what colleges and universities would look like if the principles and practices of the scholarship of teaching and learning were to take hold across academic culture, and what leaders can do to move their institutions in that direction. We conclude this first chapter with a look at the evidence we draw on in this book, followed by a return to *Scholarship Reconsidered,* and our conviction that the scholarship of teaching and learning can help colleges, universities, and the academic profession responsibly and effectively address the new realities confronting higher education today.

In short, we argue that it is time to reconsider the scope of the scholarship of teaching and learning, and see it as a set of principles and practices that are critical to achieving institutional goals for student learning and success.

THE TURN TOWARD LEARNING

The scholarship of teaching and learning is part of a broader transformation in the intellectual culture of higher education, where attention to learning has been growing steadily over the past twenty years. As Robert Barr and John Tagg put it in their influential 1995 article, "From Teaching to Learning": "A paradigm shift is taking hold in American higher education. In its briefest form, the paradigm that has governed our colleges is this: A college is an institution that exists to provide instruction. Subtly but profoundly we are shifting to a new paradigm: A college is an institution that exists to produce learning. This shift changes everything. It is both needed and wanted" (p. 13). Researchers in neuroscience, psychology, and education; funders from public and private foundations; leaders of higher education associations and policy centers; accreditors; college and university administrators; professional developers; and information technology specialists have all contributed to this shift—and so, importantly, have front-line practitioners: faculty themselves and even students. The result, if not as radical as the term "paradigm shift" suggests, has included an extraordinarily rich array of pedagogical, curricular, and assessment initiatives that often challenge familiar ways of educating college and university students.

Manifestations of this turn toward learning are everywhere, especially in renewed attention to student learning outcomes spurred by accreditation requirements that ask institutions to be more intentional about their educational programs and to determine whether they are actually achieving their goals. Colleges and universities across the country have set up committees and established offices to coordinate campus efforts to identify learning outcomes at departmental, program, and institutional levels and to devise appropriate assessment strategies and improvement cycles. Indeed, it would be hard to find faculty anywhere who have not by now engaged in such activities in at least modest ways.

Institutions' efforts in this regard are strengthened by initiatives undertaken through a variety of academic associations. The Association of American Colleges and Universities (AAC&U) has been particularly influential in seeding campus deliberations on learning outcomes for liberal education, most recently through its Liberal Education and America's Promise (LEAP) initiative. Identifying four "essential learning outcomes" (knowledge of human cultures and the physical and natural world, intellectual and practical skills, personal and social responsibility, and integrative learning) to be achieved "at successively higher levels across [students'] college studies," AAC&U has organized a host of conferences, institutes, and cross-campus projects to elucidate and elaborate what these ambitious goals might mean in theory and look like in practice (2007, p. 3).

Many other associations are also leading efforts along these lines. For example, the American Association of State Colleges and Universities' American Democracy Project, initiated in 2003, has involved 220 institutions that have set a goal of producing "graduates who are committed to being active, involved citizens in their communities." The project has brought campuses together in national and regional meetings, in a national assessment project, and in "hundreds of campus initiatives including voter education and registration, curriculum revision and projects, campus audits, specific days of action and reflection (MLK Day of Service, Constitution Day), speaker series, and many recognition and award programs" (American Association of State Colleges and Universities, "About Us"). Similarly, Campus Compact, an association of some 1,200 presidents of two- and four-year colleges and universities, offers a variety of resources and initiatives to help institutions organize, support, and assess community service, civic engagement, and service learning (Campus Compact, "Who We Are").

Disciplinary and professional fields have been no less active. The STEM fields (science, technology, engineering, and mathematics), in particular, stand out—in part due to the National Science Foundation's efforts to improve the recruitment and retention of women and minorities as science majors, and to enhance science literacy for all (Seymour, 2001). Over the past twenty years, the National Science Foundation (and other science education foundations) have funded a great number of collaborative efforts to explore curricular and pedagogical innovations aimed at helping more students learn more science at more sophisticated levels of understanding. This is not to say that the work has been without controversy, but it has helped to make conversation about teaching and learning a more familiar part of academic science, and to make promising innovations better known and more widespread (for instance, the early introduction of design experiences into engineering programs; see Sheppard, Macatangay, Colby, and Sullivan, 2009).

Indeed, the desire to engage undergraduates in disciplinary knowledge practices is a common thread running through educational reform in a wide swath of fields today. Across the disciplinary spectrum, one can find critics of older, more "passive" pedagogies, which have often emphasized mastery of content at the expense of an understanding of how that knowledge is produced and used. For example, a recent collection of essays, *Exploring Signature Pedagogies: Approaches to Teaching Disciplinary Habits of Mind*, by faculty from the University of Wisconsin System (Gurung, Chick, and Haynie, 2008) explores this shift to more active learning in the humanities (history, literary studies), in the fine arts (creative writing, music theory and performance, the arts), in the social sciences (geography, human development, psychology, sociology), and in the natural sciences and mathematics (agriculture, biological sciences, computer science, mathematics, physics). These reform ideas are the leading edge in disciplinary pedagogy, not yet the norm but opening new possibilities for undergraduate learning in many fields.

One of the best overviews of what has (and has not) been accomplished through the past twenty years of attention to learning in higher education can be found in George Kuh's study *High-Impact Educational Practices: What They Are, Who Has Access to Them, and Why They Matter* (2008). In this important report, Kuh—founding director of the National Survey of Student Engagement—discusses 10 teaching and learning practices that "have been widely tested and that have been shown to be beneficial for college students from many backgrounds" (p. 9). The list, familiar to all who follow the reform literature in higher education, includes first-year seminars; common intellectual experiences; learning communities; writing-intensive courses; collaborative assignments and projects; undergraduate research; diversity/global learning; service and community-based learning; internships; and capstone courses and portfolios. All these strategies are being used today to promote disciplinary habits of mind as well as the kinds of cross-cutting learning outcomes envisioned by AAC&U's LEAP initiative. Yet Kuh finds that these practices are not evenly distributed within or across institutions.

In fact, many high-impact practices like first-year seminars and common intellectual experiences cannot be implemented by a single faculty member or department alone; and none of them—even when they *can* be done by an individual working on his or her own—are easy to do well. As Kuh notes, these practices do not come with simple blueprints to follow, but "take many different forms, depending on learner characteristics and on institutional priorities and contexts" (2008, p. 9). As a result, whole communities of practitioners, both national and international, have assembled around each of these (and many other) promising practices, with their own conferences, workshops, publications, and web sites.[7]

Educational innovation today invites, even requires, levels of preparation, imagination, collaboration, and support that are not always a good fit (to say the least) with the inherited routines of academic life. As we'll see throughout this book, leaders and participants in efforts to improve students' educational experiences and outcomes often feel they are working against the grain. Bureaucratic barriers, financial realities, time constraints, and faculty evaluation policies can all inhibit the development or spread of promising pedagogical and curricular practices within (and among) institutions (Schneider and Shoenberg, 1999). And these factors are exacerbated by the rise in the number of faculty on contingent appointments, often without access to the support, security, and seniority that would encourage and enable them to devote the time or to take the risks associated with innovation at the classroom and program levels (Schuster and Finkelstein, 2006; Gappa, Austin, and Trice, 2007).

How, then, can higher education make good on the promise of the turn toward learning? Policies work best when they build on what is already present in a culture—even if it is only a subculture—and higher education is fortunate to have a growing number of faculty who have already intensified their engagement with teaching in significant ways. As Derek Bok suggests, "one should not be too pessimistic ... about the prospects for enlisting faculty support for a more searching, continuous process of self-scrutiny and reform" (2006, p. 342). We agree. There are professors on every campus who are looking closely and critically at their students' learning, redesigning their courses and programs, and coming together to share what they've learned with others. Broadly speaking, these are the faculty who are engaged in what is now widely called the scholarship of teaching and learning.

LOOKING CLOSELY AND CRITICALLY AT LEARNING[8]

The scholarship of teaching and learning encompasses a broad set of practices that engage teachers in looking closely and critically at student learning for the purpose of improving their own courses and programs. It is perhaps best understood as an approach that marries scholarly inquiry to any of the intellectual tasks that comprise the work of teaching—designing a course, facilitating classroom activities, trying out new pedagogical ideas, advising, writing student learning outcomes, evaluating programs (Shulman, 1998). When activities like these are undertaken with serious questions about student learning in mind, one enters the territory of the scholarship of teaching and learning.

One of the best-known programs to develop and explore the possibilities of this approach to pedagogy was the Carnegie Academy for the Scholarship of Teaching and Learning, which concluded nearly a dozen years of work in 2009. Initiated in 1998 under the leadership of Lee Shulman, successor to Ernest Boyer as president of The Carnegie Foundation for the Advancement of Teaching, CASTL included a national fellowship program for individual scholars of teaching and learning, and a succession of programs to promote the work on campuses and in disciplinary and professional associations. CASTL's reach was wide: over the years, 158 faculty members pursued classroom research projects in six cohorts of the year-long fellowship program; over 250 colleges and universities signed on for one or more of the campus program's increasingly international three phases; and some two dozen scholarly societies worked to raise the intellectual profile of teaching in their fields (see Appendix B).

The ripple effects of CASTL's work have been notable too. As participants in its various activities have moved into positions of greater responsibility in their departments, institutions, and fields, they have been able to engage others—faculty, graduate students, undergraduates. They have also begun to infuse principles from the scholarship of teaching and learning into important pedagogical and curricular initiatives. Such well-known efforts as the Peer Review of Teaching Project at the University of Nebraska (Bernstein, Burnett, Goodburn, and Savory, 2006), the Visible Knowledge Project led by Georgetown University (Bass and Eynon, 2009), and the History Learning Project at Indiana

University Bloomington (Diaz, Middendorf, Pace, and Shopkow, 2008) have had significant links with CASTL, as has the International Society for the Scholarship of Teaching and Learning (ISSOTL), founded in 2004. As long-time members of Carnegie's CASTL staff, we are not unbiased, but it is surely fair to say that CASTL has played a central role in the development of the scholarship of teaching and learning in the United States and in linking that movement with similar efforts elsewhere in the world.[9]

Like any emergent field, the scholarship of teaching and learning has grown and developed over the years. One participant in CASTL's Institutional Leadership Program mentioned to us his surprise, upon rereading the movement's early literature, at its somewhat defensive tone. And it's true: 10 years ago advocates of the scholarship of teaching and learning spent a great deal of time at meetings, conferences, and in publications discussing the meaning of the term.[10] Today, however, participants are often willing to skip the definitional prologue and dive right into the pedagogical and curricular issues with which they're concerned. This doesn't mean that definitions are unimportant, especially on campuses (and in countries) where the scholarship of teaching and learning is new. But the movement is now mature enough to live and grow within a set of tensions that inform the field.

One of these tensions can be dubbed the "theory" debate—about the work's relationship to research in education, to professional development, and to the learning sciences (see Hutchings, 2007; Hutchings and Huber, 2008). Briefly put, the question concerns the legitimacy of the literatures and methods that shape teachers' questions about learning and the kinds of evidence they seek in order to answer them. On the one hand, this debate points to the different disciplinary styles of inquiry and argument that faculty bring to the scholarship of teaching and learning (Huber, 1999; Healey, 2000; Huber and Morreale, 2002; Mills and Huber, 2005; Huber, 2006; Kreber, 2006), as well as to competing definitions of excellence in the production of knowledge that characterize different fields (see Lamont, 2009). Humanists, in particular, have felt the heavy hand of social science approaches to learning and have sought to work within, and stretch, their own disciplinary styles of inquiry and interpretation to illuminate and ultimately improve student experience in their classrooms and fields (see, for example, Linkon and Bass, 2008).

A related territorial tension concerns the appropriate roles of "experts" and "amateurs" in the study of learning in higher education *within* particular disciplines and fields. Felt most acutely in mathematics and the sciences, this involves finding space for scholars of teaching and learning vis-à-vis the growing ranks of education specialists in these fields (see Dewar and Bennett, 2010; Huber and Morreale, 2002; Coppola and Jacobs, 2002). Should pedagogical exploration be the province of those specially versed in the research literature and methods of discipline-based education research? Or is the scholarship of teaching and learning for everyone who wishes to be a reflective practitioner, especially given new opportunities for expanding pedagogical goals and repertoires? Can both contribute to knowledge building and improvement? Where do they overlap? Where do they differ?

These questions lead to an even more basic tension within the scholarship of teaching and learning: the "big tent" debate. Narrow constructionists prefer to emphasize the work's affinities with conventional academic research—though usually with modifications to accommodate the practicalities of practitioner inquiry into student learning in one's own classroom, program, institution, or field (see McKinney, 2007a; Richlin, 2001). Broad constructionists, the big tent advocates, are happy to use the term to cover a wider range of work (documentation, reflection, inquiry) in greater or lesser degrees of polish, made public in forums with nearer or farther reach. While the former emphasize the work's value as "research" within academic reward systems, the big tent view looks *also* toward elaborations within the category of "teaching," and is thus more hospitable to teachers who want to participate if only occasionally or in modest ways (Huber and Hutchings, 2005; Kreber, 2007; Phipps and Barnett, 2007).

Perhaps it's because it has these two "sides" (looking toward research, on the one hand, and teaching on the other), that the scholarship of teaching and learning can be so large, containing (with a nod to Walt Whitman) multitudes. Certainly it has proven to be a welcome destination for faculty who come to serious consideration of teaching and learning via quite different routes. To be sure, there are faculty who begin with a strong interest in making better pedagogical decisions, seeking evidence about how best to align activities, assignments, and assessments with desired outcomes—eager from the outset to engage in "hard thinking about new course designs" (Calder, Oct. 28, 2009). But teachers also enter the big tent through other doors.

Many faculty, for example, have been moved by the writing of Parker Palmer (2007) and others to attend to the emotional and spiritual dimensions of both teaching and learning (Huber, 2008a). Others come to more serious engagements with teaching and learning through concerns about weaknesses in students' mastery of a skill (say, writing), grasp of a field (say, history), or about uneven achievement among students of different ethnicities and backgrounds (say, women and minorities in the sciences). For some, the entrée has been through convictions about the importance of particular pedagogies (service learning, for example) or particular goals (civic engagement, for example). The scholarship of teaching and learning can provide common ground to develop all these passions and interests, colleagues with whom to collaborate, a growing knowledge base about pedagogy and curriculum, and a sense of community that can break through the isolation that college teachers so often feel.

Indeed, the scholarship of teaching and learning has both an individual and an institutional face today. Yes, many participants believe that the work will eventually change the ways in which faculty think and act as teachers (thus underlining the importance of welcoming all comers). And bringing faculty's inclinations and skills as scholars to questions about learning in their own classrooms is central to the movement. Yet, as surgeon and writer Atul Gawande notes of a parallel movement in medicine, those who do their best to "make a science of performance, to investigate and improve how well they use the knowledge and technologies they already have in hand" almost inevitably end up with ideas about how to make *systems* work better, as well (2007, p. 56). And the same is true of the scholarship of teaching and learning. Some of the most interesting applications and experiments to emerge in recent years are collaborative efforts focused on systemic initiatives, such as curriculum reform, program review, or assessment. This is where the scholarship of teaching and learning is being most actively reconsidered and reinvented today. It is this territory that we are especially interested in exploring in this book.

AREAS OF IMPACT, PROMISE, AND CHALLENGE

In what areas of college and university life has the scholarship of teaching and learning made the biggest impact so far? In what areas does it show special promise? What challenges does the work face in the years ahead? The four areas we examine in this book were chosen because of their strategic importance for institutional change, and because they suggest how the scholarship of teaching and learning can inform core aspects of academic life and work. These areas include: the ways in which faculty go about their teaching (Chapter 2); how professional development is understood and organized (Chapter 3); the relationship between the scholarship of teaching and learning and institutional assessment (Chapter 4); and how the work of teaching is valued and evaluated (Chapter 5). In discussing these areas, of course, we touch on many others, including the implications of the scholarship of teaching and learning for graduate education, contributions to a variety of pedagogical and institutional initiatives, effects on student learning, and what campus leaders can do (Chapter 6) to advance the work's institutional integration and impact.

Teachers and Learning

The scholarship of teaching and learning is, at its core, an approach to teaching that is informed by inquiry and evidence (both one's own, and that of others) about student learning. Its most important area of impact, then, is on how faculty conduct themselves as teachers. The scholarship of teaching and learning is not so much a function of what particular pedagogies faculty use. Rather, it concerns the thoughtfulness with which they construct the learning environments they offer students, the attention they pay to students and their learning, and the engagement they seek with colleagues on all things pertaining to education in their disciplines, programs, and institutions.

That said, many faculty members who get involved in the scholarship of teaching and learning are open to—and even seeking—new classroom approaches. They are trying to find the best ways of incorporating new media into their teaching; they are troubled by the number of students who are performing poorly in their science or math classes; or they care deeply about educating students for citizenship, and want to explore how best to build students' knowledge, skills, and confidence. The scholarship of teaching and learning, in other words, has within it a bias toward innovation, and often toward more active roles for students that engage them more meaningfully in the content, ways of knowing, and forms of practice that characterize a field.

The scholarship of teaching and learning also fosters faculty involvement with each other in ways that were not so common before. There's a public dimension built into the work, an interest in sharing pedagogical ideas and learning from one another. This takes place on campus, where innovators with interests in particular pedagogies (say, capstone projects) or programs (say, undergraduate research) find each other informally, through an office that supports that kind of teaching, or increasingly through participation in a variety of education reform initiatives. Centers for teaching are now supporting faculty inquiry, often organizing groups whose members meet to frame inquiry projects, to share results, and, not infrequently, to inspire each other with new ideas for their classrooms. In many cases, scholars of teaching and learning also form communities beyond campus, as participants and activists in their disciplinary and professional societies, pressing for more and better occasions to pursue pedagogical interests through conferences, publications, and other association forums.

Faculty who engage in the scholarship of teaching and learning also seek to discover more about their students' experience. Many begin modest projects of inquiry in their own classrooms, aimed at providing evidence to inform a next stage of instructional design. However, this effort can lead to more ambitious questions aimed at identifying common roadblocks to learning, pushing the limits of one's own disciplinary styles of inquiry, and adopting a variety of methods for making learning more visible—including methods that fall outside the field (see Jacobs, 2000). There is something inviting about a pedagogical problem that is thus reframed as a problem for investigation (Bass, 1999): as faculty are drawn further into the work, they also read more systematically in the literature on learning in their own field—a quest that can lead to the literature in neighboring fields, or even in those far away, including (for some) education and the other learning sciences.

Many participants in the scholarship of teaching and learning make a further commitment to knowledge building by seeking wider audiences for their work. They not only draw from the larger teaching commons but contribute to it as well. The opportunities for making work public continue to grow: posters and presentations at campus or disciplinary conferences, essays in campus publications or scholarly society newsletters, articles in pedagogical journals, edited collections, single- or multiauthored books. Some have pioneered multimedia genres, like electronic portfolios or repositories for teaching materials that make it possible to give fuller representation not just to inquiry on teaching and learning, but to the acts of teaching and learning themselves.

Does the scholarship of teaching and learning—all this pedagogical experimentation, study, reflection, conversation, and writing—actually improve outcomes for students? This is a question that advocates hear more and more often as they try to make the case to colleagues that the time and money necessary to support the work will be resources well spent. There are countless examples of individual scholarship of teaching and learning projects that focus directly and explicitly on learning improvement, explore students' areas of strength and weakness, and document the effectiveness (or not) of particular pedagogical strategies. But asking whether a campus commitment to this work, as embodied in a set of activities to encourage and support it, improves learning outcomes in a more general way is a harder question, in part because the higher education community is only beginning to map out the complex lines of cause and effect between faculty development programs (of any kind) and student achievement. Chapter 2 concludes with reflections on how and what to think about this "learning question."

Faculty Development

The scholarship of teaching and learning is a powerful form of faculty development. Engaging in a cycle of inquiry and improvement allows teachers to identify and investigate questions that they care about in their students' learning and bring what they've found back to their classrooms and programs in the form of new curricula, new assessments and assignments, and new pedagogies, which in turn become subjects for further inquiry. This process helps scholars of teaching and learning develop their capacities as observant, thoughtful, and innovative teachers, while making the work public contributes to pedagogical knowledge on their campuses and in their fields. It is a powerful way for faculty to grow as professionals over time.

Although this is work that faculty can do on their own, preferably in the company of a small group of like-minded colleagues from their campus or disciplinary networks, formal faculty development centers are playing increasingly important roles. They are providing programs for graduate students and for faculty new to the scholarship of teaching and learning; access to literature, methodological expertise, and other resources helpful to faculty engaged in the work; an array of forums for making teaching public in the campus community;

and, in general, a place where people can find colleagues for discussion and collaboration around pedagogical issues of common interest. Perhaps most important in light of our focus on institutional integration, faculty development initiatives—and their directors and staff—are well positioned to connect scholars of teaching and learning with educational issues of wider institutional concern.

Faculty development wasn't always this way, nor is it entirely this way yet. For many years, formal programs to promote professional improvement operated in a cultural milieu that emphasized teaching as transmission of content. Because faculty with doctorates were already presumed to command content expertise, "development" meant modest support for keeping up with disciplinary trends, while support for pedagogical purposes primarily responded to crises: assistance for faculty who were having trouble in the classroom, teaching assistant preparation, response to the learning needs of a more diverse student body, help with using new teaching technologies, and the like. Unfortunately faculty often formed a negative view of these efforts as overly remedial, technical, and generic. In contrast, the scholarship of teaching and learning, in its emphasis on pedagogical inquiry and innovation, implied a different model of development—a "narrative of growth" instead of what was frequently perceived as a "narrative of constraint" (O'Meara, Terosky, and Neumann, 2008). For this reason, scholars of teaching and learning, especially in the movement's early days, often went about their work outside the purview of faculty development centers.

Yet faculty developers and scholars of teaching and learning share a common goal: transforming teaching and learning for the better. And, over time, the benefits of partnership have become clear. Scholars of teaching and learning have gained advocates with better access to resources that can facilitate inquiry, innovation, collaboration, and knowledge building. And professional development centers have gained allies among faculty who are interested in participating in teaching initiatives that go beyond their own classrooms and programs, through which they can help raise students' levels of learning and build their own pedagogical networks and expertise.

When these opportunities are organized around issues of wide campus concern—for instance, assessment, curriculum revision, new media pedagogy, undergraduate research—then both efforts, faculty development and the scholarship of teaching and learning, gain currency and relevance. Of course, there are risks. But that is always the case when activities that have been cultivated on the margins of institutional operation move closer to center stage. Scholars of teaching and learning—along with faculty developers—have too much to offer to hold back from this chance to influence their institutions' larger educational agendas. Engaging these agendas need not be seen as a departure from the classroom inquiry and innovation that's at the heart of the scholarship of teaching and learning. Making these connections extends and enriches the work, instead.

Assessment

Assessing what students learn during college has become increasingly important for purposes of public accountability, accreditation, and for the improvement of teaching and learning. Interest in assessment picked up new life through the hearings and report of former U.S. Secretary of Education Margaret Spellings' National Commission on the Future of Higher Education (2006), the debates it sparked, and the initiatives through which the higher education community responded (see Shavelson, 2010; Ewell, 2009; Banta, Griffin, Flateby, and Kahn, 2009). Less noted in the national debate are the family resemblances between institutional assessment and the scholarship of teaching and learning (Hutchings, 2010). As we note in Chapter 4, assessment shares with the scholarship of teaching and learning a focus on student learning, a more systematic, evidence-based approach to educational quality, and a commitment to being more public about what and how well students are learning in college and university classrooms.

Yet the two movements have important differences as well. Inquiry undertaken by scholars of teaching and learning is typically motivated by questions that arise out of classroom practice, whereas assessment more often begins with concerns (both externally and internally generated) about institutional effectiveness. The scholarship of teaching and learning has typically been a "bottom-up" effort by faculty, while assessment has been a "top-down" initiative from administration. Finally, they are subject to different incentives: as Peter Ewell notes, those assessing for public accountability are inclined to present as rosy a picture of student learning at their institution as possible, while those assessing for improvement—and this would include scholars of teaching and learning—are oriented toward discovering and understanding where students have difficulties (2009).

For all of these reasons, assessment and the scholarship of teaching and learning have proceeded on more or less separate tracks—with their different histories, methods, and champions—each somewhat wary of the other. This has contributed to a troubling gap. As a recent survey of institutional practices conducted by the National Institute for Learning Outcomes Assessment has shown, assessment has become nearly ubiquitous in U.S. higher education, largely because of accreditation requirements, but the results are not used nearly as much for the design and redesign of courses and programs as one would hope (Kuh and Ikenberry, 2009). On the other side of this gap, faculty engaged in improvement efforts often lack the kinds of data that institutional assessment efforts can provide.

Our argument, then, is that it would be to the advantage of both assessment and the scholarship of teaching and learning if bridges between them could be built—a challenge that is just beginning to be addressed by administrative and faculty leaders, as they discover what each other's efforts can bring to the table. Cautious though these beginnings may (and should) be, the possibilities are intriguing. When assessment is done in ways that offer added insight into issues of student learning, and when it involves students themselves as participants in the process (as many scholars of teaching and learning have done), it is more likely to command the interest and engagement of faculty, and thus to enter more fully into the life of the institution. Likewise, when the scholarship of teaching and learning speaks to such pressing institutional agendas as student achievement and success, it is likely to receive more support and recognition—as is the better-informed teaching that this kind of scholarship underwrites.

Valuing and Evaluating Teaching

As with assessment, efforts to reconceptualize, support, and reward good teaching are also back in public discourse—certainly so in the United States. In addition to spurring new attention to the role of learning outcomes assessment for accountability, Spellings' National Commission on the Future of Higher Education urged colleges and universities to embrace a "culture of continuous innovation" in teaching and curriculum (2006, p. 5), a theme that many campuses were also voicing. Even at Harvard University, a distinguished task force sought to identify ways to foster and reward pedagogical improvement as a major professional commitment for academic scholars at all stages of their careers (see *Harvard Magazine*, 2006; Task Force on Teaching and Career Development to the Faculty of Arts and Sciences, 2007). Indeed, a consensus seems to have emerged that it's time to revisit expectations for good teaching in higher education, and to develop some common understandings about how it can be improved.

The scholarship of teaching and learning community has much to offer the larger academic world as it takes on the question: What is good college or university teaching today? To put it most succinctly, we propose the idea of the scholarship of teaching and learning itself. As Daniel Bernstein, Amy Nelson Burnett, Amy Goodburn, and Paul Savory spell it out in their book, *Making Teaching and Learning Visible*: "An excellent teacher is one who is engaged in a well-prepared and intentional ongoing investigation of the best ways to promote a deep understanding on the part of as many students as possible" (2006, p. 215). Yet even as straightforward a conception as this opens a series of difficult questions concerning the way in which teaching is recognized and rewarded in higher education today.

Since *Scholarship Reconsidered* was published in 1990, many colleges and universities have broadened or amended institutional policies to recognize and reward a wider range of faculty work, often embracing Boyer's four scholarships (discovery, integration, application, and teaching) or a version of them. Most often, however, this has involved expanding the category of "research" to give published work on pedagogy, community service, or public scholarship a place in the rhetoric—if not yet fully the reality—of the research category for promotion and tenure purposes. This has been an important development, and while there is still a lot of hard work to do to realize its promise, it has helped give visibility to the scholarship of teaching and learning in the various disciplines, and hope to people who have begun to undertake it.

But what about teaching itself? The movement started by *Scholarship Reconsidered* has always had larger aspirations: to encourage and recognize the intellectual work in teaching, and make it, in Lee Shulman's words, "an essential facet of good teaching—built into the expected repertoire of scholarly practice" (2000, p. 105). In particular, we ask in Chapter 5 what teaching evaluation would look like if it too focused on features, like those identified in the Carnegie Foundation report *Scholarship Assessed*, that characterize a wide range of scholarly work: clear goals, adequate preparation, appropriate methods, significant results, effective presentation, and reflective critique (Glassick, Huber, and Maeroff, 1997; Bernstein and Huber, 2006). We draw here on recent initiatives and experiments to supplement student evaluations of teaching with portfolio approaches, and to improve the academic community's capacity for the peer review of such materials. But this will be a long and doubtless bumpy road.

Campuses will likely make more progress on that road if they work together, developing new models and metrics for recognizing the intellectual work in teaching, and for discerning strengths and weaknesses in records of performance; doing so will be an important way of showing respect for academics as teachers. It will, in addition, give a boost to faculty who teach with a persistent focus on their students' learning and who have a willingness to engage with pedagogical literature and discussion in search of ways to create richer learning environments. The likely downstream consequences of better evaluation are also worth consideration: clearer messages to graduate programs, more serious discourse on teaching and learning in disciplinary and professional societies, and greater attention to the work of the growing numbers of non-tenure-track faculty occupying primarily teaching roles. Finally, by fostering a more collegial culture of teaching, better evaluation will encourage faculty to contribute more thoughtfully and more often to the literature and discussion on teaching and learning, increasing pedagogical knowledge and its use for the benefit of students.

EVIDENCE AND VOICE

Understanding (even measuring) the actual and potential impact of the scholarship of teaching and learning is extraordinarily difficult, but if the movement is to continue to grow and thrive, it's important to try. In this book, we draw on a wide range of evidence and experience about the inroads that the scholarship of teaching and learning has made into academic life. We hope that this effort will underline the need to document the impact of the work as its networks and knowledge develop and spread.

That, at least, has been the thinking behind the efforts that CASTL itself has made to document the movement's impact over the years. These efforts began in 2001 with an extended inventory of conditions at colleges and universities participating in the first iteration of the CASTL Campus Program (1998–2001).[11] A second survey in 2004 explored the experience of participants in the first five classes of CASTL's national fellowship program (137 at the time), seeking insights about how individual faculty members were faring in this work—what influenced their initial involvement in the scholarship of teaching and learning; what activities they had engaged in; consequences for their classrooms; support and constraints for the work in their departmental, campus, and disciplinary contexts; and their general sense of whether the work would prosper in the future (Cox, Huber, and Hutchings, 2005). We will draw on these surveys in this book.

However, our most important source of original data for this study comes from a more recent survey, designed specifically in recognition of the growing engagement of scholars of teaching and learning with institutional agendas. This 2009 survey of participants in the CASTL Institutional Leadership and Affiliates Program (2006–2009) canvassed people who have been leading efforts to promote and support the scholarship of teaching and learning within their campuses, university systems, scholarly and professional societies, or cross-campus academic initiatives. Designed in collaboration with a subset of these leaders, our survey aimed to tap these scholars' insights into the work's contributions to critical areas of institutional practice and policy.

A few words about the Institutional Leadership and Affiliates Program should be helpful in situating our respondents' authority as commentators on the institutional impact of the scholarship of teaching and learning. As described in CASTL's official statements, this program built on "influential work undertaken by colleges and universities, campus centers and educational organizations, scholarly and professional societies, and previous phases of CASTL's own work with campuses, to facilitate collaboration among institutions with demonstrated commitment to and capacity for action, inquiry and innovation in the scholarship of teaching and learning. Participating institutions were selected and organized in a distributed leadership model of 13 groupings to address specific themes and issues important to the improvement of student learning, as well as the development and sustainability of a scholarship of teaching and learning movement" (see Appendix B). The leaders of these groups, then, had experience in directing one or more initiatives in their institution, often over a period of several years—some for over a decade of CASTL-related work. And, because we encouraged respondents to consult with colleagues in answering the survey questions, the responses mentioned in our discussion are informed not only by a leader's personal experience but also by the collective wisdom of an institutional leadership team—including in several cases students, whose voices we have sought to capture as well.

The scholarship of teaching and learning has practitioners, advocates, organizers, and other supporters across the spectrum of U.S. higher education—and also internationally (especially, though not exclusively, in Australia, Canada, Hong Kong, Ireland, New Zealand, and the United Kingdom). As readers can see from Appendix B, the institutions involved in the CASTL Institutional Leadership and Affiliates Program included U.S. campuses (and systems of campuses) from all major categories of the Basic Carnegie Classification of Institutions of Higher Education, 17 institutions from outside the United States, a number of educational associations or consortia, and one discipline-based organization. To be sure, there are many colleges, universities, and academic associations with lively initiatives in the scholarship of teaching and learning that did not participate in the CASTL program. And, of course, the program also did not include institutions where interest in the work was too sparse or scattered to apply for participation. No one, to our knowledge, really knows how rare or widespread engagement with the scholarship of teaching and learning is in the United States or elsewhere. Although the answer—and in lieu of reliable numbers, people's perceptions—depends entirely on how strictly or broadly one defines the work, it is important to keep a skeptical but open mind and to neither over- nor underestimate the extent of individual and institutional involvement.

Our survey is certainly not a random sample of higher education, but it can provide, we believe, an important picture of the impact of the scholarship of teaching and learning at places where it is most established. And even there, as readers will see, we have recognized that the work is seldom evenly distributed, and have asked respondents to make a rough estimate of both the depth and extent of impact. For four key areas—how faculty approach teaching, the character of the student learning experience, the institutional culture in support of teaching, and the contribution of the work to other campus initiatives and agendas—we employed a seven-point scale designed to capture patterns of impact, from "widespread" to "localized," from "deep" to "mixed," and finally, to "no discernable impact" at all. (The scale was adapted from Eckel,

Green, and Hill, 2001.) The survey also included open-ended questions, soliciting comments, examples, reflections, and uncertainties; many of the quotes and anecdotes readers will find come from these replies or from follow-up interviews, as citations will make clear. When referring to this survey's findings, we cite the report that we wrote (with Barbara Cambridge) and distributed at the final gathering of campuses participating in the Carnegie Academy for the Scholarship of Teaching and Learning, October 21, 2009, Bloomington, Indiana (see Ciccone, Huber, Hutchings, and Cambridge, 2009). Because the 2009 report is not readily available, a lightly edited version is included in Appendix A.

At the same time, we have drawn on other surveys and studies where available—seeking, especially, perspectives that might cast a critical eye on the claims of the movement.[12] But most important, we base our understanding of the impact of the scholarship of teaching and learning on the growing literature produced by practitioners themselves. The scholarship of teaching and learning (like other kinds of scholarship) encourages a commitment to going public with what is learned, thus contributing to the teaching commons. As long-time contributors to this teaching commons ourselves, we are grateful to the many colleagues whose work has helped us obtain a fuller picture of the achievements and challenges that the movement has experienced in the past, emergent areas of engagement in the present, and critical issues for the future of the scholarship of teaching and learning.

ENGAGING INSTITUTIONAL AGENDAS

This is, of course, an anxious time in the academy. A recession as severe as the one we have been living through exacerbates and makes even more visible the vulnerability of the academic profession. In the United States, this includes the decline of the tenure-track career, the closing of teaching and learning centers, and heightened competition among institutions of higher education. Though this may seem an inauspicious time to be calling on faculty to focus on anything but survival, we have seen that the scholarship of teaching and learning provides a welcome beacon. As the experience of CASTL Scholars and campuses suggests, it is making teaching itself a more intellectually engaging, collaborative, meaningful, and energizing dimension of academic life. The work is also beginning to make good on its promise to improve the learning experience for students.

The spirit of *Scholarship Reconsidered* remains highly relevant to the academy today. The message that there's an underlying scholarly dimension to different kinds of faculty work is particularly important at a time when many colleges and universities are appointing faculty to teaching-only positions, often not on the tenure-track, increasing the danger of further separating the roles of teaching and research. We believe that the scholarship of teaching and learning is the best way for institutions to keep the interconnections between these intellectual functions alive for *individual* faculty. But, as we argue in this book, it is also possible to advance core *institutional* agendas through the scholarship of teaching and learning. This effort will involve encouraging the scholarship of teaching and learning as an approach to designing learning environments at the classroom, program, and institutional levels, supporting it through updated faculty development initiatives, engaging it in designing and conducting assessment and improvement cycles, and, finally, recognizing and rewarding it for its contributions to the institution's educational mission.

The scholarship of teaching and learning, like the other "new" scholarships of integration and engagement, will always push against the academy's specializing grain. Indeed, as we have noted in this introduction, familiar tensions between theory and practice, and even between research and teaching, are built into the very term (*"scholarship"* of *"teaching and learning"*) and into the work itself. But these are necessary tensions; to collapse one of these terms into the other, or to emphasize one side of the work over the other, would diminish the power and potential for the improvement of practice that comes from their combination.

Over the last two decades, scholars of teaching and learning have accomplished a great deal. They have pioneered approaches to classroom inquiry that provide evidence and inspiration for pedagogical improvement. They have found new ways to make teaching and learning a more collaborative enterprise, strengthening it by working together on common problems. They have helped colleagues see that pedagogy can be intellectually serious work. And, by familiarizing themselves with, drawing on, and contributing to the literature in a wide variety of forms and formats, they have enlarged the teaching commons and made it a livelier place. All these accomplishments are works in progress that continue to develop and grow. It is time now to move the work into a wider range of activities that serve the educational mission, and to weave it more firmly into the fabric of academic life.

Notes

1. This quotation is from *Scholarship Reconsidered: Priorities of the Professoriate* (p. 16).

2. Edgerton's endorsement was printed on an insert to the first edition of *Scholarship Reconsidered*. In *Scholarship Assessed*, the Carnegie Foundation's follow-up report to *Scholarship Reconsidered*, this common ground of scholarship was characterized by six standards, applicable to all four types of faculty work (giving due consideration to their various genres and audiences). These standards (as mentioned later in this chapter) included: clear goals, adequate preparation,

appropriate methods, significant results, effective presentation, and reflective critique (Glassick, Huber, and Maeroff, 1997, pp. 22–36).

3. There is a large literature on the idea of a "commons," of course. We have been influenced by Bollier's concerns (2001, 2003) about what's happening to public assets in an age of "market enclosure," especially in regard to "preserving the academic commons." We have also been influenced by the work of economists and political scientists (Ostrom, 1990, 2005; Palumbo and Scott, 2005) on the collective responsibilities that communities must take to preserve the benefits of resources held for common use, organize social cooperation in particular ways, and develop a set of practices to regularize the resource's use. (On the concept of a "knowledge commons" in particular, see Hess and Ostrom, 2007.)

4. We base this statement on a variety of markers of growth for the field, including what appear to be an increasing number of local (campus-based), regional, and national forums, programs, and initiatives that use the phrase to communicate the nature of their focus or activity. Although there are no adequate national surveys or statistics on the numbers of faculty engaged in the scholarship of teaching and learning, the 2009 Faculty Survey of Student Engagement (FSSE) offers an intriguing hint of what such a survey might show. In a special section, FSSE asked a portion of their respondents—"7,300 faculty members at 50 institutions"—about their "engagement in and perceptions of institutional support for systematically collecting information about the effectiveness of their teaching beyond end-of-term evaluations" (Faculty Survey of Student Engagement, "Other Teaching and Learning Results: Scholarship of Teaching and Learning"). According to the FSSE web site, the proportion of faculty who collected additional course information "quite a bit" or "very much" ranged from 41 percent in the biological sciences to 68 percent in education, with other fields in between: 47 percent in physical sciences, 47 percent in arts and humanities, 49 percent in social sciences, 57 percent in engineering, 58 percent in business. Further, the "findings suggest faculty tend to engage in scholarship of teaching and learning activities despite the fact they feel unsupported by their institution. The trend is consistent across disciplinary fields" ("Other Teaching and Learning Results: Scholarship of Teaching and Learning").

5. A broad agreement among educators and policymakers that too few students finish their degree or certificate programs has fueled a variety of public and private efforts to improve completion numbers and rates (see U.S. General Accounting Office, 2003; Lederman, 2010). Of course, there are complex methodological issues in how such numbers are calculated and interpreted (see Larson, 2010), and how U.S. completion rates compare to those in other wealthy countries (see Adelman, 2009).

6. Actually, the principles and practices in question (inquiry, going public, evidence-based design, and the like) are not new: each has a history in college-level pedagogy. What's new is the emphasis on bringing them together. As two of us and Lee Shulman said in sketching the history of the field some years ago, "a host of related developments gave further momentum and substance to

the work" (Huber, Hutchings, and Shulman, 2005, p. 35). See Chapter 3 for further discussion of the history of the scholarship of teaching and learning in the United States. Of course, in other countries scholars of teaching and learning have drawn on different literatures, institutional developments, and initiatives.

7. For instance, there are large literatures now on learning communities, which are widely believed to offer community college (and other) students a much-needed sense of belonging on campus (see Washington Center for Improving the Quality of Undergraduate Education; Tinto, 1997). There is also much written work on service and community-based learning, the subtleties of which matter greatly to faculty who use them to help students develop their capacities to apply knowledge to real-world problems or to hone the skills of civic participation (Colby, Ehrlich, Beaumont, and Stephens, 2003).

8. This section draws from Huber (2010a).

9. Pat Hutchings was founding director of CASTL in 1998. Mary Huber, who had been a member of Carnegie's *Scholarship Reconsidered* team and a coauthor of *Scholarship Assessed*, joined the CASTL staff at the beginning of 1999. Tony Ciccone directed CASTL's activities at the University of Wisconsin-Milwaukee from 1998 to 2007 (as we will discuss in Chapter 2), and was director of CASTL's Institutional Leadership and Affiliates Program from 2007 to 2009.

10. Over the movement's history, participants have enjoyed (and sometimes wearied of) a bumper crop of definitional discussions, yielding many fine distinctions such as those between excellent teaching, scholarly teaching, and the scholarship of teaching and learning (Hutchings and Shulman, 1999); pedagogical development, scholarship of teaching, and pedagogical research (Gordon, D'Andrea, Gosling, and Stefani, 2003); research, investigations and evaluations, literature reviews, and scholarship of teaching and learning (Prosser, 2008), and more. Many of these terms articulate boundaries that can be useful situationally, depending on one's audience, institution, discipline, or purpose. We know of a number of settings, for instance, where the scholarship of teaching and learning is alive and well but leaders of the work deliberately avoid the term.

11. In early 2001, participants in the first iteration of the CASTL Campus Program (1998–2000) were asked to prepare a "Mapping Progress Report" documenting support for the scholarship of teaching and learning. This comprehensive self-study, completed by 58 of the 190 campuses involved in the program by late 2000, included an examination of the institution's mission, infrastructure, and integration (how the scholarship of teaching and learning was represented in public documents, how it was supported through various offices on campus, and how it connected with other campus priorities and changes in campus culture helped by attention to the work); participation by students, faculty, and campus leaders, and plans for continuity; campus support, including money (internal and external) and time; faculty selection and development; faculty evaluation; collaboration (across and beyond campus); uses of technology; initiatives that didn't work or hadn't worked yet and next steps; promising signs of progress; and opportunities not yet tapped. For further information about the early work of the

CASTL Campus Program, including reflections on the "Mapping Progress" activity, see Cambridge (2004b) and Appendix B in this volume.

12. There are many sources of commentary on the movement to establish a scholarship of teaching and learning. Among the most important are reports by campus leaders at institutions involved in the work, leaders who are often well attuned to tensions and shortcomings. Some of these reports are publicly available. For example, several participants in the first iteration of the CASTL Campus Program contributed essays to *Campus Progress: Supporting the Scholarship of Teaching and Learning* (Cambridge, 2004a), and four of the groups in the CASTL Institutional Leadership and Affiliates Program have published either a book on their work (Werder and Otis, 2010), or a collection of essays in special issues of the electronic journal *Transformative Dialogues* (Kalish and Stockley, 2009; Dewar, Dailey-Hebert, and Moore, 2010; Michael, Case, Danielson, Hill, Lochbaum, McEnery, and Perkins, 2010). Surveys are also a common mode for self-assessment and a site for friendly critique. We have mentioned CASTL's own surveys (Cox, Huber, and Hutchings, 2005; Ciccone, Huber, Hutchings, and Cambridge, 2009), but smaller groups have also done them. See, for example, Dewar and Cohn's analysis of results (2010) of a survey they administered to campus leaders in their CASTL Affiliates Group, and a survey by another CASTL Institutional Leadership Group of faculty who had participated in their summer institutes for scholars new to the work (Michael, Case, Danielson, Hill, Lochbaum, McEnery, and Perkins, 2010). Larger surveys on changes in academic policy and practice, whether of faculty, students, or administrators (that is, the National Survey of Student Engagement, Faculty Survey of Student Engagement, or the survey of provosts on "Encouraging Multiple Forms of Scholarship" reported by O'Meara and Rice, 2005) help place the work in a larger context, serving as a useful brake on exaggerated or overly modest claims.

CHAPTER TWO

Teachers and Learning

There are, in human affairs, two types of problems:
those which are amenable to a technical solution and
those which are not.
—Atul Gawande[1]

Those who follow the scholarship of teaching and learning have witnessed its potential to catalyze change across many aspects of campus life, but at the center of them all is the work that faculty members do in their own classrooms with their own students. What can be said about the impact of the scholarship of teaching and learning on how faculty think about and undertake their instructional roles? Does inquiry into their students' learning actually change how teachers teach? How and what students learn? Under what conditions and in what ways? What role does evidence play in the improvement of teaching—and what kinds of evidence are most powerful? In a profession that prizes autonomy and independence, what pulls people toward community and collaboration, and what part do those play in improvement? What about disciplinary context? Campus culture? These are questions about individual improvement but also, and importantly, about how pedagogical knowledge and practices travel from person to person, site to site, and across the academic profession—and about the effects of those changes on student learning. Understandably, they are questions that matter to those who practice, support, and study the scholarship of teaching and learning, and who want to know where their investments in this work will lead.

Such questions have not, it must be said, been much on higher education's mind for most of its history; the assumption (though often castigated over the years) has been that the surest preparation for teaching was training in the conduct of specialized research and that excellence was largely a matter of personal charisma. One either had the teaching gift, or not. This view has clearly lost traction over the years, and colleges and universities today take greater responsibility for student learning, and support a wide variety of strategies to help faculty take on new challenges as teachers and bring effective new practices into their repertoires. With the White House, the states, funders, policymakers, and leaders in the field calling on higher education to achieve much higher levels of success with much larger numbers of students (Bok, 2006; Lumina Foundation, 2009; Obama, 2009), educational improvement needs all the creativity and energy it can get. Harnessing a diverse set of strategies is assuredly the right idea in a universe as large and varied as higher education: there is no silver bullet, no single best solution.

But after more than two decades, the scholarship of teaching and learning has emerged as an especially promising route to improvement, and one that offers important lessons about the ways and means through which teachers and their teaching can change, and how those changes affect the experience and learning of students. As the movement has grown larger and more multifaceted, we have drawn these lessons from campuses of all kinds, across a wide range of disciplines, in the United States and beyond. This has meant in-depth study of the work of individual scholars and their students but also—especially in the culminating stage of the Carnegie Academy for the Scholarship of Teaching and Learning (CASTL)—an examination of changes in the character and quality of teaching and learning at the program and institutional levels.

WEBS OF CHANGE

The literature about and from scholars of teaching and learning is rich with stories of transformation. Having worked in our various capacities with hundreds of scholars of teaching and learning, the three of us are hard pressed to think of one who does not report significant changes in her or his own practice; it turns out that treating one's classroom as a site for inquiry, asking and exploring questions about students' learning, can prompt a virtual cascade of effects: clearer, higher goals for students, revised course designs, more rigorous assessments, and improved student learning. But the impact of the scholarship of teaching and learning on individual practice is only a part of the picture.

Consider, for example, the following set of developments in which one of us (as the other two watched, learned, and did our best to be helpful) has been an active participant for more than a decade. In 1998, when the Carnegie Foundation and its partner the American Association for Higher Education (AAHE) launched CASTL and invited campuses to join the effort, Anthony Ciccone saw an opportunity for the University of Wisconsin-Milwaukee (UWM), but also one that spoke to his interests as a long-time faculty member in the Department of French, Italian, and Comparative Literature on that campus.

As director of the UWM Center for Instructional and Professional Development, Ciccone focused much of his energy in CASTL's early years on supporting the efforts of colleagues eager to try their hand at this new form of scholarship. But along the way he also carved out time to begin looking more closely at a course he had recently designed and begun to teach in the campus's newly established program of freshman seminars. Tantalizingly entitled "What's So Funny?" (and leavened with a generous dash of Molière), Ciccone's course aimed to develop students' capacities as complex thinkers and to foster habits of inquiry and analysis characteristic of the humanities; his scholarship of teaching and learning question, put simply, was whether and how those goals were being achieved.

Over time, and in collaboration with two colleagues who brought additional analytical skills and theories to the study, Ciccone dug deeply into that question, looking particularly at students' reflective writing as a source of evidence (Ciccone, Meyers, and Waldmann, 2008). Not accidentally, his findings both benefited from and contributed to the growing body of work by UWM "Center Scholars"—faculty given support to undertake scholarship of teaching and learning projects—who were also studying students' learning in courses designed as part of the freshman seminar program (Schroeder, 2007).

Running in parallel with these local developments was a larger effort within the University of Wisconsin System. With UWM as lead campus, the system made a commitment to CASTL and invited all 26 campuses to design scholarship of teaching and learning initiatives connected to their own needs and agendas (developing freshman seminars as at UWM, general education, course and lesson design, and so on). With coordination from the system's Office of Professional and Instructional Development, campuses learned from one another, traded ideas, and brought energy to the larger enterprise (see Ciccone, 2004). Connections were mostly bottom-up, emerging naturally from shared interests and commitments discovered along the way, but more structural connections were also put in place as emerging scholars of teaching and learning took on leadership roles in the Wisconsin Teaching Fellows Program and (for more senior faculty) in the Teaching Scholars Program.[2] Connections beyond the system were made as well, as the University of Wisconsin was selected by CASTL in 2006 as the coordinating institution for five large higher education systems[3] that were seeking ways to promote the scholarship of teaching and learning across their multiple campuses (System Group, 2009).

About the same time, the UW System was also designated the first official state partner in the Association of American Colleges and Universities (AAC&U) Liberal Education and America's Promise (LEAP) campaign to promote the value of a liberal education (2007). As noted in Chapter 1, LEAP promotes a focus on four broad "essential learning outcomes." From AAC&U's point of view, partnerships with campuses, in Wisconsin and elsewhere, were (and continue to be) a way to bring those outcomes to life, to develop concrete strategies for advancing them in actual programs and classrooms. For the UW System, the new initiative was seen as a chance to harness the power of its ongoing work on the scholarship of teaching and learning. In particular, leaders saw an opportunity to "develop the role of [the scholarship of teaching and learning] in measuring achievement of LEAP outcomes to ensure that all students get the education they need and deserve in today's world" (Karoff, Martin, Kornetsky, and Huber, 2008). Three campuses became active sites in this work: UW-Oshkosh, UW-Eau Claire, and UWM.

Returning, then, to UWM, the LEAP learning outcomes have been adopted as a framework for further work on freshman seminars, which now include a special focus on fostering student skills of inquiry and analysis. Insights about student reflection as a support for these skills—from Ciccone's project and that of other Center Scholars—have been influential in shaping next steps as the campus seeks to assess and improve the impact of the first-year experience.

In telling this story, we are aware that others who have been a part of it or observed its unfolding might start it in a different place and trace different paths; we're aware too that the story is unfinished, moving on several levels and in multiple directions. That, in fact, is precisely the point. Institutions participating in CASTL report that the impact of the scholarship of teaching and learning on "the way teachers teach and how they think about teaching" has, thus far and in most settings, been "widespread yet mixed" (Ciccone, Huber, Hutchings, and Cambridge, 2009, p. 18). The intricate web of interconnections captured in Wisconsin's story illustrates one form that such impact can take. Change has been deep and transformative for some people in some settings, more modest in others. In some cases, the scholarship of teaching and learning has been the prime mover behind pedagogical change; in others, it has been a consequence of or a companion to other developments, and an engine for advancing related agendas. Impact is both bottom-up and top-down, but it's also lateral, multilayered, multidirectional—and "widespread." In short, the scholarship of teaching and learning does its work by vitalizing a web of connections in a larger weave and process of change. Understanding the complex dynamics of this process is critical to further institutional integration and impact.

Changing Classrooms

Early on in the design of CASTL, we asked ourselves whether the program should be aimed at encouraging particular teaching approaches; in selecting CASTL Scholars, for instance, should we look for candidates committed to active learning and engaged pedagogies that many see (and mounting evidence supports) as having especially "high impact"? (Kuh, 2008). Our answer was no. The goal of the scholarship of teaching and learning, as we saw it at the Carnegie Foundation, was not to promote any particular teaching approach, but to foster habits of inquiry and exchange through which faculty could explore whatever approaches they chose to employ—including very traditional ones, like lecture and discussion—and how they affect the experience of students. Our principle was to be pedagogically agnostic.

But, in point of fact, most of the faculty who have been drawn to the scholarship of teaching and learning have also been drawn to pedagogies that actively engage students. This was true of applicants to the CASTL Scholars Program (approximately 1,000 of them between 1998 and 2005), and it appears to be true beyond CASTL as well. For instance, the 2009 conference of the International Society for the Scholarship of Teaching and Learning (ISSOTL) was packed with sessions about collaborative learning, undergraduate research, problem- and project-based learning, service learning, and new uses of technology (see International Society for the Scholarship of Teaching and Learning, 2009). For faculty employing these new, or newly discovered, approaches, the scholarship of teaching and learning is a set of practices for examining their instructional decisions and designs, finding out what is and is not working, and documenting what they discover in ways that others can learn from and adapt. The impulse for such work is partly curiosity—wanting to know more about something one cares about—but it is also pragmatic, as these scholars seek to discover whether a new approach is worth the work and energy required for change.

That said, the scholarship of teaching and learning is not simply a crucible for testing classroom innovations and experiments; its practices also *catalyze* change. A Carnegie survey of CASTL Scholars revealed, for instance, that "since becoming involved in the scholarship of teaching and learning," 93 percent changed the design of their courses; 92 percent changed the kinds of assessment they use; and 81 percent documented improvements in their students' learning (Cox, Huber, and Hutchings, 2005, p. 140). A similar survey of participants in an annual national institute modeled on the CASTL program echoes these findings (though somewhat more modestly), with 60 percent of respondents reporting that "they teach differently because of the results of their SOTL work," and over 60 percent saying that they change "both course content and course design" (Michael, Case, Danielson, Hill, Lochbaum, McEnery, and Perkins, 2010, p. 6).

Similar findings emerge when the lens moves from the individual to the institution. In CASTL's 2009 survey of participating campuses, one respondent referred to findings from a local survey showing that 90 percent of faculty reported a shift to more active learning strategies. Looking across institutions, service learning and problem-based learning were among the approaches most frequently mentioned, and many campuses reported that pedagogical changes had been particularly prominent in the science disciplines. A large research university offered an example of how change traveled in that setting: an inquiry into the use of "clickers" by a faculty member in physics led to the adoption of that technology across the department, which spread in turn to several other large courses in science, technology, engineering, and mathematics. In short, the scholarship of teaching and learning seems not only to run hand in hand with changes in teaching, but to push them along more quickly and into more places.

Catalysts for Change

What prompts such changes? Several forces are at work. Certainly one factor is that much of the work of the scholarship of teaching and learning has taken shape in carefully facilitated collaborative groups, some organized by theme, some by discipline, and some encompassing a variety of individual projects where common interests emerge more organically.[4] Individuals may enter such groups with a question that is too broad and inchoate, or their focus may be overly narrow. In either case, the interaction with others serves to sharpen or broaden the design of their study, but it also puts additional teaching practices and resources into the mix. That is, scholars of teaching and learning get ideas and inspiration from one another not simply about how to conduct inquiry, but about *teaching itself*: how they might recast an assignment to make it more diagnostic, what they might read to enrich their thinking, how such-and-such a tool or technique might support their goals for student learning. One of the reasons the scholarship of teaching and learning has taken hold is because it provides an occasion for significant exchange with others who are thinking hard about their students' learning and who come to the work with an appetite for new ideas, innovation, and practices that they can apply in their own setting.

Such exchange is a pleasure for most faculty, we have found, and most of the time a source of inspiration and excitement. But it can be disorienting as well, hearing so many different perspectives and confronting questions one had not, perhaps, thought (or dared) to ask. More than one CASTL Scholar over the years has confessed a need to "rethink everything." For such individuals, the scholarship of teaching and learning may change not only what approaches they bring to the classroom, but often their very notions about learning and its purposes. To use a phrase currently in vogue, the scholarship of teaching and learning can be not only a catalyst for change, but also a "disruptive innovation" that brings about fundamental reconceptualizations of educational means and ends.

This dynamic is especially evident when faculty turn their questioning to what they know best: their disciplines. Indeed, from the early days of the scholarship of teaching and learning, the importance of disciplinary context has been front and center. CASTL's early "sacrificial definition" of the scholarship of teaching and learning pointed to the importance of "methods appropriate to disciplinary epistemologies" (Cambridge, 2004a, p. 2). That is, humanists may choose to examine learning through close reading of student texts, whereas those from the sciences are likely to embrace more quantitative, statistical approaches; a professor of management may create focus groups to get a better sense of the student experience, whereas an experimental psychologist will want to establish control groups. A collection of essays on *Disciplinary Styles in the Scholarship of Teaching and Learning* reported on the many ways that faculty bring their field's "intellectual history, agreements, disputes about subject matter and methods" to their scholarship of teaching and learning (Huber and Morreale, 2002, p. 2). These differences make for rich exchange across fields, it is true, but they also explain why disciplinary communities are particularly fertile environments—environments in which change is not simply about doing something better, but, as U.K. scholar Lewis Elton puts it, "doing better things" (2000).

One of the more advanced developments in this regard involves a group of historians (some 300 of them as this volume goes to press) who have formed an interest group within ISSOTL.[5] The group began, as is often the case, when a few eager souls (mostly from the United States and the United Kingdom, but with growing interest in Sweden as well) found one another and realized a common interest in making the teaching and learning of history a more informed, systematic, professional practice. As is also perhaps typical in a new field of endeavor, a seminal document helped to build momentum. David Pace, a senior member of the history department at Indiana University Bloomington, published what became a much-circulated essay in the flagship journal of his field, *The American Historical Review*. With the image of the "amateur in the operating room" as foil, Pace argues that historians should bring the same levels of expertise and professionalism to their teaching that they bring to research, urging his colleagues to cultivate "a scholarship of teaching and learning history" (2004, p. 1175).

At the core of Pace's argument is the observation that teaching is a discipline-specific practice. A discipline such as history, he says, "represents a unique epistemological and methodological community, whose rules and procedures must be fully understood and made explicit before we can generate rigorous knowledge about teaching and learning in our field" (2004, p. 1175). This, then, is the driving principle for these scholars of teaching and learning history: working out the core intellectual practices that students need to succeed in college history courses, being much more explicit about those practices, and developing the pedagogies to foster them in novice learners. As members of this group will testify, the distance between this new vision of pedagogical practice and the traditional coverage model that has dominated the discipline can be vast.

History has not been alone in such rethinking. Pace's own interest took shape through his participation in the Indiana University Faculty Learning

Community—an annual two-week gathering of faculty from across the disciplines to practice new teaching strategies and serve as students for each other. With a focus on the mental operations required of students in different disciplines, the group developed a model it called "Decoding the Disciplines," a seven-step protocol that begins with the identification of a disciplinary "learning bottleneck," cycles through to questions about the design and effectiveness of approaches for breaking through that bottleneck, and—in the going-public spirit of the scholarship of teaching and learning—sharing what is learned with others who can build on it (Pace and Middendorf, 2004).

This work is harder than it may sound. Disciplinary practices—ways of reading, thinking, questioning, investigating—can become the water one swims in: invisible, just assumed, and a pretty darn nice temperature most days of the week. Dredging up one's expert practices and translating them for the learning of novices can be a painstaking process. Efforts like decoding the disciplines (and the related work around signature pedagogies mentioned in Chapter 1) illustrate the power of the scholarship of teaching and learning to bring new approaches to the classroom, but also to prompt fundamentally different thinking about learning itself.

AN APPETITE FOR (RICHER) EVIDENCE

The move to engage students with a different conception of learning raises a whole host of questions: What does it mean to understand this discipline, this interdiscipline, this field, this critical issue? What practices characterize the thinking of experts in this arena? What does it mean to think like a historian, sociologist, biologist, or engineer? What should students be expected to know and be able to do as learners in these fields? These are largely questions of conception and vision about the place of the field in the larger educational and social landscape. But progress in answering them depends on information—on drilling down into the student experience to understand its deeper dynamics. How do students actually develop new modes of thinking? Where do they get stuck? Are there stages of development? Not surprisingly, then, when asked about the impact of the scholarship of teaching and learning on teachers and learning, many campuses responding to the 2009 CASTL Survey pointed to what one described as a growing "hunger" on the part of faculty for "more information about how their students are doing" (Ciccone, Huber, Hutchings, and Cambridge, 2009, p. 6).

Clearly, this interest in evidence is part and parcel of the larger "turn toward learning" noted in Chapter 1. In many higher education settings, it has become a kind of anathema to talk about teaching without invoking evidence of learning; and the assessment movement has formalized this impulse, calling on programs and institutions to identify their contributions to student learning outcomes. In addition, of course, individual faculty members routinely generate and examine evidence of learning in the process of assignment design, grading, and giving their students feedback to guide subsequent efforts.

What the scholarship of teaching and learning has added to the mix is an appetite for types of evidence and methods of inquiry that have not tradition-ally had a place in the practice of teachers. This impulse comes in response to a recognition by many faculty making their way into the scholarship of teaching and learning that, although they are by most measures accomplished, excellent teachers, sought out by students and recognized by colleagues, their under-standing of student learning and its development feels vexingly incomplete.[6] For example, in describing the impetus for the scholarship of teaching and learning (that is, the movement in general, but also his own particular project), Georgetown University professor of English Randy Bass recalls his early—and not altogether successful—efforts to teach with new media:

> I found myself asking questions about student learning I had never asked before. For a decade I had had good success as a teacher: positive feedback, strong evaluations, evidence (anecdotal and otherwise) that students learned something in my courses. Yet, I now realized I knew very little about *why* certain students did better than others. Or, more generally, I knew very little about *how* students came to know the material I was teaching. Ever since graduate school I had taught mostly the way I had been taught, and tended to replicate the pedagogies that worked best—quite frankly—on *me* (or slight variations of me). Now that I was trying to change my teaching radically, those *naturalized* teaching methods and the assumptions behind them were exposed to be without any clear scaffolding or support by the evidence of learning, however sound or useful some of the approaches were [1999, "Section Two: A Problem I Could Live With"].

Bass is not alone in his puzzlement. Anthony Ciccone's project on student reflection, described earlier in this chapter, emerged in part from his realization that, when it came to the kind of complex thinking he wanted from students, he had more questions than answers: "I saw it, knew I encouraged it, and knew that the assignments aimed to elicit it, but I had only a vague idea of what it looked like and how it developed." He had, he says, "little understanding of the trajectory of such changes, in particular of the stages students passed through" (2008, p. 311). If learning can be likened to an iceberg, with only a portion visible above the water, the scholarship of teaching and learning challenges teachers to get at what's beneath the surface, unseen, and only vaguely understood. As such, it is work that requires (in addition to courage) not only *more* evidence of learning, but different *kinds*.

For example, there is a now a growing community of faculty, from a range of disciplines, employing "think alouds"—a protocol in which learners are asked to talk through their thought process while undertaking an intellectual task (reading a complex text, for instance, or solving a math problem). Sitting, if you will, at the far end of qualitative methods, think alouds are challenging. The records they produce are notoriously thick description, which may feel off-putting or daunting to those in fields that are more quantitative. Analyzing such data and translating them into meaningful new understandings can look like a full-time job. "I really didn't want to use them," said Loretta Brancaccio-Taras, a biologist at Kingsborough Community College whose scholarship of teaching and learning focused on the impact of writing on students' understanding of disciplinary concepts. But, she says (after learning about the method from a microbiologist who used them), "I saw what they could do for me, and I realized I had to" (May 24, 2010).

Think alouds were developed decades ago by cognitive psychologists, but the spark that ignited much of the interest in them within the scholarship of teaching and learning community was the work of Sam Wineburg, a historian who used the method to get at differences between how experts and novices read historical documents (2001), and an influential presence in the Scholarship of Teaching and Learning in History group described above. Today, think alouds show up in inquiry projects across a wide spectrum of disciplines (sometimes on web-based video) including biology (Brancaccio-Taras, 2010), history (Calder, 2006), and math (Sandefur, 2007; Stigler, Givven, and Thompson, 2009; Cho and Davis, 2008).[7]

Think alouds offer a particularly interesting, high-end instance of new methods for making student learning visible. But there are many other possibilities in the mix. Interviews and focus groups with students have given scholars of teaching and learning new access to learners' thinking and experience, as they did for Dennis Jacobs, a professor of chemistry at the University of Notre Dame, who used them to probe more concretely what he learned by tracking large-scale patterns of student success in a new model of the department's introductory course (2000). Some scholars of teaching and learning have employed sophisticated methods of discourse analysis for coding student work (Feito, 2007); others have brought new lenses and theoretical frameworks to their students' work by inviting colleagues (and sometimes students) to participate in the analysis of student writing, projects, or portfolios (Feito and Donahue, 2008; Ciccone, Meyers, and Waldmann, 2008; Drummond and Owens, 2010). And as teaching and learning have moved into online digital spaces, they leave traces (patterns of participation, records of online exchange, and so forth) that were not available in the past, making learning visible in ways it has not been, and adding yet more evidentiary grist for the mill. An important lesson here is that although most scholars of teaching and learning initially use methods that reflect the values and epistemologies of their field, working with colleagues in other areas has allowed them to learn about and try out less familiar methods as well; this is not always easy or comfortable, but the result, over time, is an expanded repertoire of approaches increasingly employed by a growing number of faculty from a full range of fields. On campuses where this kind of exchange and cross-fertilization is cultivated, the scholarship of teaching and learning can be a source of significant change.

The Turn Toward Pedagogy

But where things get really interesting is when these methods move out of the realm of a scholarship of teaching and learning "project" and begin to reshape pedagogy itself. The potential of this shift from inquiry to instruction—or perhaps, more accurately, the blurring of lines between them—is huge, as Bass and Bernstein describe: "A reciprocal effect often exists between the scholarship of teaching and learning and pedagogies designed to elicit 'data' on learning. These pedagogies often help students themselves reflect on and critique their own learning. In fact, one of the most important effects of the scholarship of teaching and learning on professional practice may be to lead faculty to consider whether additional teaching strategies and modes of assessment . . . might make student learning more accessible (or visible) to both students and faculty" (2005, p. 37). In this spirit, a think aloud may be used with a small set of students as part of a scholarship of teaching and learning project, but inviting *all* students to "talk through" their solutions to a math problem or their reading of a historical document is a formula for building powerful metacognitive and processing skills.

Student portfolios, similarly, can be a vehicle for organizing and presenting evidence, but they have spread far and wide today because of their power to help students become more intentional about their own learning and its meaning: "I have had many amazing experiences," said a third-year student at the University of Michigan whose program included portfolios, "but I didn't really know what they meant or how they all fit together. . . . Now, I see patterns and themes in the work I have been doing, how things fit together. The work I've been doing actually makes sense" (quoted in Miller and Morgaine, 2009, p. 9). Reflective writing (like this student had been asked to do as part of her portfolio), too, can provide data for a scholarship of teaching and learning project, but it can also be a tool for making students more self-aware of the learning process, and more able to monitor their own progress. Such changes can be transformational, for both students and teachers.

SUPPLY AND DEMAND

But do these changes in teaching and learning migrate in any numbers from setting to setting? Do they extend beyond a small handful of courageous faculty willing to rethink what they do? Issues of method and theory have often been invoked as keys to the impact of the scholarship of teaching and learning, and they are clearly important (see Hutchings, 2000; Nelson, 2003; McKinney, 2007a). But what has also become clear along the way is that "good evidence" is not sufficient to prompt changes and improvements in teaching practice. Faculty are, it's true, unlikely to embrace a new approach unless they are persuaded it can make a difference, but what is persuasive is very much in the eye of the beholder (often as seen through the lens of his or her discipline), and, for that matter, being persuaded does not necessarily imply a readiness to change.[8] Indeed, even as higher education has followed K–12 toward policies that privilege "scientifically based" teaching methods, and although calls for evidence are everywhere, it has become increasingly clear that the lines between data and improvement are far from straight. Data can be contradictory, disappointing, or just plain daunting (Carnegie Foundation, 2008; Bond, 2009). And just "having the data" does not ensure that what is known is constructively used.[9]

In the face of these realities, what the scholarship of teaching and learning has taught us is that whether or not pedagogical innovations travel is best understood as a function of their "social life," which is to say the networks of common interest, practice, and exchange in which new ideas (and, yes, evidence) take hold (Huber, 2009).

Historically, teaching has been short on such networks. Indeed, the need to overturn the private, often isolated nature of teaching has been a central plank in the scholarship of teaching and learning platform, with its injunction to "make teaching community property" (Shulman, 1993) and to build mechanisms for exchange and knowledge building as other professional fields have done. And the good news is that this has clearly been an area of significant impact over the last decade, as the teaching commons has gotten bigger, richer, and more diverse (Huber and Hutchings, 2005).

For one thing, faculty committed to making their scholarly work as teachers available for others to review and build on have a host of attractive choices today. Starting with the more traditional universe of publication, there are many more pedagogical journals, essay collections, and books in circulation. A number of scholarly and professional societies have created new, self-standing journals on the scholarship of teaching and learning in their field, designated sections of existing journals for such work, or hosted special issues on the scholarship of teaching and learning. *The International Journal of the Scholarship of Teaching and Learning* has recently celebrated its fifth anniversary, and, as its name suggests, its authors and audience (and its editorial board) reach far beyond the United States. More recently, Indiana University Press established a scholarship of teaching and learning series, and commercial presses (including Jossey-Bass, Stylus, and others) are working to build their scholarship of teaching and learning lists, even as individual campuses establish local journals for more local circulation. In short, though we know of no sure way to quantify the growth of published (and mostly peer-reviewed) pedagogical scholarship over the last decade, it's clear that the scholarship of teaching and learning's going-public mantra has fueled significant growth on the supply side of teaching improvement.

Publications in this narrower sense are only part of the mix, though. Thanks to the Peer Review of Teaching Project (Bernstein, Burnett, Goodburn, and Savory, 2006), faculty from scores of institutions have now created and "published" electronic course portfolios documenting their inquiry into student learning. Their efforts are posted on the project's web site[10] and can be consulted by anyone anywhere in the world with Internet access. In a similar spirit, MERLOT—Multimedia Educational Resource for Learning and Online Teaching—is a digital repository and community that invites members (more than 80,000 of them) to submit learning materials, create "a personal collection," and share online expertise (MERLOT, "Faculty Development: Personal Collections"); the collection has been expanded to include resources created through a user-friendly web-authoring service originally designed and made freely available by the Carnegie Foundation. Both MERLOT and the Peer Review of Teaching Project have, in fact, been part of a group of institutions and organizations working under CASTL's banner to "expand the SoTL Commons" (Robinson, Savory, Poole, Carey, and Bernstein, 2010). On a more modest level, but just as important in catalyzing work on campus, some institutions have now developed local repositories and online communities, working, for instance, through the library or teaching center. Happily, there are also many face-to-face opportunities for sharing one's work, as campus, regional, national, and international conferences, workshops, and institutes have been established.

On the Demand Side

With such growth on the "supply side" comes a question about demand. "Can the scholarship of teaching and learning really travel, in the sense of not only leaving home (through conversation, presentation, or publication) but also of arriving at some destination (through being heard, read, interpreted, used, by someone else)?" (Huber, 2009, p. 1). Can its practices become part of the fabric of the institution in ways that make a difference in the classroom and other settings where faculty undertake the scholarly work of teaching? Our answer is that it can—and does. Certainly there is a chicken-and-egg dynamic at work here, as more and better supply has fed the demand for these resources. Often such connections are happy accidents of surfing the Web, or of happening upon a conference session that turns out to be richly relevant to one's own scholarship of teaching and learning. But sturdier, more purposeful connections are on the rise as well, as those who get involved in such work actively seek out networks that can support and enrich their work.

Some of the most promising examples in this regard are the increasing number of disciplinary communities forming around pedagogical interests. These groups share research questions, employ similar tools and routines (for instance, the seven-step "decoding the disciplines" protocol mentioned earlier), and find one another in various outlets and venues. Examples include both the ISSOTL historians and a companion group representing a broader set of humanities disciplines that have created mechanisms (for instance, membership enrollment and rosters, bylaws, research agendas, white papers, special conferences, and the like) that serve as an infrastructure for their work. As these groups evolve and others join them, they are not only important suppliers of the teaching commons, but active consumers and users—"communities of practice," if you will, rich social networks in which new ideas grow and new practices emerge (Wenger, 1998; Brown and Duguid, 2000).[11]

Other kinds of interests, cutting across disciplines, have spawned powerful networks for improvement as well. As part of CASTL, a number of institutions coordinated by Oxford College of Emory University came together to explore their interest in the emotional and affective components of learning. Unlike, say, the historians, who as members of a discipline already shared many practices and had, at least in some cases, existing professional and personal connections, the Cognitive Affective Learning Group (as they called themselves) was obliged to start pretty much from scratch. Members came from diverse settings, did not for the most part have pre-existing relationships, and saw themselves as marching into mostly unmapped territory; even finding useful language for their interests was a challenge; and, of course, all of them had day jobs. "When we first began our work on cognitive affective learning . . . , we did so with some embarrassment or at best anxiety," writes Patti Owen-Smith, one of the group's leaders. "Would we be seen as the 'weakest' cluster [in the CASTL Campus Program], the one that lacked rigor . . . ?" (Cognitive Affective Group, 2009, p. 1). On the contrary: over time, the group developed tasks and processes that defined their work together. Based on a shared commitment to understanding the connections between the cognitive and affective elements of learning, and to developing educational theories and practices that promote such connections, each institution chose its own emphasis relative to its own particular campus needs. But each also connected to the other members of the group, which met face-to-face whenever possible, interacted online, created a journal, and undertook several ambitious collaborative writing projects.

This last point is, we believe, worth highlighting: certainly writing contributes to the "supply side" of the equation we are laying out here, but as anyone who has taken on such a project knows, nothing fuels demand more vigorously than preparing one's work for an audience. The writing process not only focuses one's attention on one's own work but has a marvelous way of lighting up the work of others, bringing what might otherwise go unnoticed into one's sphere of interest and analysis. This is presumably why writing has such a privileged position in the world of scholarship[12]—and why so many professors see writing as a key ingredient in student learning.

THE LEARNING QUESTION

The changing dynamics of supply and demand make this a rich time for pedagogical innovation and travel. As we have argued throughout this chapter, the scholarship of teaching and learning is now shaping the way teachers teach (and think about their teaching) in a multitude of ways—some modest, some ground-shifting. But a focus on teaching clearly begs another question, and it is one that we hear more and more often—from those who undertake such work, from campus leaders who support it, and from those who think about higher education policy in a broader sense: Does the scholarship of teaching and learning improve outcomes for students? The answer is yes. But it is worth thinking hard about what is entailed in answering this question.

For starters it should be said that there are countless examples of scholarship of teaching and learning projects that focus directly and explicitly on improvements in learning—and on documenting those improvements. We think of the longitudinal study by Dennis Jacobs, the University of Notre Dame chemist mentioned earlier, who designed an alternative version of introductory chemistry for at-risk students—and whose assessments showed that students in that section persisted through and did better in subsequent science courses than peers in the regular lecture section (2000, 2004). We think of the program-level studies by sociology professor Kathleen McKinney of majors in her discipline at Illinois State University—the strategies they use and believe effective in learning the field, along with the different pathways they travel from being less to more successful in the major, from surface to deep learning, and from novice to expert learners (2007b). And we think of the course-level study by Michael Smith, a historian at Ithaca College, who found that a service-learning research partnership on local environmental history helped students develop a stronger sense of themselves as ecological citizens (2010).

One campus responding to the 2009 CASTL Survey noted that faculty selected as scholarship of teaching and learning fellows "must document impact on learning," and this expectation is becoming more common. Indeed, deepening and advancing student learning can fairly be said to be *the* Project (with a capital P) of the scholarship of teaching and learning. As noted earlier, faculty self-reports reinforce this observation, with 81 percent of respondents to a survey of CASTL Scholars reporting that they had "documented improvements in [their] students' learning" (Cox, Huber, and Hutchings, 2005, p. 140).

Asking whether a campus commitment to the scholarship of teaching and learning improves student learning in a more general way (beyond individual projects, that is) is trickier. More than a third of campuses in the final phase of the CASTL program told us that such work had a "widespread but mixed" effect on the ways faculty approach teaching, and about a quarter of reporting campuses said the work has had "deep impact" on the student learning experience. Many also say that the scholarship of teaching and learning has contributed to other educational agendas and initiatives, including pedagogical innovation, general education reform, and the first-year experience (Ciccone, Huber, Hutchings, and Cambridge, 2009).

But more telling than numbers and lists is the way respondents describe the travel and ramifications of these changes. That is, while pointing out that lines of cause and effect between the doing of the scholarship of teaching and learning and the improvement of student learning are not immediate and direct, many institutions point to more web-like, multidirectional, cascading connections. "It certainly makes teachers more attuned to the question of what and how their students are learning," one campus observes. Another says, "The scholarship of teaching and learning surely is helpful if only because it prompts us to consider what we do and don't know. Intentionally and systematically asking about student learning is likely to lead to increased student learning." Indeed, as illustrated by the work at Indiana University on decoding the disciplines, faculty engaged in such efforts often end up rethinking goals and setting more ambitious expectations for student learning (Cox, Huber, and Hutchings, 2005).

On many campuses, then, the scholarship of teaching and learning in a more narrow sense has become an engine for wider engagement with and thoughtfulness about how to facilitate and deepen learning. New conversations are started, and those under way take more informed directions. New teaching practices begin to migrate through the culture and new learning outcomes begin to appear. And though many campuses have wanted to distinguish between excellent teaching (or scholarly teaching) and the scholarship of teaching and learning (Hutchings and Shulman, 1999), the fact that the latter can catalyze the former is, we believe, a crucial part of the answer to the "learning question."

Students' own voices are surely relevant here as well. A 2009 survey of member institutions by the Association of American Colleges and Universities reveals that only two-fifths of campuses believe that their students understand campus goals for their learning (p. 5). But that number is likely to shift upward as campuses find active roles for students in the scholarship of teaching and learning. Many have done so, inviting students into emerging communities of practice, seeing roles for them not as objects of study, but as co-inquirers, collaborators, and partners in formulating questions, generating and analyzing data, making sense of findings, and lobbying for change (Werder and Otis, 2010). At Elon University, for instance, students have been influential partners in course design (Delpish, Darby, Holmes, Knight-McKenna, Mihans, King, and Felten, 2010). At Western Washington University, students join faculty members and staff in conversations about educational issues that shape teaching and learning on that campus (Werder, Ware, Thomas, and Skogsberg, 2010). And graduate students were forceful voices in departmental self-studies undertaken as part of the Carnegie Foundation's Initiative on the Doctorate (Walker, Golde, Jones, Bueschel, and Hutchings, 2008).

For many faculty today the heart of the scholarship of teaching and learning is listening much more closely to students, creating occasions in which they can talk about their own learning, and encouraging them to be a force in stimulating the demand side of change. Where this has happened, students have not only made important contributions; they have had valuable experiences that support their learning, developing new language for talking about learning, broadening their repertoire of learning strategies, and reflecting on the goals and purposes of their education.

A rich compendium of undergraduates' reflections can be found in the edited volume *Engaging Student Voices in the Study of Teaching and Learning* (Werder and Otis, 2010), which features collaborative work among faculty and students on campuses in one of the CASTL Institutional Leadership Program theme groups. For example, at North Seattle Community College, one participant in a think-aloud study in a chemistry course said: "Watching [a videocapture of the think aloud] gave me an opportunity to be an observer of my own learning process. I was able to see how I took risks by saying that I was confused or making an assumption that later appeared to be inaccurate. I like the ability to brainstorm with others. I feel this experience has 'kicked it up a notch' in regard to my learning process . . . [and] helped me exceptionally grasp the concepts in this chapter" (Drummond and Owens, 2010, p. 178). Another student, Derek Herrmann, who served as an undergraduate teaching assistant at Illinois State University, commented on his experience in helping the instructor examine the development of learner autonomy among psychology majors: "Working on this grant has helped me to really think about my learning as a student and also my teaching to undergraduate students; it has only reinforced my desire to go to graduate school and to be a professor to help students learn—and hopefully to learn better" (McKinney, Jarvis, Creasey, and Herrmann, 2010, p. 89).

Clearly, the "learning question" is a critical one, and it is one that many scholarship of teaching and learning activists are struggling to address in thoughtful and responsible ways. "We want help here," one leader noted in the 2009 CASTL Survey. "We NEED help." In truth, higher education has been casual, at best, about asking whether prevailing pedagogical practices and improvement efforts advance learning. That is now changing, with the call to bring more students to higher levels of learning, and to assess and be accountable for student outcomes (our topic in Chapter 4). And though the scholarship of teaching and learning is not, all by itself, "the answer" to this growing imperative, it is a step in the right direction, providing a much-needed prompt to think more carefully about how "the learning question" can be addressed, what evidence will count, and what expectations are reasonable—in the short run and over the longer term as the demands on higher education become ever more pressing. As such, it should be of interest not only to those within academe but to policymakers and other external stakeholders who care about the future of higher education.

GETTING BETTER

In Chapter 1 we refer to the work of Atul Gawande, surgeon and author, familiar to many from his writing in the pages of *The New Yorker* about medicine and the health care system. Colleges are not hospitals, of course, and students are not patients; parallels between the health care system and education have their limitations. But many of Gawande's insights carry resonance for education, as is true for us in the epigraph to this chapter: like health care, teaching and learning do not lend themselves to a solely "technical solution." The scholarship of teaching and learning may tell us that problem-based learning is especially powerful, or that reflective writing can strengthen students' capacities for making connections in ways that really matter. It may provide compelling evidence that the use of clickers can raise students' achievement in an introductory physics course or show how to open up a bottleneck in students' understanding of American history. These are important, useful findings, and they have made their way into classrooms in significant ways. But they are not *the* solution.

"Solution" is in fact the wrong image for what is needed. Teaching is a huge profession, undertaken in staggeringly different settings. But what has been true across the board is that, as a profession, teaching has had pitifully few mechanisms to improve itself.[13] What's needed is a set of practices that have traditionally been missing, and that the scholarship of teaching and learning is now bringing much more widely into play: habits of inquiry, analysis, exchange, and knowledge building that can be harnessed to campus agendas for improvement and woven into the institutional fabric in ways that make a difference for teachers and learning. This kind of integration and impact do not take shape overnight. As we have tried to show in this chapter, promising pedagogical practices often move in unpredictable, small-scale ways; for better or worse, there is no "policy" that will suddenly transform teaching practice across the campus. But with more and more faculty turning their attention to the scholarship of teaching and learning—as investigators, collaborators, consumers, critics, and advocates of this work—the potential for widespread impact is on the rise.

Notes

1. The epigraph comes from an article by surgeon and author Atul Gawande, writing in *The New Yorker* about parallels between health care and the USDA agricultural extension system, and finding in the latter an intriguing model for evidence-based improvement (2009, p. 3). Gawande's piece drew some criticism from those who found the parallel unpersuasive, and of course education differs from health care in many ways. Nevertheless, his account of agricultural extension suggests tantalizing similarities to education, as the final section of this chapter suggests.

2. Consider the experience of Nancy Chick, a faculty member in English on the University of Wisconsin-Barron County campus. Since beginning her career in the UW System, she has risen in the ranks from the Wisconsin Teaching Fellows Program (a year-long scholarship of teaching and learning experience for pretenure faculty), to Wisconsin Teaching Scholar (the posttenure-track in the same program), and now codirects the entire UW System Wisconsin Teaching Fellows and Scholars program.

3. The five systems are City University of New York, Miami Dade College, the University of Colorado System, University of North Carolina System, and (acting as CASTL's "coordinating institution") the University of Wisconsin System. To be clear, the UW System was itself a CASTL Leadership Cluster during phase two of the Campus Program (2002–2005). Then, in phase three, the Institutional Leadership Program (2006–2009), it took on the coordinating role for the larger set of systems listed here.

4. CASTL employed this cohort-based, collaborative model in its CASTL Scholars Program. Individuals were selected with possible overlapping themes in view, be it by discipline or by educational purpose (for instance, one cohort focused on integrative learning). They were then organized in small groups (six to eight people each), which stayed together throughout a year of work and three structured residencies at the Carnegie Foundation facilitated by staff and by members of previous cohorts. Many campus fellowship programs have employed a similar model. See Appendix B for more information about the CASTL Scholars Program.

5. The International Society for the Scholarship of Teaching and Learning in History (HistorySOTL, see http://www.indiana.edu/~histsotl/blog) is technically an "External Affiliate" of ISSOTL, which also invites "Interest Groups." The latter include: a group focused on "Students as Co-Inquirers" in the scholarship of teaching and learning; a sociology group; a geography, earth, or environmental sciences group; a group focused on problem-based learning; and several other topic-based networks (ISSOTL, "Quick Links: Internal Interest Groups & External Affiliates").

6. In 1998, Carnegie Foundation Senior Scholar Tom Hatch interviewed individuals selected as CASTL Scholars. His questions—and their answers—were far-ranging, but many of these scholars of teaching and learning began to reflect on how little they actually understood about their students' learning, how unsure they were of what they did know, how many questions they had. Their uncertainties then fueled their classroom inquiry.

7. Think alouds were used by several campuses participating in a Carnegie Foundation project on developmental math and English in community colleges in order to explore aspects of student thinking that were otherwise invisible. One site referenced here (Cho and Davis, 2008) documents work at Pasadena City College, where developmental math students were videotaped working through a mathematics word problem. Viewers can see one student's full think aloud, along with faculty voiceover commentary. The site is part of the Carnegie Foundation's Windows on Learning collection, created for the 2005–2008 "Strengthening Pre-collegiate Education in Community Colleges" initiative (Carnegie Foundation, "Windows on Learning").

8. Not surprisingly, faculty in STEM fields (science, technology, engineering, and mathematics) have a particularly keen appetite for data, often demanding to "see the numbers" before entertaining the prospect of a change in their teaching practice. Yet even in the STEM community data are insufficient. Reporting on an initiative to transform science education at the University of Colorado and at the University of British Columbia, Nobel Prize winner in physics (and U.S. Professor of the Year) Carl Wieman and his colleagues observe that although "research and data on student learning are important and useful, they were seldom compelling enough by themselves to change faculty members' pedagogy, particularly when that change conflicted with their beliefs about teaching and learning" (Wieman, Perkins, and Gilbert, 2010, p. 13). At the same time (and reinforcing the value of the scholarship of teaching and learning), they note that science faculty are "more convinced by research and data on student learning from their own courses" than from other sources, either within or, especially, beyond their discipline (p. 13).

9. The challenge of using data for improvement is the focus of a research program announced by The Spencer Foundation in 2009. The intent is to question "the assumption that the simple presence of data invariably leads to improved outcomes and performance, and that those who are presented information under data-driven improvement schemes will know how best to make sense of it and transform their practice" (Spencer Foundation, "Strategic Initiatives: Data Use and Educational Improvement").

10. See http://www.courseportfolio.org.

11. Creating such communities was a central feature of the Carnegie Foundation's strategy in CASTL, as we assisted campuses to affiliate with one another in clusters and theme groups to pursue common interests and needs. Tellingly, perhaps, one of the most long-standing of these groups calls itself COPPER: Communities of Practice Pooling Educational Resources. As the name implies, member campuses traded resources around shared interests as they evolved, but

along the way the group also helped bring the idea of communities of practice to the larger scholarship of teaching and learning movement.

12. Published studies by scholars of teaching and learning can be found in field-specific journals like *Teaching Sociology*, *Teaching Psychology*, or *Arts and Humanities in Higher Education*, as well as in journals that welcome submissions across the disciplinary spectrum: *IJ-SOTL* (the *International Journal for the Scholarship of Teaching and Learning*), *JoSoTL* (*Journal of the Scholarship of Teaching and Learning*), *MountainRise*, and *Transformative Dialogues*. There are also a growing number of edited volumes, with essays by scholars of teaching and learning writing on themes of shared interest, for example, *Citizenship Across the Curriculum* (Smith, Nowacek, and Bernstein, 2010), and one in press on *Connected Science: Strategies for Integrative Learning in College* (Ferrett and Geelan, forthcoming).

13. Carnegie Foundation President Tony Bryk, writing with education scholar Louis Gomez, notes, "In fields such as medicine and engineering, spending for research amounts to about 5 to 15 percent of total expenditures, with about 20 percent of R&D expenditures going to basic research and about 80 percent to design and systematic development. In contrast, even though education is a 500 billion dollar a year enterprise, we spend well less than a billion dollars a year on educational R&D, or less than a quarter of one percent of the overall education budget" (2008, p. 1). The context in question is K–12 education, but it's safe to say that higher education's investment in educational improvement is similarly meager.

CHAPTER THREE

The Scholarship of Teaching and Learning, Professional Growth, and Faculty Development

[The] new narrative for faculty ... assumes that their
primary work, personally and professionally, is to
learn and grow.
—KerryAnn O'Meara, Aimee LaPointe Terosky, and
Anna Neumann[1]

T his book maintains that the scholarship of teaching and learning has been, and will continue to be, a transformative concept in higher education. But the work, which begins in the individual's classroom and arises from a desire to know more about one's own practice, realizes a significant part of its impact *beyond* the physical and personal spaces where it starts. The contexts where this impact is felt—individual classrooms, programs, pedagogies, discussions of student learning outcomes and institutional goals—often overlap, but may also give rise to a number of tensions. From the institutional perspective, on the one hand, the work that individuals undertake to improve their own teaching and their students' learning should also advance campus agendas and priorities; resources are finite, and administrators at all levels need to make choices about what to support. Individuals, on the other hand, may care most about classroom-based results, and may be less interested in describing the impact of their work in the broader terms of institutional advancement.

This tension can be productive, however, when each group is encouraged to speak the other's dialect of their common language—advancing learning.[2] In subsequent chapters, we examine how engagement with the scholarship of teaching and learning has affected areas where individual and institutional interests have not always been well aligned—assessment and the evaluation of teaching. In this chapter, we examine the role that the principles and practices of the scholarship of teaching and learning can play in helping advance and transform an important area where institutional and individual purposes are more clearly shared—professional growth and faculty development.

Professional growth refers to the full range of actions that individuals might take, on their own or with the support of their institutions, disciplinary societies, and so forth, in the interest of enhancing their professional capabilities. Much of the institutional support for this work is provided through *faculty development* or *teaching centers*, and that is the focus of this chapter. The terms *faculty development* and *professional development* are used interchangeably herein to refer to the opportunities provided to faculty by their institutions and centers. We acknowledge, however, that faculty increasingly find opportunities for professional growth on campus committees or in working groups formed to study particular issues—for example, teaching assistant development, retention, assessment—and are often sent as members of institutional teams to national convenings. We note also that centers play an important role in facilitating the work of these groups. Peter Felten and others have described this expanded role as *educational development,* "the profession dedicated to helping colleges and universities function effectively as teaching and learning communities," and suggest that it includes "all the areas for which we often name it: faculty development; TA development; instructional, academic, and organizational development" (Felten, Kalish, Pingree, and Plank, 2007, pp. 93–94).

Within this context, the scholarship of teaching and learning, professional growth, and faculty development as provided within and by institutions are compatible and converging priorities. We saw this among the participants in the Institutional Leadership and Affiliates Program of the Carnegie Academy for the Scholarship of Teaching and Learning (CASTL), where, in response to Carnegie's 2009 CASTL Survey, over 80 percent said that faculty development has been modestly or significantly affected, for the better, of course, by the scholarship of teaching and learning. One respondent noted that a scholarship of teaching and learning initiative led his institution to establish a faculty development workshop each term "for the purpose of sharing and discussing faculty research at the classroom level across our multi-campus system." In other places, engagement with the work's practices and principles has been more organic; for example, one teaching and learning center has incorporated its concepts into the content of workshops and communications with faculty. One of the CASTL Institutional Leadership groups even focused on using the work's principles and practices to create an "integrative structure for faculty development programs and services" (see Appendix B).

Deciding to support faculty who approach teaching "as challenging, intellectual work ... that poses interesting, consequential questions" (Huber and Hutchings, 2005, p. ix) benefits both the individual and the institution. With professional growth and faculty development, however, tension may arise between what the individual needs to grow as a scholarly teacher, and the more pragmatic needs of the institution to frame this emerging knowledge so that it can be put to work on "larger" issues.[3] Campus teaching and learning centers have often been the places where these tensions between individual and institutional needs play out. As we will argue, engagement with the scholarship of teaching and learning has helped mitigate the problem by connecting the faculty's natural interest in inquiry and improvement with the institution's ongoing need for better information about its practices and results. But the issues surrounding professional growth and faculty development are much broader. They lie in conflicting philosophies of professional growth itself, specifically in the underlying differences as to why development is necessary, where its impetus comes from, and how (or even *if*) support for it should be provided. It is important to look at these broader differences in order to understand the role of the scholarship of teaching and learning in a larger conversation that is transforming the concept of professional growth, not only in regard to institutional support, but writ large as well.

In this chapter, we will look first at two competing narratives of faculty development—a "narrative of constraint" and a "narrative of growth" (O'Meara, Terosky, and Neumann, 2008)—and situate the scholarship of teaching and learning squarely within the latter. We will examine the natural affinity between institutionally supported faculty development programs and the scholarship of teaching and learning, as well as differences in their approaches to improvement, by looking at their individual and convergent evolution toward a shared emphasis on inquiry, learning, and collaboration. We will describe how each movement and its practitioners have benefited the other, look at promising models from a range of institutional types, and conclude with a discussion of an emerging consensus about what it means—and what it takes—to develop teachers today.

COMPETING NARRATIVES

How has faculty development been understood in the culture of higher education and beyond? For many years it was often thought unnecessary, or to paraphrase one form of the argument: Didn't we hire people who were already fully developed? To this way of thinking, teaching largely meant the transmission of content. Since the doctorate certified content expertise, development—where it was offered—often meant (modest) support for enhancing knowledge of one's discipline. Consistent with this view, institutional support for development would increase mainly in response to crises: for retraining and renewal in response to the retrenchment problems of the early 1970s;[4] for teaching assistant training in response to concerns about instruction at large research institutions; for revising teaching practices that were out of touch with the learning needs of the new student population of the late twentieth century; for encouraging post-tenure review; and most recently, for training to meet the demand for more online and hybrid teaching.[5]

In their study of the past twenty years of work on faculty careers, KerryAnn O'Meara, Aimee LaPointe Terosky, and Anna Neumann view this approach to faculty development as part of a "narrative of constraint" (2008, p. 16). Within this narrative, faculty as well as their institutions are under fire to be more accountable, to increase workloads, and to relinquish some autonomy. Where these demands are particularly strong, faculty work habits and personal expectations may come to be considered part of the problem; "development," then, can come to be seen as external to the individual, provided in a climate of recalcitrance, and necessary only in times of serious external scrutiny—in short, "as something we do to faculty to get them to behave in certain (different) ways" (p. 18). Faculty development may then be forced to work in the shadow of an implied deficit model, and teaching centers may be given the conflicting tasks of evaluating and improving individuals.[6]

In contrast to the belief that institutions need to provide opportunities for faculty development only when the institution or the individual faces difficulties (and perhaps only where outside funding can be found), studies of faculty career stages based on theories of personal growth point to faculty members' own desires to grow as professionals over time (Baldwin, 1990). This willing, internal impetus, which O'Meara, Terosky, and Neumann believe has been obscured (and even suppressed) by the narrative of constraint, then fuels a "narrative of growth" that highlights how faculty "move beyond 'managing' changes brought on by external and institutional forces to composing new professional roles and work lives where they can find meaning, continue to learn, and make commitments to rigorous and meaningful research, teaching, and engagement" (2008, p. 21). In this narrative of growth, faculty work habits and personal expectations—to continue to learn, to undertake meaningful work in a supportive and collegial environment, to commit to and act upon the larger social goals of higher education—are considered essential to *institutional* growth. In this climate, professional development centers encourage the institution to understand its faculty in this way and to support their expectations. Programs that bring faculty together to learn from each other and to advance work important to both the individual and the institution are visible signs of this support.

What role has the scholarship of teaching and learning played in this emerging narrative of growth? For starters, it emphasizes inquiry—into and about practices and results—as the organizing perspective for faculty's work as teachers, and it thus aligns with the responsibility and desire of all professionals to grow in their knowledge. Further, through its emphasis on making public the intellectual work of teaching, the scholarship of teaching and learning promotes collaboration and collegiality. And finally, by grounding itself in both reflection and action, it supports faculty's commitment to ongoing improvement—of professional competence, of student learning, of the institution, and of the professoriate itself. These principles—learning through inquiry, collaboration, reflection, and action in the service of ongoing improvement—also form the basis of dramatic changes in the faculty development programs that many institutions are now starting to provide.

DIFFERENT BUT CONVERGING HISTORIES

The scholarship of teaching and learning, as a distinct concept, can be traced to former Carnegie Foundation president Ernest Boyer's seminal 1990 work, *Scholarship Reconsidered*. But as that concept began to take concrete shape in campus discussions and initiatives, it benefited from a variety of earlier (and in most cases ongoing) traditions and lines of work (see Hutchings, Bjork, and Babb, 2002; Huber, Hutchings, and Shulman, 2005). These include an important body of research on teacher knowledge (for instance, Shulman, 1987; Grossman, Wilson, and Shulman, 1989), as well as studies of the learning process from cognitive psychology and neuroscience. The student outcomes assessment movement, which took hold in higher education in the mid-1980s, underlined the value of evidence about learning. In particular, classroom assessment provided tools for faculty seeking to investigate (and to improve) the impact of their teaching on their own students' learning (Angelo and Cross, 1993; Cross and Steadman, 1996). And experiments with teaching portfolios (Edgerton, Hutchings, and Quinlan, 1991; Seldin, 1997) created an interest in documenting the work of excellent teaching. But among these several contributing developments and traditions perhaps none has been more important to the theme of this volume—bringing the scholarship of teaching and learning to the center of institutional life—than the decades of work undertaken in the name of professional development.

Faculty development in its modern institutional form in the United States is at least sixty years old. Mary Deane Sorcinelli, Ann Austin, Pamela Eddy, and Andrea Beach (2005) have pointed out that faculty development was well on its way to establishing itself as a professional field long before *Scholarship Reconsidered*. Indeed, by 1990 it had already passed through three distinct, overlapping "ages," according to these authors' useful chronology—the "Age of the Scholar," the "Age of the Teacher," and the "Age of the Developer"—and was entering, like most of higher education, the "Age of the Learner" (Cross, 1986; Barr and Tagg, 1995). That is, faculty development's goals had moved from helping scholars "maintain currency in their disciplines and enhance their content expertise," to emphasizing the "improvement of faculty as teachers," to offering broader programs that responded to the career span and changing needs of academic life (Sorcinelli, Austin, Eddy, and Beach, 2005, pp. 8, 9).

Thus, beginning in the 1980s we see, for example, the large-scale development of programs aimed at preparing graduate students for their roles as teachers. Though the original impetus for such work was concern about non-English-speaking teaching assistants in undergraduate classrooms, the programs in question quickly developed a larger vision, with preparation for teaching becoming a valued aspect of graduate training. As recounted by Leo Lambert, one of the leaders of the national "TA Training movement," this was "a change of the first order and . . . one of the most important phenomena in higher education in the last twenty years" (1993, p. vii). What makes it even more so is that on many campuses (including Syracuse University, Lambert's campus at the time), programs to prepare graduate students to teach provided an entrée for faculty themselves to focus more explicitly on their pedagogical practice.

Soon there were programs not only for graduate students, but also for faculty at various points in their careers. The Lilly Endowment Teaching Fellows Program, for instance, supported campus efforts to develop early career faculty at research-intensive institutions. Other campuses began to focus on the needs of mid-career faculty. And to support these programs, centers for teaching grew up on more and more campuses and, where they existed already, attracted further resources and larger staffs (Sorcinelli, Austin, Eddy, and Beach, 2005). Along the way, these developments took a turn that moved them more fully in the direction of the scholarship of teaching and learning.

A Focus on Inquiry and Evidence

In the history of faculty development, a speech by K. Patricia Cross at the 1986 American Association for Higher Education Annual Meeting pointed toward the emergence of the Age of the Learner. Cross proposed that teaching would be taken seriously only if faculty came to see their classrooms as research laboratories; this, she argued, would help move faculty development centers to supplement their familiar tips-and-techniques workshops with programs in classroom research or practice-centered inquiry into student learning. Her remarks struck a chord because the focus on learning and on teachers as students of learning was increasingly common. Indeed, some campuses during these years established groups of faculty undertaking classroom research (Angelo, 1998). In the early 1990s at California State University, Long Beach, for instance, the faculty development center organized a group of faculty to "start a conversation about assessment at various levels, including the classroom," notes the Center's director at the time, Susan Nummedal (1996, p. 41). The group (8–10 faculty) met over the course of several years, posing and exploring questions about their students' learning. "For most of the members, the group was key to developing deeper understandings. . . . We helped one another push beyond and probe our initial 'reading' of classroom assessment data, for instance. We reframed one another's questions, pointing to other ways of look-ing at the information and at the questions" (p. 43). Groups like these set the stage among faculty participants for the scholarship of teaching and learning.

As this approach—convening groups of faculty to explore student learning—was put in place, a new conceptual model of professional development began to emerge as well. A number of national leaders in the field had begun to argue that inquiry, often collaborative, lay at the heart of the development process itself, and that promoting inquiry fostered development. In this spirit, Nancy Van Note Chism proposed that the scholarship of teaching and learning was wholly consistent with the four "natural cycles of inquiry into teaching" that faculty go through, as they plan, act, observe, and reflect (Chism and Sanders, 1986). Understanding faculty in this way—as inquirers into their own teaching—continues to move faculty development away from the narrative of constraint and toward the narrative of growth, away from something that might have been *done to* faculty when the institution deemed it necessary, toward something faculty *did naturally with* colleagues and consultants, and increasingly closer to emerging ideas from within the scholarship of teaching and learning.

To summarize, during the 1990s significant convergences between the schol-arship of teaching and learning and professional development came into view. These included a focus not only on teachers, but also on learners and learning; an interest in bringing faculty together to create community around teaching; and commitments to inquiry and evidence as keys to strengthening the edu-cational mission of colleges and universities. Such convergences should not be surprising, for although their histories differ, the scholarship of teaching and learning and faculty development have long shared at least one common purpose—transforming teaching and learning for the better.

In this sense, faculty developers and faculty who engage in the scholarship of teaching and learning have interacted like two friendly discourse commu-nities that speak dialects of the same language. They share much of the same vocabulary and grammar, can understand each other where there are differ-ences, and can often "translate" one dialect into the other. Many have learned to speak both dialects and are equally at home in either community, as schol-ars of teaching and learning have taken on professional development roles in teaching centers, and as the reach of those centers has expanded to make a place for the scholarship of teaching and learning.

Approaches to Improvement

Despite numerous intersections between the two communities, however, there have been differences that, it must be said, have sometimes been semantic in the real sense of that word—not just about form, but about meaning. In fact, these two fields appear at times like cultures (England and the United States, or Quebec and France come to mind) that are "separated by their common language," as Mark Twain once quipped. The expression *teaching problem* is an example: Is it something to be fixed, or an opportunity to study further? (Bass, 1999). And what about *development* itself: Is it a self-directed, natural progression toward expertise (the narrative of growth), or a subtle judgment of insufficiency that implies rather than explores the necessity of change (the narrative of constraint)? (see Mills and Huber, 2005). When linguists want to understand how dialects differ or might be influencing each other, they look for places where miscommunication can occur, and, more positively, at how each discourse community responds to the problem. Examining these places over time can help linguists explain how the dialects are evolving, separately and together, as a function of their very separateness and of their contact.

Taking a cue from the linguists, then, it is useful to examine an area in which the scholarship of teaching and learning and professional development are both deeply invested yet differently inflected—and that is around the idea of improvement itself. For while both communities are committed to improving the quality of learning and teaching, they have come at that task from quite different angles.

In the case of faculty development, improvement has been the driving purpose. When the field first moved from its earliest focus on supporting faculty in their scholarly development to supporting them in their role as teachers, the teaching centers established to do this work were charged with making things better. As noted above, sometimes the need came in the form of a crisis: concerns about graduate student teaching assistants in undergraduate classrooms or the influx of new students who were more diverse and sometimes less prepared than in the past. In this spirit, "experienced" (read "older") faculty needed to learn new teaching tricks; new faculty, many of whom were hired without much teaching experience to begin with, needed to learn from scratch; and faculty "in pedagogic arrest" needed "emergency rooms" (Shulman, 2004, p. 213).

Institutions that created and funded teaching improvement centers in the 1970s and 1980s expected results, a perspective reinforced by administrators, who often recommended or even required faculty to visit such centers on the occasion of poor student evaluations. Some centers had taken on, or were forced to take on, the entire teaching evaluation process, muddying the role of the developer (counselor, physician, or police?). That said, the mandate to improve is clearly a positive one. As professional development has grown as a field, teaching centers have deployed an impressive repertoire of tools and approaches—brown-bag lunch discussions, workshops led by national experts, small grants programs for classroom innovation, and larger ongoing curricular reform projects—offered in a context of personal support, technical assistance, intellectual and financial resources, and access to colleagues. Over the years, these programs have made a significant difference on many campuses for faculty who (either) need or want to improve their teaching.

The scholarship of teaching and learning movement has clearly valued and benefited from the resources, expertise, support, and community created by professional development. But its founding premise points to a different view of improvement. That is, the problem it aimed at, in Boyer's original formulation, was not so much that teaching needed to be "developed," but that it was misunderstood—not recognized, that is, for its intellectual (which is to say scholarly) substance. The argument and the (at least implied) strategy behind the idea was that teaching, and therefore the learning of students, would be strengthened when the intellectual work entailed was recognized as such, and rewarded.

In the years after the publication of *Scholarship Reconsidered*, a number of educators elaborated on the idea in ways that reinforce this view. A second Carnegie Foundation report, *Scholarship Assessed*, begun by Boyer himself, helped situate the scholarship of teaching and learning within a broader framework of characteristics shared by all forms of scholarship (Glassick, Huber, and Maeroff, 1997). Lee Shulman, who succeeded Boyer as president of the Carnegie Foundation, argued that teaching must be reconnected with the scholarly communities of the disciplines, and, later, that the scholarship of teaching should be distinguished from excellent teaching (Shulman, 1993; Hutchings and Shulman, 1999). In suggesting how professional developers could include this scholarly notion of improvement in their work with faculty, Maryellen Weimer urged in 2006 that "the pedagogical scholarship agenda should not be motivated by any sort of need to improve" (p. 196), even though it had great potential to do so: "Rather, make the interest in pedagogical scholarship about a way of valuing teaching, a way of coming to respect its difficulty and complexity, a way of discovering how much there is yet to learn" (pp. 198–199). Clearly, the scholarship of teaching and learning and professional development were increasingly sharing a common language.

Finding Common Ground

Not surprisingly, then, much discussion took place in the early years of CASTL about the role that teaching centers and their staffs could or should play. Such centers were positioned to be key players on many campuses, and many jumped on board to provide critical leadership in the first phase of work. But, as some campuses told CASTL leaders, teaching centers were not always the right site for such work: although most teaching centers had fought long and hard against a negative perception of their role, many faculty continued to see them not as places for scholarly collaboration but as places to get "fixed." Thus, not surprisingly, when Carnegie staff (Pat Hutchings and Mary Huber) presented CASTL's early work in a plenary session at the 1999 annual meeting of the

Professional and Organizational Development Network in Higher Education (the POD Network, the organization to which faculty developers belong), the first question from the floor was about teaching centers. What was their role in this new work? Wouldn't centers and faculty development professionals have important resources to contribute?

The answer to this last question (a resounding "yes") quickly became apparent as campus teaching centers emerged as increasingly critical players in the scholarship of teaching and learning. CASTL flyers and letters of invitation were often passed from the provost's office to the director of the teaching center with a "we should get involved" note appended (as happened at the University of Wisconsin-Milwaukee)—and involved they became. Looking back on the program's almost twelve years of work, it's clear to us that these structures (they come with a variety of labels—teaching centers, teaching and learning centers, centers for teaching excellence) have provided critical leadership, creativity, and resourcefulness for the scholarship of teaching and learning on campus.

To simplify, the scholarship of teaching and learning and professional development moved into firm alignment as both communities coalesced around two basic principles: (1) that faculty do their best work as teachers when they engage in *inquiry*, and (2) that this inquiry produces its most fruitful and useful results when it is focused on *learning* and *learners*, often but not always in the context of a discipline. Constance Cook, director of the center at the University of Michigan, goes one step further: "[faculty inquiry] projects in the scholarship of teaching and learning lead not only to greater student learning, but also faculty learning" (2004, p. 11). In short, the scholarship of teaching and learning perspective, which has challenged higher education to "redefine teaching improvement in terms of student learning, is gradually becoming the *lingua franca* of professional development" (Ciccone, 2004, p. 49).

LEARNING FROM EACH OTHER

Having found common conceptual ground, the scholarship of teaching and learning and faculty development also faced the common practical problems of gaining institutional recognition and support. Faculty development centers could support the scholarship of teaching and learning by helping individuals find funding, collaborators, methodological assistance, and outlets for dissemination. But it quickly became evident that the conditions necessary to sustain the work would come only if campus leaders saw its value to broader institutional goals. At the same time, faculty development advocates were confronting a similar issue—how to bring their centers and initiatives in from the margins of institutional life (see Gaff and Simpson, 1994; Schroeder and Associates, 2010). Teaching centers had expanded their repertoire of programs and activities in response to what developers understood to be the needs of faculty (defined by career stage, teaching context, student demographics, and so forth). And yet, campus administration often argued that faculty development programs should be more responsive to the critical needs of the institution, a position underlined by the vulnerability of faculty development offices when financial exigencies required cuts.

On campus after campus, these two agendas—finding institutional support for the scholarship of teaching and learning, and making faculty development more visibly relevant to institutional concerns—have come together for the benefit of each, and ultimately for the benefit of the institutions. From their position within academic affairs, centers and their directors have advocated for their efforts to improve teaching and learning by connecting their programs to institutional agendas; the scholarship of teaching and learning, as one of these programs, has been cast in this light. Conversely, the principles and practices of the scholarship of teaching and learning have provided professional development with a conceptual framework through which faculty would be more likely to engage in advancing institutional agendas such as curriculum reform and assessment. A little more history can help elucidate this mutually beneficial relationship.

What Faculty Development Brings to the Scholarship of Teaching and Learning

As mentioned, centers for professional development had existed on many campuses since the 1970s. Because of their longer history and established place in the institution, they gave conversations about the scholarship of teaching and learning a physical and intellectual place to start. The experience at the University of Wisconsin-Milwaukee was certainly repeated elsewhere: The center director and the associate provost created an interdisciplinary group of faculty to examine documents, articles, and other materials and craft a definition of the work for the campus; a grant program supported individual work that would serve as a model for other faculty; conferences and workshops were organized to present such models; and, later, the work would become more collaborative and address other campus initiatives such as first-year instruction and general education reform. Here and elsewhere, many teaching centers have come to see the scholarship of teaching and learning as an essential part of their philosophy and practice.

Conceptually, teaching and learning centers have brought to the scholarship of teaching and learning at least three important ideas. First, in emphasizing its scholarly qualities, proponents of the scholarship of teaching and learning understandably focus on the discovery part of the work: scholars produce new knowledge about teaching and learning that advances the field because it is subject to peer discussion and review and "amenable to productive employment in future work by members of that same community" (Shulman, 1998, p. 6). Although research into teaching and learning is indeed part of the work of many centers, most have always been practical about it as well. In short, while supporting the creation of new pedagogical knowledge, they also attend to its immediate and wider application and impact. In so doing, centers have helped keep the scholarship of teaching and learning attached to the needs of the local academic community, ensured that it was immediately relevant and, thus, of course, more likely to attract positive attention from administrators.

Second, centers on many campuses in the 1990s had begun to comple-ment their individual consultations, workshops, and grants with programs that brought groups of faculty together for instructional development and collegial support (for example, creating faculty learning communities along the lines of well-established models; see Cox, 2004), or to undertake collaborative projects related to cross-curricular issues such as writing, critical thinking, technology, and diversity. Jerry Gaff and Ronald Simpson point out that this approach has "required groups of faculty to work together to see their own individual interest within the context of the department or institution" (1994, p. 167). Thus, the many campuses that already had in place structures that brought local scholars of teaching and learning together were well positioned to connect that work to the institution's goals, and thus to fulfill its promise of wider impact.

Third, the turn in faculty development toward classroom assessment, in-quiry, and learning has produced a strong cadre of potential partners, who offer faculty interested in the scholarship of teaching and learning knowledge of the literature on learning and expertise in methodology. Chism, for instance, has urged professional developers to join faculty at their moments of challenge, namely as they face a teaching problem, by "suggesting instruments or meth-ods for collecting good information and creating peer networks that encourage reflection" (2008, p. 6). Even further, she argues that "when professional de-velopers support the scholarship of teaching and learning, they are working harmoniously with the natural way in which faculty grow and develop. They reinforce an activity that promotes faculty growth, results in better student learning, and adds to the literature on college teaching and learning. These multiple and important outcomes make work in this arena extremely valuable" (p. 7). Teaching centers that have reconceptualized their work in this fashion have realized much of the promise of Shulman's urging for structures that pro-vide "support systems, sanctuaries, and learning centers for scholars across the disciplines, interdisciplines, and professions pursuing the scholarship of teaching seriously" (2004, p. 147).

What the Scholarship of Teaching and Learning Brings to Faculty Development

What does the scholarship of teaching and learning bring to faculty develop-ment? Randy Bass suggests that the scholarship of teaching and learning has provided faculty development centers with a language that can complete the shift begun by the new literature on learning: the move toward disciplinary thinking. By inviting faculty to study the learning in front of them, the scholarship of teaching and learning directs attention to questions about how students come to acquire the knowledge and skills of the discipline in various combinations, at differing levels of sophistication, and so forth. It gives them, in Bass's words, "a way to work *outward,* from where they [are]" (Nov. 24, 2009). Faculty need no longer feel that they are working on or implementing generic ideas about learning, as interesting as those ideas might be. Nor would they necessarily have to begin with the question of how these ideas applied to them and their students. Instead, discipline-based questions could come first, and the more general literature on learning could be used in support. Questions about how students acquire the skills and habits of mind of various disciplines—of making historical arguments (think of the work of the International Society for the Scholarship of Teaching and Learning History group featured in Chapter 2), or of dealing with complexity and ambiguity through reflection in a humanities course (Ciccone, Meyers, and Waldmann, 2008)—provide inviting entrées into undertaking pedagogical changes and studying their results.

What has the scholarship of teaching and learning brought to the focus on inquiry that faculty development had initially acquired from the classroom assessment/classroom research and faculty learning community models? An early definition of the work made reference to *"methods appropriate to disciplinary epistemologies"* (Cambridge, 2004a, p. 2), thus pointing to one major contribution: a broadening of the methodologies that could be brought to bear on the problems posed. Confronting an unfamiliar object of study such as student learning, faculty might look first to familiar research methods—experimental design for scientists and social scientists, more qualitative methods of close reading and analysis of student work for the humanists. But they might also look to the methodologies of other fields, because systematically studying the problem that had been posed would invite, indeed require, multiple perspectives (Huber and Morreale, 2002; Huber, 2006). Professional developers have made progress in engaging faculty in teaching and learning questions not when they have tried to extend social science methodology to faculty inquiry, but when they have helped faculty in the humanities and natural sciences see the possibilities of that methodology within the universe of approaches that their own fields can bring to the question.

Further, the scholarship of teaching and learning has emphasized the practitioner's responsibility not only to use knowledge to improve one's own classroom, but also to improve the field (Shulman, 1993; Hutchings and Shulman, 1999). Many scholars of teaching and learning have become activists in their scholarly and professional societies, pushing for more forums in which rigorous and innovative work on teaching and learning in their disciplines can be shared. But this push toward going public extends to the local institution as well, and has helped make teaching and learning centers key players in the development of the campus as a teaching commons (Huber and Hutchings, 2005). Scholars of teaching and learning have become contributors to local center newsletters and publications, to workshops and speaker series, and to the conferences that so many centers sponsor—important stages in the journey by which findings in particular classrooms and programs travel to enrich the repertoire of colleagues teaching other students other things (see Huber, 2009).

Finally, the scholarship of teaching and learning reaffirms one of the core principles of faculty development—the importance of the self as a source of reflection and action. Parker Palmer emphasizes this principle in *The Courage to Teach*, urging readers to look for insight into teaching and learning by asking first "Who is the self that teaches?" (2007, p. 4). But this perspective on faculty development can be lost in the flurry of workshops on evidence-based practice, on high-impact practices, or even on the goals of teaching and learning. In legitimizing the individual classroom as the source of interesting, consequential questions about teaching and learning, and in recognizing the teacher as the person best suited to formulate and study these questions, the scholarship of teaching and learning reinforces the possibility of the kind of professional growth that comes from within, in response to a felt need. The most effective forms of faculty development thus help faculty discuss their teaching and learning concerns collaboratively before providing prescriptive "solutions."[7]

MODELS TO LEAD THE WAY

Today, and looking ahead, it is clear that professional development and the scholarship of teaching and learning can be very good company for one another. Yet they retain their separate identities, and there is no single model for how to ensure that the connections are sustained and mutually enriching. A look at the various ways such work has come together on different kinds of campuses can show what has been accomplished, and what may be possible in the future.

Dedicated Programs

For starters, some campuses have created structures that put the scholarship of teaching and learning front and center. One such is the Center for the Scholarship of Teaching at Michigan State University. Housed in the College of Education, the MSU Center "aims to encourage university-wide discussions and scholarship about teaching and learning," providing resources for studying one's own teaching, training in "action research," and links to other organizations committed to such work (Michigan State University College of Education, "Home"). Indiana University Bloomington (IUB) has also created a special program to advance the scholarship of teaching and learning. Established in 1998 by the dean of faculties and academic affairs and currently operating under the auspices of the Office of the Vice Provost for Undergraduate Education, the program provides multiple resources for emergent and established scholars of teaching and learning, including grants to support such work, a speaker series (featuring IUB faculty as well as national and international leaders from beyond the campus), and community-building initiatives in the scholarship of teaching and learning such as the annual Writing Retreat, the Spring Poster Sessions, in addition to funded faculty collaborations known as Communities of Inquiry, some of which focus on decoding the disciplines (Indiana University Bloomington). We describe the latter in Chapter 2.

The IUB program acknowledges that students, colleges, and universities are best served when teachers practice scholarly teaching, and that no one is better situated to conduct the scholarship of teaching than those engaged with students on a regular basis. Premised on the belief that teaching is a scholarly activity to be valued as community property, one of the most important goals of the program is to foster significant, long-lasting learning for all students while simultaneously bringing recognition and reward to teachers who practice evidence-based teaching. Aimed squarely at improving undergraduate education, the program's mission is to encourage, support, and disseminate course-focused research projects that are faculty defined and implemented, while working to build both disciplinary and interdisciplinary conversations locally, nationally, and internationally as well. The program has engaged large numbers of IUB faculty and is seen as a key component of the research mission of the university, one that draws on faculty research talents and dedication and directs these toward the interplay of teaching and student learning. More recently, the program director, working with the vice provost, has been exploring ways to connect this work to other institutional initiatives, including a major implementation of general education requirements, and a growing push for institutional assessment—our topic in the next chapter (Rehrey, June 29, 2010).

A further, highly successful element of IUB's model is a funding program for local scholars of teaching and learning; faculty apply for peer-reviewed grants to support new or ongoing studies into issues of teaching and learning. Funding opportunities begin at the $1,500 level for individual and initial (seed) research projects and scale up to grants as large as $35,000, available to teams proposing a scholarship of teaching and learning initiative that promises to have a sustained impact upon instructional development and education and that could serve as a model for others on campus (Rehrey, June 29, 2010).

Similar initiatives (albeit not all so well funded) have, in fact, now become a centerpiece of professional development programs. For instance, the Maricopa Community Colleges created the Maricopa Institute for Learning (MIL), a one-year fellowship opportunity for faculty "in any discipline who are interested in examining significant issues in their teaching fields and contributing to the scholarship of teaching and learning through classroom research projects" (Maricopa Center for Learning and Instruction, "Home"). Explicitly modeled after the CASTL Scholars program, the MIL issues a call for proposals, selects a small number of fellows (six in 2010), and supports their inquiry projects through a summer retreat, fall and spring seminars, release time, and—perhaps most important—through a community of like-minded colleagues doing similar work. Seeking to build knowledge that can travel through the system's 10 campuses, participants have also created online multimedia "snapshots" of their work.

The fellowship model is also employed at St. Olaf College (whose story we will tell in Chapter 4), where the Center for Innovation in the Liberal Arts (or CILA, as the campus teaching center is called) selects a group of "CILA Associates" each year and supports their work on a scholarship of teaching and learning project through regular meetings, and through the creation of faculty learning communities that form around their work.[8] The University of Wisconsin System Office of Professional and Instructional Development (OPID) creates yearly cohorts of 20–25 faculty and adjunct staff through its Wisconsin Teaching Fellows and Scholars Program. Each participant undertakes a significant scholarship of teaching and learning project, records the project's progress on an electronic poster, collaborates with other Fellows and Scholars in project design, and shares the project and its results in public forums.[9]

Programs such as these pose challenges. Participants are busy people, and it takes time to build a critical mass of activity and examples. There are costs—of money, staff time, and other opportunities that cannot be pursued. And yet, it is clear on the many campuses taking this tack that the experience is a powerful one for the individual participants and for the larger initiatives in which they participate.

Integrating Key Principles

Most centers of teaching and learning provide a variety of services and supports useful to scholars of teaching and learning. Programs (such as fellowships) explicitly aimed at the scholarship of teaching and learning are often only a small part of the picture. What's interesting, however, is how the principles, practices, and (often but not always) the language of the scholarship of teaching and learning have begun to inform and shape the larger set of opportunities. For instance, Mary Savina at Carleton College reports that the principles of the scholarship of teaching and learning underlie the planning for many of the Perlman Learning and Teaching Center events, such as workshops that focus on how to collect and use data about student learning. And, to repeat a theme we are hearing more and more often, Savina notes that "some of the other academic-initiative-related faculty development events are organized on scholarship of teaching and learning principles, notably the writing and quantitative literacy initiatives" (Mar. 1, 2010). Further, many centers have had small-grants programs for faculty undertaking a teaching innovation in their classroom; with the scholarship of teaching and learning in view, some grantees are now being asked to document the impact of the innovation on student learning. Similarly, the idea of reading groups has caught on in some settings, with centers convening faculty and staff to discuss one or more books that bear on teaching and learning, an approach that parallels the research "journal club" model one finds in many science departments (see Walker, Golde, Jones, Bueschel, and Hutchings, 2008), and that brings a greater level of scholarly engagement to the process of improvement.

The work of Lin Langley (Douglas College) and Nancy Randall (Vancouver Island University) on "integrative faculty development" suggests progress toward facility in the scholarship of teaching and learning as one way to organize development activities, a model of professional development (as they call it) that builds on the concept of faculty growth as learners about learning. In their thinking, faculty development can guide individuals through the stages of reflective practice and scholarly teaching to the scholarship of teaching and learning (Faculty Development Group, 2009). Douglas College reconceptualized its faculty development offerings in this way. In so doing, not only did its faculty development office provide multiple entry points into the work; it also infused the principles of the work at every point. Similarly, Vancouver Island University's teaching center makes explicit the link between individual faculty inquiry work on learning and broader institutional agendas: "The VIU Teaching and Learning Centre team believe that investing in the Scholarship of Teaching and Learning will provide staff and faculty with substantive evidence of key elements supporting student learning, enabling everyone in the VIU community to make evidence-based decisions to modify their teaching and learning processes where needed" (Vancouver Island University, "Networks and Initiatives: Scholarship of Teaching").

Professional development programs for graduate students have been shaped by the scholarship of teaching and learning as well. Some campuses offer a full course on the topic, typically open to graduate students across fields. At George Mason University, for instance, students enrolled in CTCH (College Teaching) 604 in the spring of 2010 worked toward six goals, aimed at giving them a sense of the history and possibilities of this kind of work (see Exhibit 3.1, adapted from Cambridge, 2010).[10] But more "modularized" approaches—that is, less than a full-blown course—are also on the rise. The Center for the Integration of Research, Learning, and Teaching (CIRTL) based at the University of Wisconsin-Madison is a network of six institutions offering graduate students and postdocs in the sciences an opportunity to turn their skills and habits as scholars and researchers to the study of their students' learning. Those who complete the program receive a certificate. "The certificate program has been

---

Exhibit 3.1 CTCH 604, The Scholarship of Teaching and Learning

George Mason University, Spring 2010

Learning Outcomes

1. Students will learn about the SOTL movement in higher education (primarily in the context of the Boyer/Rice models of scholarship).

2. Students will consider major perspectives on how students learn, including different learning styles, and how to improve student learning.

3. Students will develop an ethic of inquiry (problem-based thinking) in which to explore aspects of teaching and learning.

4. Students will explore various methods and approaches for undertaking and assessing SOTL.

5. Students will become familiar with how to do research in the area of teaching and learning: how to formulate questions, how to use various resources, and how to publicly disseminate scholarship in this area.

6. Students will develop a taxonomy of questions regarding teaching in one's own discipline: what works, what it looks like, and possible opportunities for learning.

---

quite popular," says CIRTL leader Robert Mathieu, an astrophysicist at UW-Madison. "It is interesting," he adds, "because in the end the certification per se doesn't mean so much. It's a bit like a PhD—what matters is the CV and letters of recommendation that you generate as you obtain the certificate/PhD. But students find it very useful as an organizational device for their professional development and commit to its completion" (June 22, 2010).

Similar opportunities are now part of the mix beyond the United States as well. Ireland's National Academy for the Integration of Research and Teaching and Learning (NAIRTL), modeled on CIRTL, offers fellowships and other opportunities for faculty in the six participating institutions, but graduate education is a special focus of work.[11] A five-credit module entitled "Learning to Teach in Higher Education" was first offered on a pilot basis for graduate students in 2006–2007, providing "a combination of practical advice and initiation into theoretical work, inquiry and the scholarship of teaching and learning" (Graduate Education Group, 2009, p. 8). With a little luck, the graduate students who participate in such experiences will "pay it forward" by bringing a similar spirit and set of commitments to their future work as faculty, be it with colleagues or with their own students—some of whom will become teachers themselves.

Building Collaborative Communities

In all of the preceding examples, a key dynamic is support for collaboration and conversation. If, as we argue repeatedly in this volume, the scholarship of teaching and learning is to engage a larger group of faculty, it must move beyond the individual classroom and constitute itself in collaborative communities and networks of improvement (Gomez, 2010). The embrace of collaborative work is, clearly, not the exclusive province of the scholarship of teaching and learning, but its emphasis on going public with the work has certainly helped to encourage and shape this aspect of professional development. Like many in higher education, we have particularly admired the faculty learning communities (FLC) movement pioneered by Milton Cox and Laurie Richlin—groups of faculty "who engage in an active, collaborative, year-long program with a curriculum about enhancing teaching and learning and with frequent seminars and activities that provide learning, development, the scholarship of teaching, and community building" (Cox, 2004, p. 8). Such groups can direct their focus in a variety of ways—Cox points to cohort-based and theme-based models—but on campuses engaged with the scholarship of teaching and learning, they provide ideal vehicles for the support of inquiry projects. At Georgia Southern University, for instance, where the Center for Teaching, Learning & Scholarship established an FLC program in 2006–2007, goals for such groups include emphasizing "that teaching is serious intellectual work" and encouraging "scholarly teaching and the scholarship of teaching and its application to student learning" (Georgia Southern University, "Goals of FLCs at Georgia Southern").

Additionally (sometimes connected to faculty learning communities or to scholarship of teaching and learning fellowship programs), many campuses are building the campus teaching commons through collaborative writing projects, where emerging work on pedagogy can benefit from connection to larger groups, local and beyond. In some cases, faculty who are writing for these collections are convened (typically by the teaching center) in a retreat or workshop where they can share drafts, critique one another's work, and form relationships that then shape next projects. But collaboration and networking need not be face-to-face, and products can be as important as process. We think, for instance, of LaGuardia Community College's local scholarship of teaching and learning journal, *In Transit*, and of occasional collections of pedagogical inquiry issued by Eastern Michigan University, Illinois State University, Middlesex Community College, Indiana University, and many other campuses; publication is, after all, a way of joining the conversation.

This focus on building scholarly community around teaching has not only strengthened the scholarship of teaching and learning, it has also helped to energize and revitalize the professional development function on many campuses. As one campus leader told us, the scholarship of teaching and learning increased the teaching center's reputation for "gravitas and rigor." Jokes about locating the center for teaching in a place where faculty can come and go without being seen are a caricature, to be sure, but one with a grain of truth, no matter how hard faculty developers have fought against it. In contrast, many teaching centers are now exciting places for faculty, places where they find like-minded colleagues interested in important campus and disciplinary teaching and learning issues. As they support these communities of practice, centers continue to shake off any lingering perceptions of faculty development as remediation, and position themselves more fully within the core work of the institution.

These new directions have shaped the experience not only of faculty who participate in professional development programs and opportunities, but also of those who run them. In the view of Peter Felten at Elon University, the scholarship of teaching and learning has fundamentally changed the way center directors and staff understand and practice faculty development. Like many faculty (his discipline is history), Felten came to faculty development without training, and he did so at a time—the early 1990s, the "Age of the Developer" (Sorcinelli, Austin, Eddy, and Beach, 2005)—when faculty development was rapidly becoming a field unto itself. Felten reports that he often felt he had to learn a new discipline. The scholarship of teaching and learning, with its focus on inquiry and collaboration, he explains, broadened the range of approaches one might take as a faculty developer. No longer did developers need to function solely as "experts" in pedagogical practices; rather, they could bring their significant skills and experience in teaching a discipline to help colleagues ask and study questions about their students' learning (Nov. 23, 2009). Not surprisingly, Felten moves effortlessly between his work in the scholarship of teaching and learning and in faculty development. Indeed, he became president of the POD Network in 2010.[12]

WHAT IT MEANS—AND TAKES—TO DEVELOP TEACHERS TODAY

How can the scholarship of teaching and learning continue to contribute to a narrative of growth for faculty, faculty developers, and for their institutions? O'Meara, Terosky, and Neumann make the argument that since "higher education is centered on learning, learning should be considered at the center of how faculty grow throughout their careers" (2008, pp. 27–28). By proposing inquiry as the organizing principle, the scholarship of teaching and learning encourages a perspective on faculty as engaged learners. This has many potential benefits, chief among them a more promising idea of what it means to develop as a teacher, and of what it takes to develop teachers today.

The scholarship of teaching and learning suggests a particular developmental trajectory for faculty in their role as teachers: one that includes attention to emerging pedagogies and serious work on curriculum and assessment, but which also means continuing to develop as a *learner about learning* along the way. In this spirit, faculty would develop expertise in asking good questions about how teaching practice connects with student learning; investigating those questions in increasingly sophisticated ways; using the information gathered to improve one's immediate results; and reaching broader conclusions that ultimately contribute to what is known about teaching and learning in higher education. In keeping with this model, faculty developers can become learner-centered themselves, as many now encourage others to be. That is, their work can build upon the faculty member's existing knowledge (of teaching, of students, of areas of difficulty, of disciplinary methodology) to forge true partnerships that raise knowledge about learning from anecdotal to systematic. What we have learned about the value of engagement in learning for *students* can and should apply to how we help *faculty* engage in learning about themselves as teachers.[13]

The notion of faculty as engaged learners carries with it a vision of the institution as a true learning environment. In this view, faculty are not seen as obstacles to change (as they tend to be within the narrative of constraint), but as crucial sources of information about their own and their students' learning, and as advocates for changes in policy and practice to support that learning. In becoming advocates for faculty inquiry, faculty developers too can support these changes.

The early premise of faculty development was exactly this. Although later lost in the emphasis on research products (for example, publications and grants resulting from sabbaticals), the underlying view was of faculty as lifelong learners, albeit solo ones. In that era of teaching as telling, and learning as listening, this meant maintaining currency in faculty members' disciplines and enhancing their content expertise. In the era of the scholarship of teaching and learning, lifelong development also means strengthening the skills not only to teach better, but also to understand the teaching and learning dynamic more fully, to reflect on that new understanding, and to bring all of this to one's colleagues and one's institution, often in collaboration with others. In continuing to move institutional faculty development away from the narrative of constraint, then, scholarship-of-teaching-and-learning-informed faculty development can recreate "a new old model" of individual professional growth, one that connects the personal acquisition of knowledge about teaching to what we now know, and still should find out, about student learning.

More important, perhaps, organizing faculty development in this way sends the message that learning in higher education is not just for students.[14] No longer is learning seen as something that we make students do, often passively; rather, students become active partners in their own learning and in providing useful information about it. For example, when faculty study student learning more deeply, they often realize that the summative information available from the usual sources (tests, quizzes, papers) isn't rich enough to answer the more interesting questions about what students are learning and at what level, whether they are able to use that learning in novel contexts, and how they think about and manage their own processes as learners. In seeking this "closer to the bone" information, faculty realize that they need to create formative assignments and activities that reveal progress toward learning goals and invite students to reflect on that progress (see Ciccone, Meyers, and Waldmann, 2008). In other words, by thinking of themselves as learners, faculty are more likely to think of their students as informed consultants who take their own learning just as seriously. This evolution from seeing the student as empty vessel to engaged learner to informed consultant leads naturally to the idea that students can become participants and co-investigators in the study of teaching and learning (Werder and Otis, 2010).

The narrative of growth reminds us that "faculty learn, grow, and make contributions through professional relationships embedded in communities" (O'Meara, Terosky and Neumann, 2008, p. 171). Faculty development work in support of the scholarship of teaching and learning has often brought individuals together in a community of scholars. In responding to the challenge to have an impact on institutional priorities, however, scholarship-of-teaching-and-learning-informed faculty development has begun to include organized, collective work on programmatic or institutional questions about student learning that are best studied by groups of committed learners: How do students in first-year seminars develop critical thinking? How does the use of e-portfolios support student and instructor reflection on learning? Collaborative investigation and collective scholarship, to use Richard Gale's terminology (2008, pp. 45–46), thus has the potential to join the faculty's desire for colleagueship—an essential part of the narrative of growth—with the institution's need for better information about student learning and faculty development's goal to promote both purposes. When coupled with the scholarship of teaching and learning, faculty development can support *institutional* learning by increasing the institution's capacity to study itself and its important practices (Felten, Kalish, Pingree, and Plank, 2007).

At the beginning of this chapter, we noted that although the scholarship of teaching and learning arises from the desire to know more about one's practice, it achieves its true impact when it affects the work of others. The scholarship of teaching and learning movement has always aspired to having an impact on how students, faculty, and institutions learn and improve. The same can be said for professional development. As educational developers continue to promote faculty learning; as faculty continue to study their practice; and as students continue to reflect on and improve their own learning while collaborating with faculty, both movements come closer to their shared goal of advancing learning. The web of inquiry and collaboration that the scholarship of teaching and learning and professional development create when joining forces provides both individuals and institutions with the perspectives and structures needed to succeed in that endeavor.

Notes

1. This quotation is from "Faculty Careers and Work Lives: A Professional Growth Perspective" (2008, p. 178).

2. "Retention" is a case in point. Institutions may look at the correlation between a high-impact practice, for example, and student retention. Faculty are more inclined to look for the correlation between a high-impact practice and student learning. Research on high-impact practices, then, might connect retention to learning.

3. Leaders of the CASTL program at Buffalo State College of the State University of New York took on this tension by intentionally supporting work that studied the impact of institutional initiatives on student learning, funding fellowships for examining service learning, writing across the curriculum, critical thinking, undergraduate research, learning communities, and oral communication electives.

4. Where campuses needed to close or significantly reduce certain programs, faculty were often given support to develop new expertise and new courses.

5. Much of the support for pilot professional development programs in these areas has come from outside funding agencies, for example, from the Danforth Foundation, the U.S. Department of Education's Fund for the Improvement of Post-Secondary Education (FIPSE), the Lilly Endowment, and the Bush Foundation. While providing essential resources, this type of "outsourcing" of what many have argued is a core institutional responsibility did not often lead to systemic institutional change.

6. It bears mentioning that the scholarship of teaching and learning risks becoming part of this narrative of constraint whenever institutions cast it as an imperative for all faculty, who thus come to view it not as a professional aspiration, but as "one more thing they'll make us do to change the way we want to work."

7. In "Teaching Excellence and the Inner Life of Faculty," Robert Craft makes this point about effective leadership for a seminar on teaching for faculty: "Above all, the leader must avoid being answer-person or advice-giver. Connection, after all, is what faculty are after, not someone else's 'right' answers. Faculty won't return weekly for patronizing advice" (2000, p. 52).

8. See http://www.stolaf.edu/depts/cila/associates.htm.

9. See http://www4.uwm.edu/sotl/.

10. CTCH 604 was originally designed and taught by John O'Connor, then adapted by subsequent instructors Victoria Salmon and (in the version represented here) Darren Cambridge, all at George Mason University.

11. University College Cork is the lead institution in NAIRTL, which also includes the National University of Ireland, Galway; Trinity College Dublin; Waterford Institute of Technology; and Cork Institute of Technology (Graduate Education Group, 2009, p. 5).

12. It is also important to note that many center directors and senior staff moved into these roles as faculty engaged in the scholarship of teaching and learning. The CASTL program alone has offered many examples: Randy Bass (Georgetown University); Spencer Benson (University of Maryland); Daniel Bernstein (University of Kansas); Jacqueline Dewar (Loyola Marymount University); Linda Hodges (Princeton University); and Kathy Takayama (Brown University).

13. Arguing from the premise that knowledge is socially constructed by the learner, Thomas Angelo encourages faculty to make students active participants in the construction of their own learning. Just as important, however, he extends this advice to faculty developers, who "must engage colleagues in constructing new, shared, contextually relevant concepts, rather than presenting faculty with imported prefabricated mental models for adoption" (2001, p. 100).

14. O'Meara, Terosky, and Neumann speculate on the benefit of representing faculty to the public in this way, that is, as learners. They believe this will help counter the public perception of faculty as often detached experts—certain, all-knowing, and sometimes set in their ways: "A narrative of faculty as learners positions faculty as master learners who purposefully open themselves to learning more than they know already" (2008, p. 168).

CHAPTER FOUR

The Scholarship of Teaching
and Learning Meets
Assessment

We will be continuing to look for ways to build
bridges between the scholarship of teaching and
learning and institutional assessment.
—St. Olaf College[1]

Like members of an extended family, the scholarship of teaching and learning and institutional assessment clearly share some DNA, but they have their differences as well. Both put a spotlight on student learning and on bringing a more systematic, evidence-based approach to questions of educational quality. For scholars of teaching and learning, this move is typically motivated by questions that arise from experience in their own classrooms, whereas assessment more often begins with concerns about institutional effectiveness and accountability. The former brings faculty's habits and values as scholars to their work as teachers; the latter is more likely to reflect administrative needs.

Both the scholarship of teaching and learning and assessment are dedicated as well to being more public about the learning that happens (or does not) in college and university classrooms, and to making that learning visible. But the publics they have in view can be quite different. The scholarship of teaching and learning is, if you will, work "of the faculty, by the faculty, and for the faculty," who use its findings to improve the experience of their own students in their own settings. Assessment's audiences, in contrast, often include trustees, policymakers, parents, and others who want to know if higher education is meeting its promises to students and society.

Care must be taken here; it's easy to overdraw the distinctions between these two educational movements.[2] Both are multidimensional, taking various shapes in various settings. The scholarship of teaching and learning looks

different when done by historians than it does, say, in the chemistry department; different, often, on a research university campus than at a liberal arts
college. Similarly, with assessment: on some campuses it is driven mainly by
external reporting demands; on others it prompts rich faculty discussion of goals
for student learning and new designs for curriculum and pedagogy to achieve
those goals. And in some settings these approaches even manage to coexist.

Nevertheless, and at some risk of overgeneralization, the scholarship of
teaching and learning and institutional assessment can fairly be seen as mirror
images, both shining a powerful light on student learning, but with the former
being faculty-driven, bottom-up, close to the classroom, and, yes, scholarly,
whereas the latter is driven by administrative needs, top-down, typically focused on institutional effectiveness, and shaped by outside requirements including, especially, accreditation. In short, the scholarship of teaching and
learning and institutional assessment may belong to the same extended family,
but their origins, methods, contexts, and champions differ in significant ways.

Not surprisingly, then, the two movements have proceeded on more or
less separate tracks. From its early days in higher education, assessment was
"consciously separated from what went on in the classroom," Peter Ewell
explains—a move intended to "increase the credibility of the generated evidence" and to distinguish it from grading, which was seen as suspect and
inflated (2009, p. 19). Meanwhile, the emerging scholarship of teaching and
learning community sought to distance *its* approach and language from that of
assessment, concerned that getting too cozy with an institutional or administrative agenda could put at risk the grass-roots, intellectual impulse behind the
work. Indeed, many faculty we have worked with in the Carnegie Academy
for the Scholarship of Teaching and Learning (CASTL) have looked with mixed
feelings, and even with alarm, at signs of buy-in from the provost or president,
fearing that such work could become yet another requirement, or be co-opted to
meet someone else's goals. "It can't be something thought up by administrators
and adopted accordingly," one campus leader told us.

Cautions like these have not disappeared; nor should they. But our review of
the trajectories of assessment and the scholarship of teaching and learning over
the last decade suggests that the family feud may be starting to cool.[3] In this
chapter, we reconsider the relationship between these two important developments in higher education, looking, as suggested in the chapter's epigraph from
St. Olaf College, at "ways to build bridges between the scholarship of teaching
and learning and institutional assessment." In particular, our focus is on the
possible benefits to be had—on both sides—from stronger and more strategic
connections. For assessment, building bridges to the scholarship of teaching
and learning may help solve the movement's most enduring challenge: making
a difference in the classroom. For the scholarship of teaching and learning, a
closer connection with assessment may help embed the work more deeply in

institutional life, raising the chances for long-term viability. Our argument is that the two movements stand to gain from the work of the other, but also, and more important, that higher education *needs* their combined strengths.

BUILDING BRIDGES

In the Carnegie Foundation's recent survey of campuses in the CASTL Institutional Leadership and Affiliates Program, connections between the scholarship of teaching and learning and institutional assessment were a prominent—and, frankly, surprising—theme. Asked about an array of "wider institutional agendas" to which the scholarship of teaching and learning might have contributed, respondents ranked assessment fourth from the top of the list—and third in a version of the question focused on departmental and program agendas (Ciccone, Huber, Hutchings, and Cambridge, 2009, p. 19). Indeed, the theme of impact on (or sometimes from) assessment ran through the responses to virtually every question on the survey. Given the sometimes uneasy relationship between the two movements, it's worth asking: What's going on here, anyway?

Consider, in this regard, developments at St. Olaf College. A private liberal arts college in Northfield, Minnesota, St. Olaf became officially engaged with CASTL in 2003, but interest was longer standing. "Our work has been to support faculty in exploring ways we can improve teaching and learning," says David Schodt, director of the Center for Innovation in the Liberal Arts (CILA), as the campus teaching center is called. "What can I do in my classroom tomorrow, or next semester, that will help me do things better?"[4] Toward this end, in 2000, Schodt and his colleagues established a program of "CILA Associates"—individuals selected for a year-long experience with a scholarship of teaching and learning project at its center. In 2005, an additional feature was added, with learning communities organized around each Associate's project, a model intended to expand faculty engagement with such work. CILA Associates also participate in "Faculty Conversations" and in other events where they share their work with the broader campus and academic community.

Several years ago, as CILA Associates spread the word about the scholarship of teaching and learning, St. Olaf was also sharpening its focus on institutional assessment in preparation for a required progress report to its regional accrediting commission. At first, says Schodt, his instinct was to keep that work—housed in the Office of Evaluation and Assessment, and directed by a faculty member—as distinct as possible from the scholarship of teaching and learning. Institutional assessment, as he saw it, "was never something faculty are going to be interested in," and he didn't want its shadow darkening enthusiasm for the classroom inquiry projects being undertaken by CILA Associates and their learning community colleagues.

But here's the surprise: looking back on the larger trajectory of campus work, Schodt reflects, "It seems to me that our efforts on campus over the past 10 years or so to support faculty in the scholarship of teaching and learning have acquired some useful synergy from recent national assessment efforts." He points, for instance, to the campus's use of the Collegiate Learning Assessment (CLA), an instrument designed to measure the institution's contribution to students' critical thinking and problem-solving skills. Though the CLA does not provide results at the level of individual students or courses, its use of performance tasks and scoring rubrics resonated with what faculty know and do as teachers, and the instrument thus turned out to be a useful "complement to local work in the scholarship of teaching and learning," Schodt says. "We recently used our students' performance on the CLA as a way to invite faculty to consider ways to design assignments to improve critical thinking and to assess the consequences of these assignments for student learning."

The dynamic has worked in the other direction as well. Not only has assessment contributed to the scholarship of teaching and learning; Schodt believes that "engagement with the scholarship of teaching and learning has contributed to faculty acceptance of institutional assessment." In particular, he says, "We've noticed that those departments that have had faculty engaged with the scholarship of teaching and learning tend to have the best understanding of how to [identify learning outcomes]." Because they have assessed student learning in their classrooms as part of their scholarship of teaching and learning, faculty "understand much better why an institution might want to do that and what are useful ways of doing it, and what are some ways that aren't so useful."

Connecting classroom inquiry to institutional assessment has not been easy. "I spent a lot of time thinking about how you could scale up from the scholarship of teaching and learning and scale down from institutional assessment," Schodt recalls. The connections sometimes feel fragile, and the purposes are often different, even at odds; and, in short, "it has been harder" than he expected. But as our 2009 CASTL Survey responses show, bridges *are* being built—and not only at St. Olaf.

At a large public research university, for example, the climate created by the scholarship of teaching and learning has meant that "assessment is no longer a four-letter word"; faculty have begun to understand "that it can be done 'from the inside' according to their curiosities and remaining within their control." At a private master's level institution, participation in the scholarship of teaching and learning movement has helped to make "the assessment of student learning... an institutional priority." At a public comprehensive university, "discussions of assessment (at all levels) have become more sophisticated." And among two-year institutions in a state system, "assessment conversations have connected to the scholarship of teaching and learning to generate more meaningful assessments." Indeed, in some settings the two movements have been so intertwined as to be inseparable. A leader of CASTL work from Miami Dade College reports, "It is impossible to separate the College's initiative to map and assess newly adopted learning outcomes from the presence of the scholarship of teaching and learning initiative as they span the same timeframe and are both aimed to make the process of teaching and learning visible."

Where then does the scholarship of teaching and learning leave off and assessment begin? How are they different—in motivation, methods, and results? Is it a good thing for them to be subsumed into each other? What do these two major movements in higher education have to offer one another? What does each, individually and "bridged" to the other, contribute to higher education's mission in a time of heightened expectations for student learning and growing calls for institutional accountability?

AN ETHIC OF INQUIRY

Throughout its several recent decades of activity in higher education, assessment's critics, as well as its champions, have worried about the weak link to classroom teaching and learning. "Just because an institution assessed student learning outcomes relative to a general education goal [does] not mean that the assessment information was used," quips Derek Bok in *Our Underachieving Colleges*, "nor is there much indication these evaluations affect how professors teach their courses" (2006, p. 317). Indeed, the National Institute for Learning Outcomes Assessment (NILOA) reported that assessment is often seen on campus as "redundant," duplicating already existing processes and not yielding additional benefits (Kuh and Ikenberry, 2009, p. 9). Similarly, in 2009 the Faculty Survey of Student Engagement revealed that although 75 percent of respondents saw their campuses as involved in assessment "quite a bit" or "very much," only about a third had positive views of the dissemination and usefulness of assessment findings (National Survey of Student Engagement, 2009, pp. 21–22).

This disconnect is not altogether surprising. The kinds of data generated by many of today's most widely used assessment instruments and approaches can feel distinctly distant from the daily life of teaching and learning. Assessment, coming as it typically does from a central office, often reporting to the provost, tends to live "up there," generating data about the institution's general effectiveness in fostering, say, critical thinking, while faculty are busy "down here" planning activities for the next class session, grading exams, and meeting with students. Given the distance between the two activities, faculty may have a hard time seeing how institutional scores and results relate to their plans for Monday morning's class or for their department's curricular redesign.

Questions at the Classroom Level

Against this backdrop, it is intriguing to see growing numbers of faculty working under the banner of the scholarship of teaching and learning. Their efforts comprise a number of practices, but the movement's defining feature, its sine qua non, is inquiry into the learning of one's own students. Indeed, for many faculty (often because they are trying something new in the classroom that raises questions about what works and how), it is the desire to understand much more deeply what and how their students are learning that propels them into such inquiry (Bass, 1999; Ciccone, Meyers, and Waldmann, 2008). Again and again in reports from scholars of teaching and learning about what motivates them to do this work, we see this impulse: the need to be "as discerning about what is learned as we are about what is taught"; "unprecedented attentiveness to students' work, their cultural capital, and their learning" (Salem and Salvatori, respectively, quoted in Huber and Hutchings, 2005, p. 127);[5] and, as one campus put it in responding to the 2009 CASTL Survey, "a hunger for more information about how their students are doing" (Ciccone, Huber, Hutchings, and Cambridge, 2009, p. 6).

Not surprisingly, the shapes that this impulse to inquiry takes are sometimes far afield from the kind of work that occupies the institution's office of assessment. The scholarship of teaching and learning encompasses a wide range of methods, drawn from a full range of disciplines, and may, for instance, focus on a very small number of students, sometimes even a single learner whose development is traced over time. Projects may yield densely qualitative data that do not resolve into neat findings; indeed, some have proposed that "messiness" be recognized and valued as a feature of classroom inquiry (Bass and Eynon, 2009, p. 5). And many scholars of teaching and learning see themselves in the business not simply of providing data for improvement (or reporting), but of building new knowledge and conceptions of learning (Hutchings and Huber, 2008; Riordan, 2008; Ciccone, Meyers, and Waldmann, 2008). In all of these ways, and more, the scholarship of teaching and learning differs from assessment, but the two movements overlap around one deeply generative shared notion: that the experience and learning of college students can and should be a site for investigation; that there are good questions to be asked about what, how, how much, and how deeply students are learning. Seen in this way, the scholarship of teaching and learning can help nourish the ethic of inquiry that assessment depends upon but has been hard-pressed to establish in ways that reach down into the work of faculty and students.

Mary Savina at Carleton College has watched this connection emerge. On her campus, she tells us in the 2009 CASTL Survey, the scholarship of teaching and learning has brought about "an increase in the number of faculty who want to see actual data about, say, the types of students who presently take lab courses, rather than relying on anecdotal information.... It's clear that ideas from the scholarship of teaching and learning, most importantly the idea that data from assessments can be used to improve student learning, have filtered into these discussions." What she sees is, in short, "a change in the intellectual climate," a new attention to data as a key to improvement. And while the scholarship of teaching and learning is only one of a number of forces that have pushed in this direction in recent years, it has been a powerful impetus, one that invites faculty involvement; stirs interest in results (as CLA findings did at St. Olaf); prompts further inquiry, experimentation, and improvements for students; and provides an entrée to assessment that did not otherwise exist. For campuses that see and carefully cultivate this connection, assessment may begin to look more appealing and much more likely to make a difference where it matters most—in the classroom.

LOCATION, LOCATION

What makes this possibility even more intriguing is that it has a flip side. Whereas the scholarship of teaching and learning can help move assessment "down" toward the work of teachers and teaching, assessment, for its part, can help pull classroom-based inquiry "up" toward more cross-cutting program and institutional agendas. This does not mean letting go of the classroom focus, which most observers (we among them) would agree is a defining feature of the scholarship of teaching and learning. What it does mean is looking for ways to locate and embed that work in the wider context of the discipline, department, program, and institution.

This move is under way, as a growing chorus of voices has arisen around the possibilities for more collaborative, cross-cutting scholarship of teaching and learning (see, for instance, Gale, 2008) and for inquiry at the program and department level (Schroeder, Brooke, and Freeman, 2006). The design of CASTL in its final phase also aimed to promote collaboration, organizing campuses around shared institutional agendas to which the scholarship of teaching and learning could make a contribution.[6] This move toward attention to shared agendas makes particular sense at a time when so many campuses (spurred largely by accreditation) are moving to articulate student learning outcomes at the program and institutional levels (Association of American Colleges and Universities, 2009, p. 3; Kuh and Ikenberry, 2009, pp. 2–3).[7] Such outcomes are a promising focus for collaborative inquiry. Imagine, for instance, a group of faculty from different fields investigating students' progress toward critical thinking, writing, problem solving, or quantitative reasoning, as some campuses are doing through the use of portfolios (Bierman, Ciner, Lauer-Glebov, Rutz, and Savina, 2005).[8]

Sometimes collaborative work emerges organically, as in the Visible Knowledge Project (VKP), a national scholarship of teaching and learning initiative that brought faculty from diverse institutional settings together to explore the impact of new media on the learning and teaching of the humanities. As individual projects evolved and took shape, so did a sense of the larger whole. VKP leaders Randy Bass and Brett Eynon explain: "That is, what emerged from each individual classroom project was a piece of insight, a unique local and limited vision of the relationship between teaching and learning that yet contributed to some larger aggregated picture,... our own 'teaching commons' in which individual faculty insights pooled together into larger meaningful patterns" (2009, p. 11).

In other cases, attention to collective work is "designed in" from the beginning. At the University of Kansas, for example, the Center for Teaching Excellence has adapted the course portfolio—originally designed for individual faculty to document and examine learning in a particular course—to program-level inquiry. Thus, over the past few years, faculty teams from art history, journalism, electrical engineering, and more than 20 other fields have created "program portfolios" that capture and explore their goals for student learning. "It has been fascinating," Center director Daniel Bernstein says, "to see how the work of an entire program has the same feature of scholarly inquiry that can be seen in an individual teacher's work" (2008a, p. 2). The program portfolio initiative was spurred in part by a comment from Bernstein's provost, who suggested a move from "retail to wholesale" (Bernstein, Bunnell, and Collins, 2008), and Bernstein believes that "extending the focus of the scholarship of teaching and learning to the program level has brought significant gains for our campus. When individual faculty members see their department engage an ongoing cycle of inquiry and improvement, they are more inclined to import that practice into their own courses" (July 5, 2010).

These two approaches—letting shared interests emerge organically, on the one hand, and, on the other, situating the scholarship of teaching and learning as a collaborative venture from the beginning—are not mutually exclusive, certainly. Mount Royal University in Calgary, Alberta, has deliberately created opportunities for both through its Institute for Scholarship of Teaching and Learning. Individuals selected to participate in the Institute's Teaching and Learning Scholars Program each undertake a research project aimed at improving practice in the teaching and learning of his or her discipline. But in addition, the Engaging Departments Initiative aims to bring the tools and habits of the scholarship of teaching and learning to "campus-wide and emerging degree programs," writes Miriam Carey, a faculty member in policy studies. "Our belief is that systematic scholarly inquiry into student learning will provide significant data on student learning that can, when organized and aggregated around common institutional or programmatic themes, lead to systemic improvements within specific academic departments and throughout the university as a whole" (2010, p. 13).

The time is right for such work, as Mount Royal recently changed status from a two-year college to a university, and new degree requirements and programs must be put in place. Seizing this opportunity, four faculty members teaching in the newly designed general education program are collaborating to study "critical reading" in four different first-year "foundations" courses they teach within the new program, working with a shared definition (critical reading is defined as reading for academic purposes and social engagement), common methods and sources of evidence, and a jointly designed rubric for analyzing results. This effort promises to help advance thinking about critical reading and how to teach for it in the new general education program, but the four scholars are committed as well to undertaking their collaborative inquiry in a way that other programs and departments—at Mount Royal and beyond—can use as a model (Carey, Gale, Manarin, and Rathburn, 2010).

Looking Across Levels

One last example of how the scholarship of teaching and learning can be extended beyond the individual classroom is the Carnegie Foundation's recent project "Strengthening Pre-collegiate Education in Community Colleges" (SPECC). As part of a commitment to improving learning in developmental mathematics and English programs, SPECC campuses created vehicles for collaborative scholarship of teaching and learning called Faculty Inquiry Groups (FIGs). These groups bring educators together—including full-time faculty, adjuncts, and others, such as counselors, who work closely with students—to confer about their goals for student learning and to design and test out strategies for accelerating progress toward meeting those goals. Sometimes groups are diverse in interests and backgrounds, with membership from different departments and roles, drawn together by a general commitment to inquiry. More often, however, and in our view especially important for changes that "add up," FIGs bring together educators who work in a particular setting and share specific goals for student learning. For instance, faculty teaching a multisection developmental English course at City College of San Francisco met regularly to review student work, to rethink and revise course design and assignments, and to create new assessments, which, in turn, spurred a next cycle of inquiry and action (Huber, 2008b; Carnegie Foundation for the Advancement of Teaching, 2008).

Particularly relevant to our themes in this chapter is the power of FIGs to create an appetite for types of evidence that were not otherwise at hand, and an occasion for bringing different kinds and levels of evidence together in order to meet new pedagogical challenges. As vehicles for practitioner research, FIGs depend first and foremost on careful examination of evidence generated in the regular routines of teaching and learning: student exams, projects, papers, problem sets, office consultations, and grades. But what participants often discover is that inquiry at the classroom level, though necessary, is not sufficient. Teachers need a chance to step back from their own practice and see their students' work, and their own, anew, from a different angle and altitude. Thus, an important lesson of SPECC's work is the power of viewing evidence from the classroom (the province of the scholarship of teaching and learning) through the lens of larger trends and patterns (from institutional assessment and research): data about student demographics, enrollment, retention, results from instruments like the Community College Survey of Student Engagement, and so forth.

The value of bringing these different perspectives together is nicely illustrated by a story from Los Medanos College, where the Developmental Education Committee realized that their efforts to reshape curriculum and pedagogy needed to be informed by evidence that faculty members did not have, including—and especially—patterns of students' course taking and success beyond the level of individual courses. The committee approached the Office of Institutional Research, and the two groups worked together to develop a data-gathering plan that would address the questions faculty wanted to understand more fully. The result was a report tracking students from precollegiate courses into the first level of transfer English and math courses. This was not the kind of information institutional research staff members were in the habit of preparing; nor was it a perspective that faculty as scholars of the teaching and learning in their own classrooms were accustomed to seeing. But it turned out to provide a powerful rationale for redoubling efforts to keep Los Medanos students moving through the developmental sequence.[9]

This example is a suggestive one, we believe, because it underlines the value of pursuing inquiry across multiple, interconnected levels, linking classroom-based scholarship of teaching and learning to issues at the curricular, department, program, and institutional levels where assessment typically finds a home. Faculty Inquiry Groups are one mechanism for facilitating such links, but of course they are not the only one. Campus teaching centers—prominently featured in Chapter 3—can play a key role in facilitating cross-level, data-based conversations, providing leadership not only for the scholarship of teaching and learning, but for assessment—an enterprise that many of them were once eager to keep at arm's length (Hutchings, 2010).[10] And, to pick an example from abroad, we are intrigued by the potential of "innovation labs" at Bournemouth University in the United Kingdom, where a course team identifies a problem that needs to be tackled, and then works with campus scholars of teaching and learning to design solutions. Whatever the structure or particular process, the idea is to get richer and more varied kinds of information into the mix and "talking to each other."

New Roles for Students

In Chapter 2, we highlight the experience of students who are, on many campuses today, taking active roles in the scholarship of teaching and learning—not as objects of inquiry, that is, but as co-inquirers, helping to shape key questions, gather and analyze data, and then push for change where it is needed. This may mean working with an individual faculty member to conduct a study of his or her classroom, but it may also entail participation in projects on course design, curricular reform, and the creation of new campus structures and communities for strengthening learning and teaching. As it turns out, these kinds of student involvement in the scholarship of teaching and learning constitute a further point of intersection with assessment. In both arenas, new roles for students, and new ways to give voice to student perspectives and experiences, have emerged as a promising resource for improvement—at the classroom level and beyond.

One particularly interesting development has recently taken shape as part of the Wabash National Study of Liberal Education, a multiyear effort, employing a variety of instruments and data sources, to determine how much students change during their time in college. As explained by the study director, Charles Blaich, a critical goal of the current phase of work is to translate assessment results into "actionable" ideas that lead to real improvement (Nov. 4, 2010). That's a common enough goal, and certainly one that many institutions have found challenging, but the study's approach is an *un*common one: to invite students into the process. Student participation can take many forms, from student government meetings focused on local Wabash Study results, to informal conversations in which students talk about where and when they learn the most.

One recent approach asked participating campuses to identify a "specific point of assessment data that would be more fully understood and actionable with student input" (Blaich and Wise, 2010, p. 1). Student-faculty and student-staff teams then worked collaboratively to put together appropriate processes for capturing student perspectives—including surveys, interviews, focus groups (run in some cases by students themselves), and Town Hall gatherings—and plans for sharing their results with faculty, staff, administrators, and students on their campuses. The approach has turned out to be especially useful, Blaich says, in interpreting results from standardized surveys and instruments, which are necessarily framed in general terms that do not capture particular circumstances and realities on any given campus, thus masking problems but also missing important opportunities to build on what's working (Nov. 4, 2010).

The 49 institutions engaged in this work are a diverse group, including liberal arts colleges, two-year institutions, regional comprehensive campuses, and large public research universities. Certainly they will develop different approaches to student involvement as their efforts evolve, but the possibilities are nicely illustrated by North Carolina A&T State University, a participant in the Wabash National Study and also, not coincidentally, a member of the CASTL Institutional Leadership and Affiliates Program. Using campus results from the Wabash National Study as their foundation, Karen Hornsby, a faculty member in philosophy, and Scott Simkins, director of North Carolina A&T State University's Academy of Teaching and Learning, developed the Wabash-Provost Scholars Program to "dig deeper" into their assessment results. Now in its third year of implementation, the program "trains undergraduate students to conduct focus group sessions with their peers, obtain and analyze qualitative and quantitative data, develop written summary reports, and lead scholarly presentations on their work and experiences. Wabash-Provost Scholars directly contribute to the knowledge base regarding the student learning environment at NC A&T State University while developing valuable research and presentation skills" (North Carolina A&T State University Academy for Teaching and Learning).

Over the past three years, Wabash-Provost Scholars have conducted student focus group sessions on the campus learning environment and classroom teaching practices, on the impact of student-led versus faculty-led Supplemental Instruction, and on ways to enhance the intellectual climate on campus. In addition, the Scholars have assisted with campuswide national assessments, conducted surveys, and overseen a comprehensive weeklong time-diary study including over 200 students. Hornsby and Simkins have trained over 35 Wabash-Provost Scholars, who receive "service hour" credit for participation, learn about human subjects issues, and carry out their work with full institutional review board approval. These students not only provide context for campus-based institutional research through reports and presentations to the campus community (including, in what is now an annual event, to senior administrators), but also share their experiences through presentations at regional and national conferences, workshop leadership, and even consultations with other campuses. Their work has been especially consequential in highlighting practices and policies that impede student success on campus, outlining the characteristics of effective Supplemental Instruction practices, and illuminating issues regarding students' use of out-of-class time. Results of their scholarship are being used to inform faculty, staff, students, and administrators of students' perspectives on academic and institutional concerns and to shape campus efforts to improve retention and graduation rates.

Both assessment and the scholarship of teaching and learning embrace values of evidence and inquiry. And both must seek out ways to make the evidence they generate as powerful as it can be if higher education is to meet society's goals for student learning and success in the twenty-first century. For assessment, the challenge typically lies in turning "high-level" data (such as survey findings or retention statistics) into information that educators care about "on the ground" and can act upon in the ways they teach and design their courses, work with colleagues on curriculum, and contribute to institutional practice around advising, retention, and graduation. For the scholarship of teaching and learning the challenge typically lies in the other direction—turning findings about a particular classroom into information that is meaningful at the level of program and curriculum design. What's needed is more conversation between the two communities; more "brokers," including students, who can help make connections across levels; and more structures and tools for an integrated, top-to-bottom approach to educational quality.

ACCOUNTABILITY

Our thesis in this chapter is that building bridges between the scholarship of teaching and learning and institutional assessment, finding common cause, can strengthen the work of students, faculty, programs, and campuses; that the two movements can do more good together than alone. But as St. Olaf's David Schodt and many others have discovered, making these connections is easier said than done. Creating an integrated web of evidence for improvement, and a collective will and capacity to use it, will always be a work in progress. And like many things, it is harder yet in the current climate of accountability.

Some not-so-distant history may be relevant here. In the 1980s, before the term "assessment" was widely heard on most college campuses, the National Governors Association released a report tellingly entitled *Time for Results* (1986). The impulse behind that report—an impatience, on the one hand, with higher education's perceived complacency and sense of entitlement, and, on the other, an urgency about quality spurred by the critical examination of K–12 education in *A Nation at Risk* (National Commission on Excellence in Education, 1983)—was played out in several ways.

For starters, states began issuing higher education assessment mandates, some with teeth (and high stakes for students), some relatively gentle and permissive. Over time, and in the face of budget exigencies and competing agendas, many of those mandates fell by the wayside or were simply let slip. But accountability did not go away. Indeed, by 1989 assessment was already institutionalized, written into federal requirements for accrediting agencies, which were—and still are—required to ensure that campuses gather and use evidence of student learning for improvement. Those requirements took time to take shape and make their way into self-study guidelines and protocols for visiting teams, but they are now for the most part taken for granted. "The majority of academics now realize that engaging in assessment has become a condition of doing business," Peter Ewell observes in a review of the movement's evolution over twenty years. "All of them may not want to engage in assessment themselves, but they are willing to accord the activity a legitimacy that was not forthcoming two decades ago" (2009, p. 6). This view has no doubt been helped along by the fact that accrediting groups have been able to hold off the twin specters of standardized testing and institutional comparisons, which were widely feared in the movement's earlier years.

Then, just when it seemed safe to go back in the water, the Spellings Commission hearings brought the testing agenda rushing to the surface. Though its final report (National Commission on the Future of Higher Education, 2006) set that prospect aside, the message was heard, and several national education associations jumped into action to create the Voluntary System of Accountability through which institutions can report a range of data, including results on a menu of possible assessment instruments.

The point here is that the pressure for accountability has waxed and waned and taken different forms, but it has remained a looming presence on the higher education landscape for the last twenty-some years—and that landscape, for better or worse, is the one on which the scholarship of teaching and learning has landed and taken root. Where then, one must ask, does such work sit relative to assessment-as-accountability?

For many, the hoped-for answer is certain to be "as far away as possible." But what we have seen from our CASTL perch is a growing sense that if the scholarship of teaching and learning is to have a lasting place—and make an enduring difference—in academic life and work, it must connect to other institutional agendas, including those that matter to the public and to policymakers: retention, completion, writing, problem solving, critical thinking, and so forth, all of which come with an accountability edge.

An important moment in CASTL's own history comes to mind here. From 2006 through 2009, the Carnegie Foundation periodically gathered the coordinators of the multicampus groups that comprised the CASTL Institutional Leadership and Affiliates Program. At one of these gatherings, this group of leaders was having dinner at the hotel restaurant, enjoying good food and a chance to catch up before we turned to the formal meeting agenda the next morning. But one of our guests had something serious on her mind. At Middlesex Community College in Massachusetts, where she has spent her career as a psychology professor and leader of numerous institutional initiatives, Donna Duffy saw the writing on the scholarship-of-teaching-and-learning wall. If we want this work to stick in a place like mine, she told the group, it has to connect to high visibility, public agendas for higher education—in particular (in her case), raising levels of student retention and completion among learners who are underprepared and underserved. How, she challenged the dinner group, do we talk to campus presidents and to those outside the scholarship of teaching and learning movement about its contribution to these larger institutional and social imperatives?

That challenge has very much informed our thinking in recent years, and it has begun also to shape the way institutions have framed the scholarship of teaching and learning. Working with five other CASTL campuses in a group called COPPER (Communities of Practice Pooling Educational Resources), Duffy and her colleagues organized a conference that brought together scholars of teaching and learning along with presidents, provosts, and deans who attended a special workshop to discuss the work's relevance to campus goals and agendas, and to core processes around retention, the assessment of general education outcomes, strategic planning, institutional effectiveness, and accreditation. The work has also been presented to the Middlesex Community College's board of trustees and to the Massachusetts Secretary of Education, to whom Duffy described "the value of the scholarship of teaching and learning for faculty and why it is a good investment" (Duffy, Feb. 6, 2009).

Middlesex is certainly not alone in the move to give the scholarship of teaching and learning a more visible, public face. Workshops to help campus administrators understand more about the institutional role and power of the scholarship of teaching and learning have become standard fare at an annual institute sponsored by a group of former CASTL campuses and hosted most recently by Creighton University. And we know of a number of campuses that have showcased the scholarship of teaching and learning at meetings with trustees. Accreditation too has created an occasion for giving such work more prominent, public visibility; about a quarter of our 2009 CASTL Survey respondents identified accreditation as an institutional agenda to which the scholarship of teaching and learning had contributed. At the University of Cincinnati, for instance, Wayne Hall, vice provost for faculty development, reports that in materials for an April 2009 reaccreditation visit, the campus was "able to refer to scholarship of teaching and learning areas of focus within our undergraduate general-education curriculum as evidence of assessment of student learning." At Truman State University, the scholarship of teaching and learning has been used in five-year program reviews, and, says Julie Lochbaum, director of the campus teaching center, "it will probably be natural then to use scholarship of teaching and learning data in our next accreditation round" (Aug. 25, 2009).

Such forays into the public arena may still be the exception rather than the rule, but they speak to a new stage of work in which the scholarship of teaching and learning is seen not (or not only) as a set of discrete projects or as a special institutional initiative (always one among many), but as a set of practices that can be brought to bear in achieving widely valued goals and purposes. Seen in this way, its relevance to accountability becomes clearer. Indeed, it is integral to the powerful vision set forth by the Association of American Colleges and Universities in *Our Student's Best Work: A Framework for Accountability Worthy of Our Mission,* which urges commitment to four essential learning outcomes, locally owned goals for student learning, and "a campus-wide commitment to faculty inquiry and educational improvement" (2008, p. 12).

One important argument for this connection is that the scholarship of teaching and learning can help to mitigate the narrow view of evidence that has so far held sway when it comes to educational accountability in the United States. The Voluntary System of Accountability, arguably this country's largest and most visible higher education accountability initiative, invites institutions to report scores on standardized assessment instruments, data about retention, and the like. But its image of accountability is relatively narrow (see, for example, the critique by Adelman, 2008, 2009),[11] making no place for the more fine-grained, in-depth examinations of how and why students learn, which often characterize the scholarship of teaching and learning. And that's a loss. Particularly as new pedagogies take hold—pedagogies that are not simply new ways to accomplish old goals, but approaches that bring with them new goals for learning—higher education needs the wider array of evidence that the scholarship of teaching and learning can offer. In short, the scholarship of teaching and learning suggests a wider approach to accountability.

In saying this, we recognize the need for caution—for not undoing the distinctive character of the scholarship of teaching and learning, rooted as it is in intellectual curiosity, in a desire to know, in an impulse not to prove but to *im*prove and to understand. It is important to be clear here. We are *not* recommending that the scholarship of teaching and learning become a wholly owned subsidiary of external and administrative pressures, by whatever name. What we *are* suggesting is that the inquiry undertaken by growing numbers of faculty in their own classrooms has something important to contribute as the institution thinks about how to represent its work—and that campus leaders should be actively open to this possibility. Such connections can be especially fruitful where scholars of teaching and learning are working collaboratively to explore questions in which they have a shared interest—especially questions with implications at the departmental and program level: What can we learn, for instance, about the experience of students in first-year seminars designed to prepare them more fully for work in their major? Or how might student engagement with new media change the department's vision of goals for learning? Seeing scholars of teaching and learning as contributors to more meaningful forms of accountability for the institution strikes us as delicate business but also as a possible "win-win," giving the former a firmer place in the campus culture, and the latter a source of fresh evidence to demonstrate responsibility for student learning.

Notes

1. The epigraph comes from the Carnegie Foundation's 2009 survey of campuses participating in the CASTL Institutional Leadership and Affiliates Program. St. Olaf's survey was completed by David Schodt, director of the campus's Center for Innovation in the Liberal Arts.

2. Peter Ewell's observation about the difference between assessment for improvement and assessment for accountability pertains to the distinction we're

making as well. "As with all ideal types," Ewell writes, "the differences between these two contrasting, opposing paradigms of assessment are exaggerated, and rarely does an existing assessment approach fully conform to either one" (2009, p. 3). He suggests a variety of ways to reconcile the two and bring them closer, as we do with assessment and the scholarship of teaching and learning in this chapter.

3. Reinforcing Schodt's observation, Ewell notes that although assessment "remains distasteful for many faculty members, it is angrily rejected far less frequently than it was 20 years ago" (2009, p. 6).

4. All quotes from Schodt, here and throughout this section, come either from the 2009 CASTL Survey or from a telephone interview with Pat Hutchings on Aug. 17, 2009.

5. The first quote is from Anita Salem, a faculty member in mathematics at Rockhurst University; the second from Mariolina Salvatori, professor in English at the University of Pittsburgh. Their comments come from the 2004 Carnegie Foundation survey of CASTL Scholars (see Huber and Hutchings, 2005, p. 127).

6. The move toward more collaborative kinds of inquiry has been central to CASTL, the final phase of which (2006–2009) brought institutions together around "theme groups," in which participants could bring the scholarship of teaching and learning to bear on shared institutional agendas. One group, for instance, working under the leadership of Vancouver Island University (formerly Malaspina University-College), focused on using the scholarship of teaching and learning to advance good practice in the area of undergraduate research (see Beckman and Hensel, 2009). Another group organized around a shared commitment to finding new roles for students in the scholarship of teaching and learning (see Werder and Otis, 2010). A full list of the 13 groups, with participating institutions, can be found in Appendix B in this volume.

7. A survey commissioned and published by the Association of American Colleges and Universities reports that nearly four in five of the organization's 1,200 member institutions have established a set of common learning outcomes for all undergraduates (2009).

8. Such work has been supported by a number of foundations in recent years, including the Teagle Foundation, which has taken a leadership role in pushing the assessment agenda ahead in ways that connect to teaching and learning, as reflected in a statement on its web site:

> The Teagle Foundation's Outcomes and Assessment program is based on the belief that nothing has the potential to affect students' educational experience as much as the systematic assessment of what they learn, along with the use of such assessment to frame discussions on learning and to drive continuous improvements in teaching practices. High priority is given to faculty-driven, ground-up assessment of student learning outcomes in the liberal arts and sciences, especially as they are achieved in academic courses, majors, institutions, and whole sectors of higher education. Our approach to assessment has been shaped by Listenings with college and

university administrators and faculty, leaders of higher education associations and consortia, assessment experts, and others. It continues to be informed by ongoing conversations with these stakeholders ["Outcomes and Assessment"].

Grants for such work have gone to individual campuses, consortia (for instance, the Great Lakes Colleges Association), special centers and institutes (for instance, the Center of Inquiry in the Liberal Arts at Wabash College), scholarly societies, and higher education organizations. Beginning in 2007, in partnership with a number of other groups (including the Association of American Colleges and Universities and the Council on Higher Education Accreditation), Teagle organized a series of meetings to work toward new approaches to assessment and improvement. Emerging consensus among participants led to the establishment of the New Leadership Alliance for Student Learning and Accountability, incorporated in March 2009 (New Leadership Alliance for Student Learning and Accountability, "History").

9. This passage draws from *Basic Skills for Complex Lives* (The Carnegie Foundation for the Advancement of Teaching, 2008, pp. 30–31), a report on the Carnegie Foundation's work with 11 California community colleges.

10. Ed Nuhfer, a long-time leader in the faculty development community, notes: "Many administrators don't have a sense of what faculty development is or how to make the best use of it," adding that "college leaders too often lack a strong sense of how to use teaching centers to complement the work of their campuses' assessment programs" (quoted in Glenn, 2009). On some campuses, however, this connection is beginning to emerge, as suggested by examples in this chapter.

11. In a report on the Bologna Process, Clifford Adelman, a senior associate with the Institute for Higher Education Policy, takes the United States to task for promoting "accountability light": "Even the 'voluntary system of accountability' adopted by a large segment of higher education—which tells the public how many pieces of paper colleges and universities hand out (to whom and when), how much students liked different aspects of their experience at any institution, and how much scores on tests of something called 'critical thinking' improved for a sample of students between entrance and senior year—is more show than substance" (2008, p. 1). Some will see this characterization as overly dismissive, but Adelman's focus on the need for evidence of *learning*, and for forms of accountability that are helpful to *students*, reinforces our sense that the scholarship of teaching and learning can help to reframe thinking about accountability.

CHAPTER FIVE

Valuing—and Evaluating—Teaching

An excellent teacher is one who is engaged in a
well-prepared and intentional ongoing investigation
of the best ways to promote a deep understanding on
the part of as many students as possible.
—Daniel Bernstein, Amy Nelson Burnett,
Amy Goodburn, and Paul Savory[1]

Along with faculty development and the assessment of student learning outcomes, teaching itself has moved up the agenda on many campuses across the United States. Signs of its rising importance appear in many sites of institutional life. It is now common for graduate programs to provide training for doctoral student teaching assistants, and for colleges and universities to expect job candidates to have real teaching experience and elaborated statements of teaching philosophy. There is more support for teaching through centers, sabbaticals, course development grants, certificate programs, external funding, and special initiatives. New criteria for teaching awards reflect today's more sophisticated understandings of "excellent teaching," and it is no longer unusual to find pedagogical publications, presentations, and leadership highlighted on academic CVs. This is progress.

Yet from the perspective of many participants in the scholarship of teaching and learning movement, there remains a troubling gap between rhetoric about teaching's value and the realities of teaching's recognition and reward. It's not that teaching hasn't made great strides in this regard. Guidelines governing academic advancement at many institutions allow and even invite consideration of a wider range of teaching activities than ever before. Considered in all their complexity, however—not just as policies, but as evaluation practices applied to particular cases—these systems have miles to go before they adequately acknowledge the scholarship of teaching and learning in any of the traditional categories of faculty work. Indeed, improving this situation involves everyone: administrators who can signal changes in what should count in their institutions and programs, faculty in their roles as gatekeepers and reviewers of each other's accomplishments both on and off campus, and students in their capacity as evaluators of their teachers' efforts on their behalf.

The issues surrounding recognition and reward are complicated by the variety of activities that the scholarship of teaching and learning can involve. It may be helpful to think of the work as a continuum, with phases (and products) pertaining to each of the familiar faculty roles in teaching, service (to the institution or profession), and research.[2] Like the other new scholarships of integration and engagement, which share this same hybrid character, the scholarship of teaching and learning is vulnerable to the risks associated with each role, in addition to the burdens that its very novelty imposes.

Consider the "teaching" side of this continuum. Classroom innovation is always risky. The teacher must learn the ropes of the new pedagogy or curriculum, and the new approach may offend pedagogically conservative colleagues or run afoul of student expectations for their own levels of engagement and work. Intensifying one's involvement in teaching also tends to take more time, and is not usually confined to new course design and delivery. It easily leads to new lines of work ("service") in support of students, curricula, assessment, or pedagogy—and to the committees and communities that form around these interests and initiatives. And, if one adds inquiry ("research") to the picture, time commitments can multiply. Colleagues may question one's choices, especially when they lead too far beyond one's own classroom, program, or students, because (this is where novelty comes in) they may have little experience or understanding of this kind of work.

More questions arise when it's time for the formal evaluation of a faculty member whose portfolio includes accomplishments in the scholarship of teaching and learning. What part of the work gets presented as teaching, research, or service? Can pedagogical publications, presentations, and grants be considered under the category of research in fields where teaching and learning is not a recognized subject of study? How will their quality be judged, and by whom? Will there be space to submit evidence of the intellectual work that has (presumably) enhanced the scholar's service and teaching? Will that evidence be taken seriously? And—beyond meeting a modest threshold of competence and effectiveness—do the scholar's accomplishments in service and teaching actually matter for purposes of promotion, tenure, retention, or annual review?

The answer to all these questions is, of course, "It depends." It depends on the type of institution one is talking about; on the guidelines of the particular institution in question; on the "evaluative cultures" of individual departments, programs, or disciplines;[3] and on the commitment and skills of the leaders in each of these institutional, departmental, and disciplinary corners of the academic world. To be sure, a great deal of work by scholars of teaching and learning gets done under the radar of formal faculty evaluation.[4] But that is untenable if the scholarship of teaching and learning is to become an integral part of the pedagogical landscape in higher education. This work must be recognized and rewarded in systems of faculty evaluation if it is to influence what larger numbers of faculty (not just heroes, saints, and martyrs) see as possible and desirable to do in their roles as teachers, citizens of their institutions and disciplines, and contributors to knowledge.

This is not to deny or diminish the many other rewards that accrue to faculty members who intensify their engagements with pedagogy and become involved in the scholarship of teaching and learning. At many community colleges, there is precious little recognition or reward to be won through formal faculty evaluation, so the benefits to participants come almost exclusively in other forms: the intellectual pleasures it brings, the sense of professional fulfillment, opportunities for collegiality and instructional leadership, the satisfaction of helping students succeed. The same may be true for the increasing number of faculty who work as adjuncts or in teaching-only positions off the tenure-track in four-year institutions. But this situation is a shame. These faculty, whether they teach in two- or four-year settings, have a great deal to offer from their participation in the scholarship of teaching and learning, and their students, programs, and institutions have much to gain. One might expect that recognizing and rewarding this kind of pedagogical inquiry and innovation would be a priority for institutions that call themselves "teaching colleges," or that depend on faculty in teaching-heavy positions to do the institution's core educational work. But that is not always the case.

The campus leaders we surveyed in our CASTL Institutional Leadership and Affiliates Program strongly agree that important questions about the value and evaluation of the scholarship of teaching and learning are yet to be resolved. Of course, the right promotion and tenure guidelines are needed. But adequate recognition *also* requires better strategies for assessing the quality of the work, weighing its value, and gaining peer acceptance. If, indeed, the scholarship of teaching and learning is contributing positively to a shift (as one leader put it) "in the prevailing understanding of what is expected of professors as teachers," the most important questions concern not only how to evaluate the work's rigor, but also how to expand its reach. "How," another respondent asked, "do we continue to increase understanding of the scholarship of teaching and learning and its value in the reward system?"

THE NEW SCHOLARSHIPS ENTER FACULTY EVALUATION

Since the publication of *Scholarship Reconsidered* in 1990, the "new" scholarships of teaching, application (or engagement), and integration have made real headway into campus systems of faculty evaluation. It's true that they entered what was already a lively field of revision and debate. The Carnegie Foundation's 1994 survey of provosts at four-year institutions found that within the previous five years over four-fifths had completed such a review, had one still under way, or were planning to do one soon (Glassick, Huber, and Maeroff, 1997, Table 1). *Scholarship Reconsidered* gained an audience among faculty and administrators involved in these deliberations because it picked up on an issue of widespread concern: at 86 percent of these colleges and universities "redefining faculty roles" was a major focus of policy review (Table 4). Over three-fourths reported that "the definition of scholarship is being broadened to include the full range of activities in which faculty are engaged," and just over 60 percent said that *Scholarship Reconsidered* itself had played a part in the discussion about faculty roles and rewards at their institution (Tables 5 and 56).

In fact, the scholarships of application and teaching (at least as then understood) had already gained a place on institutional reform agendas by the early 1990s.[5] At institutions where policy reviews were planned, under way, or recently completed, over half the provosts stated in the same survey that "applied scholarship (outreach) is being clearly distinguished from campus and community citizenship activity," while four out of five agreed that "the definition of teaching is being broadened to include activities such as curriculum development, advising, and conducting instructional and classroom research" (Tables 7 and 6). Respondents also reported that they were using or considering a wider set of methods for the evaluation of teaching (for example, about one quarter said they already took account of evidence of student achievement, and some 40 percent more were considering doing so); and that for purposes of faculty advancement, teaching counted more than it had five years before—a change most marked at research universities, where four out of five noted this upward trend (Tables 23 and 35).[6]

Over the next decade, the new scholarships continued to make headway in campus guidelines, in documentation and evaluation practices, and in value or weight, as institution after institution attempted to update its mission and align it with their system of faculty roles and rewards. The effort was given a center and some measure of coordination by the American Association for Higher Education (AAHE) through its annual conferences, its editorial oversight of *Change* magazine, and especially its Forum on Faculty Roles and Rewards, which met every January from 1993 through 2002. Of course, many other associations and initiatives also played important roles in what became a vigorous national conversation about academic priorities. For example, a 1994 report on *The Work of Faculty* by the American Association of University Professors directed "attention to total faculty workload rather than classroom hours" (p. 35).

The new scholarships made sense in different ways (as they still do) to people from different fields and institutional types. At a time when expectations for research were rising across the spectrum of four-year institutions, tensions were rising too. Many faculty in professional fields with strong clinical components saw the scholarship of application as a way to legitimize clinical research and to explain it to faculty from other fields who were more familiar with the rigors of basic discovery research. Some found the idea of a scholarship of integration useful in building the scholarly profile and reputation of efforts to engage a broader public with the findings, methods, and significance of university-based research. Many were intrigued with possibilities of a scholarship of teaching, which, some thought, might be a useful direction for those liberal arts colleges and master's colleges and universities that were expecting faculty with heavy teaching responsibilities to become more productive scholars.[7] And, of course, the scholarship of teaching was a notion that also appealed to faculty in master's and doctoral universities who were interested in focusing more of their intellectual energies on pedagogy.

The early to mid-1990s was, in fact, a productive period of exploration and experimentation in the documentation and evaluation of all kinds of scholarly work. Highlights included: reports from an initiative orchestrated by Robert Diamond of Syracuse University to engage disciplinary associations in thinking about how different kinds of scholarship might be regarded in their fields (Diamond and Adam, 1995, 2000); a set of important reports on the scholarship of application or engagement (Lynton, 1995; Driscoll and Lynton, 1999); and the AAHE's Peer Review of Teaching Project (see Hutchings 1996, 1998). While these efforts all focused on how faculty reward systems might be broadened to better recognize the unique characteristics of the new scholarships, the Carnegie Foundation's own follow-up report to *Scholarship Reconsidered* argued for a focus on qualities that the old and new scholarships *shared*.

Specifically, *Scholarship Assessed* examined the intellectual arc that characterizes scholarship on any topic or of any type, and proposed using the phases of that process to define standards of excellence (Glassick, Huber, and Maeroff, 1997, p. 36; see Exhibit 5.1 on the following page). In other words, work is scholarly to the extent that it exhibits clear goals, adequate preparation, appropriate methods, significant results, effective presentation, and reflective critique—characteristics that can also be used as guides for documentation and standards for evaluation. This was not a completely new formulation; it was drawn from studying the existing standards and criteria recommended by publishers, journals, granting agencies, and colleges and universities for the evaluation of research, teaching, and community engagement. However, many institutions found the synthesis helpful, and *Scholarship Assessed*, too, found its way into the maze of campus discussions and guidelines about the review of faculty work.[8]

Exhibit 5.1 Summary of Standards

Clear Goals

Does the scholar state the basic purposes of his or her work clearly? Does the scholar define objectives that are realistic and achievable? Does the scholar identify important questions in the field?

Adequate Preparation

Does the scholar show an understanding of existing scholarship in the field? Does the scholar bring the necessary skills to his or her work? Does the scholar bring together the resources necessary to move the project forward?

Appropriate Methods

Does the scholar use methods appropriate to the goals? Does the scholar apply effectively the methods selected? Does the scholar modify procedures in response to changing circumstances?

Significant Results

Does the scholar achieve the goals? Does the scholar's work add consequentially to the field? Does the scholar's work open additional areas for further exploration?

Effective Presentation

Does the scholar use a suitable style and effective organization to present his or her work? Does the scholar use appropriate forums for communicating work to its intended audiences? Does the scholar present his or her message with clarity and integrity?

Reflective Critique

Does the scholar critically evaluate his or her own work? Does the scholar bring an appropriate breadth of evidence to his or her critique? Does the scholar use evaluation to improve the quality of future work?

Source: Glassick, C. E., Huber, M. T., and Maeroff, G. I. 1997. *Scholarship Assessed: Evaluation of the Professoriate.* San Francisco: Jossey-Bass and The Carnegie Foundation for the Advancement of Teaching. Exhibit 2.1, p. 36.

Local Interpretation

Help was certainly needed. Reflecting on what had and had not been achieved by the movement to broaden definitions of scholarship in systems of faculty roles and rewards, Russell Edgerton (president of AAHE during the movement's heyday) pointed out that the "initial presentation of the idea in *Scholarship Reconsidered* was rather thin" (2005, p. xiii). Indeed, Boyer's restraint had been both a plus and a minus for the faculty committees charged with revising campus rules and regulations. On the positive side, the light touch of *Scholarship Reconsidered* invited—even required—a great deal of local interpretation, allowing campuses inspired by the book to tailor their revised guidelines to local circumstances. On the negative side, as Edgerton notes, there was "lots of confusion at the campus level about what the various dimensions of scholarship really entail, and how these should be documented and evaluated" (2005, p. xiii).

A thousand flowers bloomed as educators, entrepreneurs, and advocates worked to bring faculty evaluation systems up to date. Important monographs were published, proposing comprehensive approaches to faculty evaluation that could better capture the scholarly (and other professional) dimensions of different kinds of faculty work (see, for example, Arreola, 2000; Arreola, Theall, and Aleamoni, 2003; Braskamp and Ory, 1994; Cashin, 1996; Centra, 1993). Portfolio approaches to facilitate the documentation and evaluation of teaching and community service were developed (Edgerton, Hutchings, and Quinlan, 1991; Hutchings, 1996; Seldin, 1997). New instruments for the student evaluation of teaching were developed, marketed, studied, and refined. Scholarly associations began responding to the challenges that digital scholarship posed to traditional habits of faculty evaluation.

More significant, perhaps, though less widespread, were changes to the language of college and university guidelines. O'Meara's study of the archive of policies collected in 1998 through Harvard University's Project on Faculty Appointments found that *Scholarship Reconsidered* had "had a significant influence on the way in which higher education defines and evaluates faculty work" (2000, p. 156). Although few campuses used the occasion to introduce a completely new set of categories, O'Meara noted that the impact of *Scholarship Reconsidered* was widely evident in the expansion of work mentioned within the familiar terms of teaching, research, and service—especially, the Harvard study found, in "the category of research" (2000, p. 156). Of the 163 institutions that had policies with detailed descriptions, "70 (79%) ... have expanded research definitions to encompass Boyer's work" (p. 158).[9] Because many institutions had long used the term "scholarship" as a virtual synonym for "research," redefining that category to include certain kinds of achievement in interdisciplinary study, community engagement, and pedagogy seemed the obvious way to go.

The AAHE's 2001 survey of chief academic officers at four-year colleges and universities confirmed these trends. Over two-thirds of these provosts "reported that their institutions had changed mission and planning documents, amended faculty evaluation criteria, provided incentive grants, or developed flexible workload programs to encourage and reward a broader definition of scholarship" (O'Meara, 2005, p. 261). And among these reform-minded campuses, over three-quarters reported "expanding the definition of scholarship in faculty evaluation policies"—the most popular change (O'Meara, 2005, p. 261). Interestingly, this is remarkably similar to the proportions reported from the Harvard (79 percent) and Carnegie Foundation (78 percent) studies in earlier years.[10]

By the early 2000s, the new scholarships had entered the official world of faculty roles and rewards, with the scholarship of teaching and learning particularly well served. To summarize, the major developments included (1) revised guidelines at a growing number of institutions (especially, but not only, at baccalaureate colleges and master's colleges and universities), permitting pedagogical projects, presentations, publications, and grants to be considered as research for purposes of tenure, promotion, and annual review; (2) richer, more elaborated ways of documenting teaching at a wider array of colleges and universities; and (3) greater weight assigned to teaching across higher education, for its own sake, no doubt, but also as part of a general trend toward everything counting more. It seems that service on behalf of undergraduate education had also become more important, as opportunities increased for faculty to contribute to (and become known for) pedagogical innovation and inquiry on a wider scale.

Not surprisingly, though, cautious observers could see that although real progress had been made, there was still a long way to go. Surveying the scene in 2002, Braxton, Luckey, and Helland noted that the new scholarships had all been institutionalized at a basic, structural level and that the scholarship of teaching—at least in its guise as a more intentional approach to pedagogical design and improvement—had attained a "procedural level" of institutionalization as a regular part of the workload (pp. iv–v). Yet none of the new scholarships had attained the same level of "incorporation" enjoyed by the scholarship of discovery. In other words, according to these researchers, the new scholarships were not yet fully accepted by faculty as part of academic culture in their institution or field (see also O'Meara, 2005).[11]

THE SCHOLARSHIP OF TEACHING AND LEARNING AS "RESEARCH"

The dilemmas posed by the under-institutionalization of the new scholarships have become most evident to scholars of teaching and learning in the quest to gain recognition for their work as "research." On the positive side, faculty have made successful cases for promotion and tenure based on pedagogical projects and publications—even at research universities—as documented through the case studies of the four pathfinders featured in *Balancing Acts: The Scholarship of Teaching and Learning in Academic Careers* (Huber, 2004). There is also evidence that policy revisions have prompted a growing number of faculty to include such work in their dossiers.[12] Still, campus leaders are quick to point out that recognition for the scholarship of teaching and learning as research is by no means yet assured—and that this uncertainty remains a barrier to wider faculty engagement.

The problems are typically not in the language of the faculty evaluation policy documents themselves. True, many colleges and universities have very general guidelines defining research and creative work at the institution-wide level—but at least these guidelines don't rule out pedagogical scholarship. Even policies that explicitly include pedagogical scholarship have usually been through a lengthy and painstaking vetting process and are very cautiously worded.[13] Two Canadian institutions provide examples with contrasting degrees of specificity and elaboration. Queen's University has a straightforward statement: "Writing and research with respect to pedagogy and innovative teaching shall be assessed as scholarly activity" (Leger, Van Melle, Mighty, and Stockley, 2009, p. 8), whereas the University of British Columbia, officially open to a wider range of products, frames its *Agreement on the Conditions of Appointment for Faculty* with an eye toward clarifying when these products count as scholarship, and when they do not: "For example, textbooks and curriculum reform that changed academic understanding or made a significant contribution to the way in which a discipline or field is taught might constitute useful evidence of the scholarship of teaching, whereas textbooks or curriculum revision of a routine nature would not" (2006, Section 4.03, "Scholarly Activity," under Article 4, "Criteria for Appointment, Reappointment, Tenure and Promotion").

Many policy statements include criteria for the evaluation of scholarship that are—like typical definitions of research and creative work—quite broadly cast. For example, the University of British Columbia's *Agreement* also includes: "originality or innovation, demonstrable impact in a particular field or discipline, peer reviews, dissemination in the public domain, or substantial or sustained use by others" (2006, Section 4.03, "Scholarly Activity," under Article 4, "Criteria for Appointment, Reappointment, Tenure and Promotion"). Thanks, in short, to the high level of generality of such documents, and to the extreme care with which they are written and revised, whatever problems scholars of teaching and learning face in getting their published pedagogical work recognized as research don't usually lie in the formal rules themselves. The problem is in the interpretation and implementation.

Disciplinary Differences

The most general issue, in fact, concerns the interpretation of the rules by particular departments and divisions within the institution, because colleagues in these units make the first, and usually most important, call in recommending (or not) a colleague for tenure and promotion, as well as for ordinary merit review. This important feature of the peer review process allows for variation in the scholarly and evaluative cultures of different fields, but it can also cause problems for scholars of teaching and learning because understanding of this kind of pedagogical work is simply not that widespread. Thus, when leaders of the CASTL program at Queen's University surveyed department heads to find out how the work "was represented as part of the pathway to academic advancement," they found some confusion and resistance. Even though, as we have noted, university rules for scholarly activity clearly included "writing and research with respect to pedagogy and innovative teaching," there were chairs for whom "the predominance of discipline based research as the traditional vehicle for promotion seemed to overshadow any consideration of SoTL affiliated activities" (Leger, Van Melle, Mighty, and Stockley, 2009, p. 10).

These differences in interpretation are not always the simple result of individual understanding and preference. Many institutions formally invite academic units to write their own specifications for what counts as scholarship in their discipline or professional field. Cheryl Albers, a leader of CASTL's work at Buffalo State College, provides a good example of the range of discussions and results that one could find at many colleges that have sought formally to acknowledge the value of the work:

> Policy revision was accomplished through a collaboration among the significant campus structures for faculty governance (the College Senate), academic planning (the Academic Council), and support for SOTL (CASTL Campus Programs Advisory Committee). The document that emerged from campuswide debate and negotiations stresses: the credibility of multiple forms of scholarship; identification of characteristics that unite and those that distinguish various forms of scholarship; acknowledgement that not all faculty will undertake SOTL; the premise that the criteria for assessing scholarship are more important than its classification; and preservation of departments' rights to determine acceptable products of, and criteria for, assessing the quality and significance of scholarship [2004, p. 1].

This means that at Buffalo State (and the same is true elsewhere), departments develop their own statements to guide implementation of the general policy. Albers notes further that some, such as the Computer Information Systems Department at Buffalo State, had actually included the scholarship of teaching and learning in their "Definition of Scholarship" before this campuswide approach was enacted (2004). So, clearly a great deal depends on how these departments' intersecting connections both to institutional and disciplinary norms play out—including, in this case, not just what products of the scholarship of teaching might be acceptable as research, but also by what criteria their quality will be judged, and even whether pedagogical work will be countable as research at all. A particularly informative case study from Western Carolina University notes differences among departments at that institution in regard to "load balance" among different types of faculty work, the value attributed to various outlets for scholarship (regardless of type), proper forms of peer review, and variation in the official value accorded the scholarship of teaching and learning at different career stages (Cruz, Ellern, Ford, Moss, and White, 2009).

The good news is that disciplinary cultures themselves have become friendlier to pedagogical concerns over the past twenty years, with scholarly societies devoting more air-, column-, and cyberspace to teaching and learning in their conferences, journals, and web sites. The sciences, especially, have been encouraged by National Science Foundation programs to strengthen science education. But other fields too—sometimes spurred by the drive from accrediting bodies to articulate student learning outcomes—have stepped up to the plate. As mentioned in Chapter 1, faculty in all fields are now exploring ways to engage undergraduates in disciplinary ways of knowing (Gurung, Chick, and Haynie, 2008). Indeed, the disciplines are now finding themselves home to faculty exploring the possibilities of a wide variety of new pedagogies. Of course, the intensification of interest in matters pedagogical is not evenly spread across fields, but it is probably safe to say that nowhere are teaching and learning still considered marginal or minor concerns.

This is not to say that the scholarship of teaching and learning looks the same or is valued the same across the various disciplines and fields—a fact that complicates institutional efforts to recognize at least some work in the scholarship of teaching and learning as research. Scholars of teaching and learning often draw from familiar disciplinary repertoires of method and argument when undertaking classroom inquiry, which is, of course, a good way to get started. Yet, as Huber and Morreale have pointed out, "the resistance of these [pedagogical] problems to the discipline's familiar modes of inquiry, conceptualization, and research procedures can limit interest in the scholarship of teaching and learning, and even undermine its legitimacy" (2002, p. 16). These problems are somewhat different in the sciences, social sciences, humanities, and professional fields—and so, too, is the response of disciplinary colleagues to inquiry that deals with what is often seen as alien subject matter (teaching and learning), makes use of "stretched" or borrowed methods to look more closely at learning, draws from a different literature, cites different authorities, and is made public in often unfamiliar outlets (see Huber, 1999; Huber and Morreale, 2002; Huber, 2004). Clearly, these considerations can color the opinions of colleagues both inside and outside the scholar's institution, affecting tenure and promotion proceedings directly (committee members and external reviewers), but also indirectly through the evaluation of proposals for grants or conference presentations and of manuscripts for journal or book publishers.[14]

Questions About Quality

When faculty submit the scholarship of teaching and learning as a component of their research and creative activity, they must (like anyone else engaging in new and less familiar lines of work) be prepared for special scrutiny. Some, like Brian Coppola, a chemist from the University of Michigan, and his advocates, believe that the best strategy for making the case is "the standard metric." The goal is to show that the work—however unusual the subject matter (issues in learning), genre (a new curriculum), or methods—can be measured by the same criteria usually applied to research: external funding, peer-reviewed publications, evidence of impact, and support from prestigious peers (see Huber, 2004). In fact, most guidelines, like those mentioned earlier, with their invocation of such criteria as innovation, impact, and leadership, explicitly invite the standard metric approach.

Yet this approach has a downside, especially when it comes to the evaluation of new kinds of work. When Sheri Sheppard, a mechanical engineer from Stanford University, was up for tenure and promotion, she found that the journals, conferences, and external reviewers for her work on engineering education, though respected in that emergent subfield, were not well known to the colleagues on her tenure committee. Her funding did not come with the same prestige; the methods seemed soft; the graduate students did not move on to the "best" positions. Most troubling of all was the fact that even her most successful teaching innovations tended to become public property without her name attached—making it hard to trace, much less lay claim to, the impact of her work (Huber, 2004). She was successful, but it took special effort to make the case on her behalf.[15]

Unfortunately, similar problems can dampen the reception of work on teaching that's presented in genres beyond traditionally peer-reviewed conference presentations, journal articles, and scholarly books. Textbooks, though more likely to be regarded as works of scholarship in some fields than others, have long been problematic when submitted as research for purposes of faculty evaluation. And so have new media projects. Can elaborate web sites created with pedagogical purposes in mind be seen as the equivalent of a book? Can such work be peer reviewed? In the view of one observer, "getting academe's gatekeepers to take digital work seriously" is still a problem, even with sites designed as interactive archives for traditional scholarly research: "If the members of your tenure-and-promotion committee don't have the skills to judge your dazzling visualization of Republican Rome or your fluid-text edition of *Rasselas*, and if it's not getting written about in the journals they read and respect, how likely are they to give you full points for your work?" (Howard, 2010).[16]

New college and university guidelines allowing work in the scholarship of teaching and learning to be submitted as research have opened many doors. But variation among departments in their regard for pedagogical work, and the standard metrics problem highlighted here by cases in engineering education and new media resources, are still challenges to address. Nor are they unique to the scholarship of teaching and learning. For example, a 2008 report on *Scholarship in Public: Knowledge Creation and Tenure Policy in the Engaged University* notes that public scholars tend to organize their work around projects "carried out by a purpose-built team organized for a finite period of time in order to bring about specific results or to create particular events or resources" (Ellison and Eatman, 2008, p. 8). Thus, to be appropriately responsive to community-engaged scholarship, the authors argue that "project-friendly" policies are needed. The evaluation of locally or regionally focused endeavors should "not use national or international scope to define intellectual quality," but rather attend to the project's "complexity, creativity, and rigor," and promotion and tenure policies should also recognize the variety of roles (project management and leadership), results (a new program or curriculum), and products (public presentation) that "may flow from project-based academic work" (Ellison and Eatman, 2008, p. 8).

Clearly, there is a lot at stake in finding ways for the faculty evaluation system to "see" the genres native to particular kinds of work, if that work is to maintain its integrity and even count as research. Of course, there is always the possibility of submitting work in the scholarship of teaching and learning as teaching or service, but these alternatives raise difficult issues as well.

THE SCHOLARSHIP OF TEACHING AND LEARNING AS "TEACHING"

Although demands for research and creative activity in U.S. higher education have generally risen over the past twenty years at all kinds of campuses, the standards for quantity, visibility, and impact still vary considerably by institutional type. However, virtually all faculty teach, and though course loads vary, the expectation that faculty will do a good or excellent job as a teacher is common. Moreover, what counts as teaching has been broadened, and the definition of "good" or "excellent" has become more sophisticated in ways that are consonant with principles from the scholarship of teaching and learning. Some very important experiments in the evaluation of teaching, under way today, show promise as ways of institutionalizing these principles in the tenure and promotion process. And, at the farther end of the tunnel, we can see developments, both in the United States and abroad, that intimate a future where pedagogical accomplishments are weighted more heavily for all and even, for some, recognized as the principal pathway to faculty advancement.

The 1994 Carnegie Foundation survey of provosts at four-year colleges and universities suggested that the evaluation of teaching was even then undergoing considerable change, with over 70 percent reporting that new methods had been developed for this purpose (Glassick, Huber, and Maeroff, 1997, Table 9). At that time, nearly *all* respondents said that student evaluations of classroom teaching were in common use (Table 21). Other commonly used methods included personal statements or self-evaluations (82 percent); peer reviews of syllabi, examinations, and other teaching materials (62 percent); and the peer evaluation of classroom teaching (58 percent). Less frequently cited, but interesting nonetheless, were evidence of continuing student interest (34 percent); alumni opinions (31 percent); student achievement (24 percent); and student evaluations of advising (24 percent).[17] Of course, one might question how carefully and systematically such methods were used. For example, Carnegie's 1997 National Survey of Faculty produced figures that roughly agreed with the provosts about which methods of evaluation were in general use, but between 70 and 80 percent of faculty at four-year institutions strongly or somewhat agreed that "at this institution we need better ways to evaluate teaching performance" (Huber, 1998, Table 77).[18]

This persistent theme—that teaching evaluation has simply not been up to the job—may reflect faculty dissatisfaction with what many see as an over-reliance on the quantified measurements (and distinctions in performance) allowed by student evaluations. Certainly, there has been a great deal of useful discussion about techniques for student evaluations of teaching, especially that most important topic of what aspects of a faculty member's teaching performance students are best qualified to assess—and what aspects are better represented and reviewed in other ways.[19] This discussion has also led to wider appreciation of the full arc of teaching—a view inherent in the scholarship of teaching and learning. As Lee Shulman points out: "Too often teaching is identified only as the active interactions between teacher and students in a classroom setting (or even a tutorial session). I would argue that teaching, like other forms of scholarship, is an extended process that unfolds over time. It embodies at least five elements: *vision, design, interactions, outcomes,* and *analysis*" (1998, p. 5, italics in original).

Richer Representations

A desire to represent richer views of teaching than student course evaluations can afford is widespread across U.S. higher education today, and can be seen even at the nation's top research universities. The 2007 report from Harvard University's Faculty of Arts and Sciences, for example, recommended that procedures be found to "account for and assess all important aspects of teaching, advisement, and efforts at pedagogical improvement" (Task Force on Teaching and Career Development to the Faculty of Arts and Sciences, p. 3). The task force suggested that annual activity reports "should include opportunities for accounts of faculty goals and achievements, along with fuller information" about all pedagogical activities, and that in promotion reviews, "senior colleagues should be prepared to offer an informed assessment of the *full trajectory* of the junior member's teaching" (p. 4, italics in original). In other recommendations that also resonate with principles from the scholarship of teaching and learning, the report connects the evaluation of teaching with improvement, including seeking ways to assess student learning that would allow faculty to make "midcourse corrections" (pp. 2–3).

The course, as a meaningful unit in which to evaluate instructional materials, pedagogy, and connection to the larger curriculum, holds particular promise as a way to recognize and reward teaching that is informed and enriched by the scholarship of teaching and learning. Indeed, Lee Shulman and Pat Hutchings, designers of the Carnegie Academy for the Scholarship of Teaching and Learning (CASTL), had earlier developed a model for course-based documentation while collaborating on an AAHE project, "From Idea to Prototype: The Peer Review of Teaching." Looking for ways to make teaching visible to colleagues that could convey the thinking behind instructional choices and the student learning that resulted, Shulman, Hutchings, and a team of talented faculty collaborators were drawn to William Cerbin's concept of a "course portfolio." The purpose was to create a genre that would allow faculty to improve their courses based on critique and conversation about the materials with colleagues, learn from each other's experiences in more systematic ways, and provide a platform for further work in the scholarship of teaching and learning (Cerbin, 1996; Hutchings, 1998).

Developing the idea further, Daniel Bernstein and colleagues at the six universities participating in a later Peer Review of Teaching Project distinguished between benchmark and inquiry portfolios—the former providing full documentation for a particular iteration of a course, and the latter focusing on a question that led to course revision. Their efforts resulted in guidelines for creating course portfolios "that parallel those used to explore a research question or creative project" (Bernstein, Burnett, Goodburn, and Savory, 2006, p. 214). Bernstein and colleagues also adapted and elaborated the evaluative categories of *Scholarship Assessed* as a way to guide both creators and evaluators of this new genre. Such guidance is critical: the best portfolio in the world will not be useful unless colleagues read it and know how to discern levels of quality in the work (see Bernstein, Addison, Altman, Hollister, Komarraju, Prieto, Rocheleau, and Shore, 2009; see also Bernstein, 2008b; Bernstein and Huber, 2006).

Some of today's most innovative developments in the formal evaluation of teaching by peers are moving in similar directions; while they look broadly at a faculty member's complete teaching repertoire, they also aim for richer documentation by focusing on a smaller sample of courses—including a selection of student work. At some institutions, as at the University of Kansas, these ideas have informed new nomination and review processes for annual teaching awards: "One award committee asked nominators to follow the outline of a SoTL account of teaching. The protocol requested a peer review of teaching materials, including samples of student work. That review focused on intellectual content, course design, depth and breadth of student performance, and evidence of growth in teaching from consideration of students' learning" (Bernstein, 2010, p. 6).

Efforts to enhance the quality of teaching evaluation for tenure and promotion are also taking a closer look at course design, pedagogy, and student learning. For example, at the University of Notre Dame, faculty are now implementing such a plan. Rather than base the teaching component of these decisions predominantly on student course ratings, the institution now requires in-depth documentation of selected courses over a three-year period, which departmental committees of peers examine for course design, implementation, and evaluation of student work, as well as for student perceptions (University of Notre Dame, 2007). Also worth watching is a recent policy change at the University of Western Florida. According to Claudia Stanny, director of the institution's Center for University Teaching, Learning, and Assessment, "An important element of the [new] teaching rubric for the highest rating is that the faculty member documents his or her use of assessment evidence to inform teaching strategies, course design, selection of assignments, etc." (Feb. 5, 2010).

Approaches like these have real potential to raise the level of knowledge within a department about how students are doing, to enrich pedagogical discourse on campus, and to reverberate back into practice, rewarding the kind of classroom innovation, informed by literature and evidence, that is encouraged by the scholarship of teaching and learning.

Extent and Weight of Teaching Contributions

These experiments suggest the possibility of real progress in the evaluation of course-based teaching and learning—the heart of an institution's educational work. Yet what about faculty contributions to education that extend beyond the classroom? This is where slippage among the categories is most problematic. As we have seen, in the research category some institutions explicitly allow faculty to submit publications and presentations that bring pedagogical inquiry to a wider audience, and some allow textbooks or major curricular innovation there as well. Unfortunately, as one campus leader noted in the recent CASTL Survey, there is often no space for the documentation of the scholarship of teaching and learning that is "not specifically defined as part of the research component" (Ciccone, Huber, Hutchings, and Cambridge, 2009, p. 13). Many of these would be listed simply as "additional contributions to teaching" in the teaching category itself.[20] And it is still common for work on committees and task forces (such as the kind that leads to new guidelines!) to appear in the category of institutional service; contributions to educational committees and associations within one's discipline are often included under professional service; and educational activities that connect campus and community appear as community or public service. If this sounds too scattered to really add up, today's widely required personal statements about teaching (and research) provide space for faculty members to explain the ways in which their various contributions to teaching and learning support each other, draw from (or contribute to) an educational philosophy or agenda, and connect to other scholarly interests as well.

The real trick, though, is "weight." How much does teaching, as a category in tenure, merit, and promotion reviews, and the facts behind it, count? Are those who excel in these accomplishments rewarded at the same level as those with strong records in research? Most institutions ask that merit in the various categories of work be evaluated separately and then specify standards for different levels of recognition and reward. For example, at one state university in the Midwest where a candidate's teaching, research, and service are rated either "excellent," "meritorious," "adequate," or "inadequate," tenure now requires a judgment of at least "adequate" in all three areas and at least "meritorious" in two, one of which must be teaching (Eder, July 21, 2010). Clearly, the exact definitions of different degrees of merit and their formal weighting will depend on the kind of institution and department where one is working, but doubts about whether teaching accomplishments are *really* accorded sufficient weight or reward are widespread.

In our survey of CASTL participants, this concern about weighting was captured concisely in a complaint about official documents that "mostly pay lip service to teaching" (Ciccone, Huber, Hutchings, and Cambridge, 2009, p. 8). For many leaders this gap between rhetoric and reality is the crux: "Even though there is a great deal of rhetoric around the importance of teaching, it is clear that departmental cultures still rate scholarship above teaching and service. Thus, if integration is regarded as the scholarship of teaching and learning's parity with other kinds of work as conceived by those 'on the ground' within individual departments, then we still have work to do in changing culture" (Institutional Culture Group, 2009, p. 6).

One way through this dilemma—a designated teaching pathway—is emerging both in the United States and abroad. In some cases, as at the University of Colorado at Boulder and the University of British Columbia, tenurable positions are possible for faculty whose principal scholarly interests lie in the teaching and learning of their field (typically, though not only, the sciences).[21] At some institutions, as at Indiana University Bloomington's College of Arts and Sciences, individuals can choose the primary basis for their promotion—research or other creative work, teaching, service (in exceptional circumstances)—or they can present a balanced case. For example, candidates for promotion to full professor who select teaching as primary "must have demonstrated a superior ability and interest in stimulating in students (at all levels) a genuine desire for study and creative work. [They] should also provide evidence of a significant educational impact on their particular discipline, both inside and outside of Indiana University" (Indiana University College of Arts and Sciences Policy

Committee, 2006, criterion no. 2).[22] Another possibility includes creating a distinct track for faculty who are focused on teaching. While such tracks are often not tenurable in the United States, institutions in Australia are designing new pathways that are meant to be fully comparable to traditional faculty positions.[23]

The more elaborate and nuanced view of pedagogy envisioned by the scholarship of teaching and learning should, we believe, justify more than the creation of special career paths. If the ultimate goal is to improve teaching and learning more widely, then this new view of teaching should also give greater weight to the pedagogical achievements of all faculty. A recent news article reporting criticism of the tenure system at The Ohio State University by the institution's president, Gordon Gee, cited a common objection to the possibility of taking greater account of teaching. In the words of an English professor who is preparing for her own tenure case three years hence: "There's a feeling, I think, that good teachers are a dime a dozen. . . . I'm not sure what you'd have to do to distinguish yourself as a teacher to get tenure" (Welsh-Huggins, 2010).

But what if faculty members understood that their teaching would be evaluated by peers (including pedagogically knowledgeable colleagues from outside their own institution) using a general framework such as that provided in *Scholarship Assessed*, perhaps elaborated and refined as a rubric as Bernstein and colleagues have done? For example, in a recent iteration of this rubric, prepared for a task force on the teaching of psychology for the American Psychological Association, the authors identify four levels of expertise (entry, basic skill, professional, and advanced) for the six dimensions of scholarly work identified in *Scholarship Assessed*. Adapted specifically to teaching, these include: "goals of the course or other learning activity"; "preparation for the course or learning activity"; "methods used to conduct the teaching"; "evidence gathered to demonstrate the impact of the teacher's work"; "reflection on the teaching and its impact on student learning"; and "communication of teaching results to others" (Bernstein, Addison, Altman, Hollister, Komarraju, Prieto, Rocheleau, and Shore, 2009, p. 39, Table 2.1). If faculty were asked to submit materials that documented each of these phases in the intellectual arc, evaluators should be able to identify different types and levels of distinction in teaching, and teachers would be better informed about what they might do to distinguish themselves in this area.

More important, this approach to evaluation would invite all faculty to regard teaching as an occasion for inquiry into learning, for becoming familiar with the relevant pedagogical literature, for finding colleagues to work with, and for joining a community that can understand, evaluate, and support their contributions. Clearly, though, moving further in this direction will require a comprehensive undertaking, one in which all who care about learning in higher education have critical roles to play.

CHANGING THE CULTURE OF TEACHING

Cultural change seldom moves easily or evenly through complex systems; it can take years of advocacy, activism, and experience to reach that Gladwellian tipping point (Gladwell, 2002) where "victory by incorporation" can be declared.[24] Certainly this is true of the efforts to achieve recognition for the new scholarships as research, scholarly, and creative work. The expansion of the research category to include certain kinds of achievement in pedagogy and community engagement has been a slow but significant change. Developments in evaluation that recognize a more elaborated and fine-grained view of teaching have also advanced the scholarship of teaching and learning. But there is a great deal more to be done.

First, there is the challenge of improving guidelines and monitoring their effects. It's important for scholars of teaching and learning to claim a strong voice in these proceedings, to make relevant cases public, and to work with colleagues to address shortcomings in the formal rules and their implementation. For example, colleagues from the CASTL program at the Open University in the United Kingdom are "influencing university committee practices in supporting promotion of academics engaged in scholarship of teaching and learning activities, by being elected members of the committee that determines academic promotions." They are now working to "develop a timeline and progression pattern that recognizes scholarship in promotion from junior faculty member through to full professor," hoping to change criteria for promotions and specify ways of documenting and evaluating scholarship that will foster "cultural changes in the acceptance of the scholarship of teaching and learning as a valued and rewarded form of scholarship" (Institutional Culture Group, 2009, pp. 7–8).

A second challenge for the scholarship of teaching and learning community is to be sure that what's presented for evaluation is truly worthy work. On the research end of the continuum, that means efforts to clarify standards both within and across disciplines and to develop appropriate and appealing genres and outlets. On the teaching side, this means continuing to hone practitioners' pedagogical imagination and to tighten the cycle of inquiry, so that good questions lead to promising innovation and back again. Moving toward the service spectrum of the continuum, it is important to show how the scholarship of teaching and learning can enhance a wide range of collaborative educational processes, such as professional development, assessment, and program review. CASTL colleagues at Buffalo State College, for example, have "increased the visibility and demonstrated the value of the scholarship of teaching and learning" by designing a fellowship program "to systematically document the student learning outcomes" of "high impact and high priority" campus initiatives such as service learning, writing across the curriculum, critical thinking, undergraduate research, and the like (Institutional Culture Group, 2009, p. 5).

Finally, there is the challenge of expanding the reach of the scholarship of teaching and learning. It is a truism to say that sophisticated pedagogical practices and products will not be adequately recognized and rewarded without colleagues who use them, or without evaluators (internal and external) who understand what they are about. However, we suspect that the situation will prove to be very much as it is in core areas of research: in order to read and critique such materials with the requisite discernment, one needs the experience of producing them oneself. Some of our CASTL program colleagues refer to this as the "critical mass problem"—how to get enough people involved to "engage widespread and ongoing conversations" (Ciccone, Huber, Hutchings, and Cambridge, 2009, p. 13). And thus one comes full circle, because to expand participation, there must be recognition and reward.

Some leaders, eyeing soft spots in their campus cultures, have wondered whether it might be time to reconsider the Boyer categories themselves. Certainly it can be difficult to explain the scholarship of teaching and learning to faculty and draw them in. For instance, in the 2009 CASTL Survey, one community college leader thought it important to "reframe classroom research so that faculty would not be intimidated or turned off by the idea of engaging in meaningful exploration of teaching and learning." And a doctoral university colleague suggested that the term "scholarship of teaching and learning" not be used: "engaging faculty in intellectual inquiry into what they care about in their student's understanding is a welcome invitation in ways that having added expectations in 'scholarship' is definitely not." Some have also raised the delicate question of whether the effort to recognize the work as research in faculty guidelines might, as one campus warns, serve "as a barrier to more robust recognition of [other] SoTL activities" (Robinson, Gingras, Cooper, Waddell, and Davidge, 2009, p. 10).

Though these issues all deserve careful deliberation in particular institutional contexts, it's important to recognize them, fundamentally, as questions about means toward an end. The movement to broaden the meaning of the term "scholarship" has always had its eyes on the larger academic culture and its values. Will we recognize it when we get there? What would a culture that truly values—and discerningly evaluates—teaching look like? Advocates for the scholarship of teaching and learning at each institution should be asking what a "SoTL Utopia," as John Draeger and Linda Price (2009) call it, would look like in their setting, and how their system of faculty roles and rewards might be improved to move them toward that goal.

Notes

1. This quotation is from *Making Teaching and Learning Visible: Course Portfolios and the Peer Review of Teaching* (2006, p. 215). This chapter has benefited from

timely information and advice from many colleagues including: Michael Burke (College of San Mateo); Constance E. Cook (University of Michigan); Douglas Eder (Emeritus, Southern Illinois University Edwardsville); Jean Mach (College of San Mateo); Kathleen McKinney (Illinois Sate University); Gary Poole (University of British Columbia); Linda Price (Open University); Duane Roen (Arizona State University); Mark Searle (Arizona State University); Mary Ann Shea (University of Colorado); and Claudia Stanny (University of West Florida).

2. The idea that the new scholarships involve work that covers a range—or a continuum—of intellectual tasks is central to the report on promotion and tenure for public scholarship in the arts, humanities, and design (Ellison and Eatman, 2008). The authors argue that "the idea of the continuum structures four key domains," citing "a continuum of scholarship," "a continuum of scholarly and creative artifacts," "a continuum of professional pathways for faculty," and "a continuum of action for institutional change" (p. ix).

3. In *How Professors Think*, sociologist Michele Lamont uses the term "evaluative cultures" to refer to the characteristic ways in which scholars from different disciplinary communities judge excellence in academic work (2009, pp. 4–5). In her study of the deliberations of peer review panels as they discuss which proposals to recommend for funding, Lamont argues that "making judgments about excellence is a deeply interactional and emotional undertaking, rather than a strictly cognitive one" (p. 112).

4. As we mentioned in a note to Chapter 1, the 2009 Faculty Survey of Student Engagement (FSSE) asked a special set of questions about how often faculty systematically collected information about the effectiveness of their teaching, beyond end-of-term course evaluations. Results from 7,300 faculty in 50 institutions suggested that "faculty tend to engage in scholarship of teaching and learning activities despite the fact [that] they feel unsupported by their institution" (Faculty Survey of Student Engagement, "Other Teaching and Learning Results: Scholarship of Teaching and Learning").

5. The survey did not ask about the scholarship of integration or about closely related areas of intellectual endeavor, such as interdisciplinary work or public scholarship.

6. It's important to point out that this didn't necessarily mean less attention to other kinds of faculty work. As the Carnegie Foundation's 1997 survey of faculty indicated, 27 percent of *all* the nation's college and university professors said that both teaching and research count more than they did five years earlier, or that one counts more while the other counts the same. (See Huber, 1998, Tables 83 and 86, for results on research and teaching separately; this information on intersecting demands is from a special analysis of the data.)

7. These shifts in institutional mission and faculty priorities, sometimes referred to as "mission creep," continue today, propelled in part by the ever more competitive landscape in higher education (see, for example, Wildavsky, 2010). In some circumstances, these shifts also respond to the increasingly sophisticated demands of work in today's economy.

8. Writing in 2002, higher education scholar Carol Colbeck noted that the two books—*Scholarship Reconsidered* and *Scholarship Assessed*—"have had profound influence on the conduct and evaluation of faculty work" (p. 1).

9. The Harvard study supports Edgerton's observation about the variability with which the expanded categories of scholarly work have been defined. According to O'Meara, additional areas of research found in FAPA [Faculty Appointment Policy Archive] policies include creative work (for example, recitals, artistic creation, publicly demonstrated performance) (51, 73 percent); grant-writing, reviewing, directing (22, 31 percent); postdoctoral fellowships, academic awards, and honors (15, 21 percent); textbook publications and pedagogical publications (12, 17 percent); publication of research in nonacademic outlets including nonrefereed professional magazines aimed at segments of the general public and unpublished [sic] or scholarship in progress (11, 16 percent); incorporation of new disciplinary developments into courses or the development of experimental programs such as distance education (10, 14 percent); inventions, designs, innovations, and patents (9, 13 percent); innovative use of computers and the development of computer software (7, 10 percent); applied, theoretical or basic, and clinical research (5, 7 percent); initiation of new pedagogical methods (5, 7 percent); and keeping abreast in one's discipline including educational travel (2000, p. 159).

   On the same page, O'Meara goes on to note that 15 institutions include the scholarship of application in the research/scholarship category, and that a couple of others include collaborative work with students, even when it doesn't lead to publication.

10. It is worth reiterating that, in each case, the proportion reporting definitional change in faculty roles and rewards policy was not a proportion of the whole sample, but of that portion reporting any change at all (approximately two-thirds for the Carnegie Foundation or AAHE studies), or that provided definitions of the categories themselves (about four-fifths of the sample in the Harvard study).

11. Braxton, Luckey, and Helland credit Curry (1991) with identifying the three levels of institutionalization they use in this analysis. Here are their definitions: (1) "At the structural level ... there is a basic knowledge of the behaviors associated with the innovation, and those involved understand how to perform the behaviors. There is also some form of measurement in place for assessing how individuals perform each behavior. ... It is also possible that the organizational structure will have changed to accommodate additional personnel to administer the new program" (2002, pp. 5–6); (2) "At the procedural level, behaviors and policies associated with the innovation become ... part of the standard operating procedure of the disciplinary department or the entire institution. As for individuals in the organization, this level shows their preferences for the behaviors identified at the structural levels" (p. 6); and (3) "The most in-depth level of institutionalization is incorporation, where the values and norms associated with the innovation are incorporated into an organization's culture. With this normative consensus comes an awareness of how others are performing the behavior as well as an agreement on the appropriateness of the behavior" (p. 7).

12. For example, CASTL program leaders at Buffalo State College of the State University of New York surveyed all 118 faculty who had been tenured, promoted, or had a contract renewed since their tenure policy was revised in 2001. Of the 76 surveys returned, over half (40) indicated that "they had included work categorized as Scholarship of Teaching and Learning in their review materials" (Institutional Culture Group, 2009, p. 6).

13. Many institutions form task forces periodically to review official criteria for appointment, reappointment, tenure, and promotion. These task force reports often propose excellent new language around the new scholarships, but the process of adoption is conservative—probably for good reasons—and much of this new language never sees the light of day. Kathleen McKinney, professor of sociology and Cross Endowed Chair in the Scholarship of Teaching and Learning at Illinois State University (ISU), wrote to say: "We don't make major changes to this language in these documents very often," but as ISU's definition of the scholarship of teaching and learning does "fit under our formal institutional definition and example products under research, creative products, and scholarship," she has "spent time on supporting and helping make the work public and getting it to count case by case under research when necessary." Although the "fit" is "open to interpretation," McKinney says that getting this kind of recognition for published work is "usually not a problem" (June 21, 2010).

14. The perceived distance of classroom inquiry from one's disciplinary inclinations and expertise can be an impediment to doing the work, not just to evaluating it (Huber, 2010b). As Mills and Huber have pointed out (2005), this can be a special problem in humanities-oriented disciplines, where the epistemological stance (and not just the methods) of educational inquiry can seem off-putting and strange. Sherry Linkon and Randy Bass concur: "For many literary scholars, staking a claim for a disciplinary practice of SoTL has been difficult," they write, "because the standard approaches used in SoTL, borrowed from the social sciences and educational research, seem foreign to literary scholars" (2008, p. 246). Indeed, many of their colleagues don't see their *own* field's research culture as particularly friendly to the scholarship of teaching either, but Linkon and Bass make a strong case for the applicability of the interpretive practices of close reading to texts of student learning (see p. 257).

15. This passage draws on a description presented in Huber, 2005, p. 52, which in turn summarizes lessons from the case studies presented in *Balancing Acts* (Huber, 2004).

16. The Modern Language Association's December 2006 task force report on evaluating scholarship for tenure and promotion observed: "While publication expectations for tenure and promotion have increased, the value that [modern language] departments place on scholarly activity outside monograph publication remains within a fairly restricted range" (2007, pp. 10–11). Refereed journal articles were still valued, but "Translations were rated 'not important' by 30.4% of departments (including 31.3% of foreign language departments), as were textbooks by 28.9% of departments, bibliographic scholarship by 28.8% of

departments, scholarly editions by 20% of departments, and editing a scholarly journal by 20.7% of departments. Even more troubling is the state of evaluation for digital scholarship, now an extensively used resource for scholars across the humanities: 40.8% of departments in doctorate-granting institutions report no experience evaluating refereed articles in electronic format, and 65.7% report no experience evaluating monographs in electronic format" (Modern Language Association, 2007, p. 11). Though the MLA has long supported the legitimacy of digital scholarship, the problems besetting its evaluation are not trivial (Borgman, 2007), nor, according to recent reporting like Howard's (2010), are they by any means yet resolved.

17. These figures can be found in the series of tables on the evaluation of teaching (Tables 18–27) in Glassick, Huber, and Maeroff, 1997.

18. The actual figures were: 76 percent of faculty at research universities (40 percent strongly; 36 percent somewhat); 78 percent at doctoral colleges and universities (43 percent strongly; 35 percent somewhat); 76 percent at master's colleges and universities (39 percent strongly; 37 percent somewhat); and 70 percent at baccalaureate colleges (32 percent strongly; 38 percent somewhat). Community college faculty were only a little less dissatisfied: 67 percent said better ways of evaluating teaching performance were needed (26 percent strongly agreed; 41 percent somewhat).

19. For example, one study identified seven dimensions important to capturing the complex nature of faculty teaching performance, and argued that students could appropriately evaluate four of them: "delivery of instruction, assessment of instruction, availability to students, and administrative requirements" (Cashin, 1988, as summarized by Paulsen, 2002, p. 9). Of course, others see things differently. Elaine Seymour and her colleagues at the University of Colorado, concerned that science faculty were reluctant to innovate because of possible negative effects on their student evaluation scores, thought students might more usefully report on their own views regarding how much they learned in a course and which aspects of a course were most helpful to their learning. Their new instrument, the Student Assessment of their Learning Gains (SALG), is now widely used, though often in addition to the more conventional student evaluations of teaching required by institutions (Seymour, Wiese, Hunter, and Daffinrud, 2000; Glenn, 2010).

20. Consider Notre Dame's "additional contributions" category. One could see that any of these entries could be the subject of inquiry as well as of innovation: "facilitating student participation in experiential learning opportunities, such as research, fieldwork, or scholarly or creative endeavors; directing students' theses; and the introduction of significant innovations within the curriculum" (2007, pp. 10–11). Notre Dame's guidelines ask that "contributions that lead to noteworthy student achievements (for example, publications, performances, exhibitions, placements, and awards) should be highlighted" (p. 3). Perhaps they could also request highlighting contributions that lead to noteworthy faculty achievements as well!

21. At the University of Colorado at Boulder, tenurable positions like these now exist in physics, chemistry, and biochemistry, according to Mary Ann Shea, director of the University's Faculty Teaching Excellence Program and the President's Teaching Scholars Program (June 24, 2010). But, as the case study of Brian Coppola at the University of Michigan shows, gaining recognition for such positions has not always been easy (Huber, 2004). According to Gary Poole, then director of the University of British Columbia's Centre for Teaching and Academic Growth:

> The language of our collective agreement allows for the physicist [for example] to advance through the professorial ranks on the strength of physics education research. In practice, this has much to do with the culture of a given department. In other words, if Physics thought such a path was viable, they could put their candidate forward for the next step in the process—the Science Faculty-level tenure and promotion committee. If the case was strong, it would then go forward to the University-wide committee. Cases have moved forward in this way, though there are departments that simply don't see scholarship of teaching and learning research as being viable ... regardless of what the collective agreement might say [June 21, 2010].

22. Of course, this leaves open the possibility that a person choosing to be evaluated primarily on work in the scholarship of teaching and learning might be reviewed under the rules for "research or other creative work." This rule simply states: "If research or other creative work is the primary criterion for promotion, we expect the candidate to have achieved a position of leadership in a substantial field. This must be demonstrated by evidence of letters, both internal and external, and by other pertinent documentation" (Indiana University College of Arts and Sciences Policy Committee, 2006).

23. The University of Queensland (UQ) has recently introduced "teaching-focused positions," parallel to the "teaching-research" positions for faculty. In addition, UQ policy now recognizes "Scholarship of Teaching activities as a dimension of the academic role for both teaching-research and teaching-focussed [sic] positions; including a set of related criteria for appointment, confirmation and promotion." Documentation for this work is mandatory for faculty in teaching-focused positions, but optional for others (O'Brien, Goos, and members of TEDI/HERS Team, 2008, p. 2). An effort similar in spirit to Indiana University's at the University of New South Wales allows applicants to "nominate teaching as their main criterion for promotion," although a subsequent change of leadership may have made this more difficult in practice (see Lee, 2009, p. 11).

24. This is simply a positive way of naming what Robert Merton dubbed "obliteration by incorporation" (1968, pp. 27–28, 35–37), where the sources of an idea are forgotten as it becomes more integral to the culture.

CHAPTER SIX

Getting There: Leadership for the Future

Ultimately, investigative work into teaching and learning will not be an intriguing aside, or add-on, but an essential facet of good teaching—built into the expected repertoire of scholarly practice.
—Lee S. Shulman[1]

When we first began thinking about this book, we set ourselves the task of imagining what academic life would look like in 10 years if the principles and practices of the scholarship of teaching and learning were to take hold at a deep level of institutional "incorporation" (Braxton, Luckey, and Helland, 2002, p. 7). For starters, this thought experiment brought to mind former Carnegie Foundation president Lee Shulman's answer to the same question a dozen years earlier. His vision was simple and elegant: "When one faculty member meets another on campus or in the hallway and [says] 'What are you up to these days?' instead of the answer always being, 'Well, I'm doing this experiment in my lab,' just as often it will be 'I'm experimenting with this new course and it's *so interesting*'" (Carnegie Foundation for the Advancement of Teaching, 1999).

There's still a lot to love in that answer, capturing, as it does, the most fundamental transformations we have been discussing in these pages: that teaching is understood as intellectual work; that it is, indeed, "work" in the richest, most generative sense of the word; that it can be improved through inquiry and investigation; and that it's a fit and proper subject for exchange with colleagues who just might be interested themselves, or doing related work and eager to learn from the experience of others.

At the same time, we have pushed ourselves to imagine a future that stretches beyond Shulman's, by looking ahead yet another decade. Although on many campuses the scholarship of teaching and learning has, as yet, only a fragile hold, and many obstacles to deeper integration remain, significant progress has been made. There are now many more teachers engaged in the study of their students' learning, more outlets for what they discover, and a growing demand for what these outlets make available. Campus policies are evolving to create space (and rewards) for such work, disciplinary and professional fields have promoted it, and notions of inquiry and evidence are integral to an impressive range and number of national and international teaching improvement initiatives.

Building on these developments then, what visions of a possible future can we offer? How might academic life be changed by the scholarship of teaching and learning? What lasting impact can be expected—and planned for? What difference will it make for campuses, for faculty, and, most important, for students?[2] And what can campus leaders do to realize the best of these possibilities?

ONE VISION OF THE POSSIBLE

Let us then imagine a campus, and, for fun, let's call it Utopia University (UU).[3] The place: somewhere conducive to futuristic thinking. The time: a decade hence.

For the past several years, Utopia U has been much talked about among those in the know about higher education. This is not because of national rankings (the institution stopped responding to *U.S. News and World Report* some years ago), but because UU has become a place where virtually everyone, top to bottom, is a connoisseur of learning.

The engine behind this development is an expectation, woven into everything the institution does, that students become "expert learners." Of course, they must learn about their field of study, and they must develop the cross-cutting skills (critical thinking, for instance, and teamwork) needed in an increasingly complex, interconnected, fast-moving world. But they must also develop the capacity to understand, monitor, and direct their own learning. This ability to "go meta," to be "intentional learners," is an essential learning outcome at UU, central to the student experience.[4] For instance, the required first-year seminar introduces students to basic principles about the different ways people learn, and begins to equip them with a language of learning. (After all, faculty have had to hash out the meanings of critical thinking, civic engagement, and other important outcomes—students need a chance to do so as well.) In addition, every department offers a course, typically taken during the junior year, in which students learn about the distinctive habits of mind, modes of questioning, and conceptions of evidence and argument that characterize the field. Students' growing expertise as learners is also the organizing principle of the e-portfolio that serves as a centerpiece for their required interdisciplinary capstone course.

This ongoing focus on learning has not come easily. Not all faculty members felt equipped (or disposed), at first, to teach in this way; certainly their graduate programs had not trained them in the fine points of the learning sciences. Recognizing this gap, UU has made professional development an increasingly high priority, and an area of significant institutional rethinking; the emphasis today is not on "improving teaching," but on creating occasions for faculty, like students, to "go meta" about their own development as scholars and teachers, and to do so in ways that build communities of shared interest and practice among colleagues.

For instance, the Learning Institute (formerly the teaching center but reconceived and renamed a few years ago) works with each department to "decode the discipline," teasing out and making explicit the modes of thinking that characterize the field and translating those understandings into designs for teaching and assessment.[5] This work feeds into the departmental seminar described earlier, but it plays out in broader ways as well, shaping courses and teaching across the curriculum, and catalyzing a wide variety of projects in which faculty work together across disciplines to study the impact of their new approaches to student learning. Interestingly, many faculty report that the focus on how novices become expert learners has also informed, even transformed, their research. Meanwhile, retirements, along with increased enrollment, have made it possible to hire a top-notch crop of new faculty who developed a serious taste for teaching, curriculum design, and assessment in graduate school, and who see UU as a place to continue that work.

When it comes to promotion and tenure, special value is placed on integration, as faculty prepare dossiers that explore the connections between their development and accomplishments as disciplinary and interdisciplinary scholars, the learning of their students, and their engagement with institutional and professional agendas. In short, like students, faculty are expected to be expert learners. "I know that sounds corny," says Provost Leaderlee, "but the best, most accomplished scholars have always been those who have the skills to build on what they've done previously and push into new territory." Faculty work hard to meet the institution's expectations, but there's a sense of professional integrity, cohesion, and community that seems to keep spirits high at UU.

Like the rest of higher education, UU has had to provide evidence of learning for accreditation for more than a decade. Early on, the necessary information was largely generated and managed by a central office of institutional research and assessment. Several years ago, however, a task force was convened to design new ways to frame key questions and to bring information together across levels, from the classroom to the president's office. As a result, faculty questions about their students' learning shape data gathering "at the top," and the resulting information, in turn, shapes innovation and inquiry at the program and classroom levels. This kind of coordination takes effort, but habits of communication and collaboration have now been established and built into processes like program review, institutional assessment, and curricular reform.

Some newer members of the faculty believe the campus has not gone far enough in its turn toward learning. But clearly progress has been made, and those, like Professor C. F. Castle, who have been at UU over the long haul, take pleasure in the way one thing has led to another. Castle enjoys thinking back—maybe 20 years ago now—to the institution's participation in a national initiative on the scholarship of teaching and learning. Some of his colleagues were skeptical, it's true, but over time a diverse and growing group of faculty—on campus and beyond—found one another and worked together exploring questions about their students' learning. One of their touchstones, Castle recalls, was "making learning visible," and that process of going public prompted important changes in teaching and curriculum. Interestingly, the language of the scholarship of teaching and learning has gradually disappeared at UU, as the practices behind it became second nature, built into the regular routines of institutional work and life. That's probably a good thing, in Castle's view, a natural progression, a process of integration and change... though sometimes, he thinks, it would be good to revisit that history, to share it with those who weren't part of it. Maybe it would even yield lessons for the future!

LESSONS FOR LEADERS

Utopia University is, of course, a construction. To some readers it will seem overly optimistic, and to others perhaps insufficiently bold. Its hypothetical setting skips over important issues about institutional type, history, and culture, and clearly the direction and details of the story would play out in different ways at a small liberal arts college, at a major research university, on a regional comprehensive campus, or at a community college, as accounts of progress in this volume and elsewhere (see, for instance, Cambridge, 2004a) make clear. The point of our "utopia" is not to prognosticate or prescribe (and certainly not to prescribe a one-size-fits-all model), but to reiterate our central message, our "reconsideration": that the scholarship of teaching and learning should increasingly be seen not as a discrete project or special initiative, but as a set of practices that are critical to achieving the institution's core goals for student learning and success. In this sense ours is an integrative vision, one in which the scholarship of teaching and learning is woven into the institutional fabric in ways we have highlighted throughout this volume. Such integration is critical if the scholarship of teaching and learning is to deliver on its promises, but it is needed too if higher education is to meet today's growing imperatives around student learning.

This integrative vision cannot be achieved by individuals acting in isolation. There will, we hope, always be a place for the individual faculty member to dive into a study of student learning in his or her classroom, but the most significant, deep (UU-like) transformations require action and advocacy by campus leaders—committee heads, chairs, deans, professional development leaders, assessment officers, provosts, and presidents—who understand how the scholarship of teaching and learning can strengthen life and work in their setting. Toward that end, we offer eight recommendations, mindful that they are necessarily broad and must be tailored and adapted to each campus's distinctive mission, history, and culture.

Recommendations

1. Understand, communicate, and promote an integrated vision of the scholarship of teaching and learning. There are many ways to support the scholarship of teaching and learning, and all of them depend on leadership's own understanding of the character of such work, and why it matters. This understanding must be informed by the views of faculty and staff who have embraced this new form of scholarship, and it must be communicated, in turn, to the broader campus community, a task that requires both vision and translation skills.

On most campuses the scholarship of teaching and learning typically arrives as one of a number of special reform and improvement initiatives. But its real power, as we have argued throughout this volume, comes from understanding how its values and practices—seeing teaching as intellectual work, treating classrooms as sites for inquiry, and using what is learned to improve student learning—can be applied more broadly: in course design, curricular development, professional development experiences, assessment activities, and so forth. Indeed, it is hard to think of an area of institutional priority or responsibility today where habits of inquiry and the use of evidence for improvement are not needed.

One of the central challenges in this recommendation is terminology. On the one hand, it's clear that the language of "the scholarship of teaching and learning" can be a rallying point, and that, at least for some people in some settings, being part of a "new thing," with a distinctive language and identity, is an important source of energy, group cohesion, and sustainability (see Ewell, 2002). On the other hand, special language can work against the kind of integrative vision we are arguing for here. "Never use the term [the scholarship of teaching and learning], it only starts fights you can't win," one CASTL survey respondent told us; the language is "cumbersome and misunderstood," another reported. In short, leaders must decide when to keep the special identity of the scholarship of teaching and learning intact and when to find alternative ways to talk about it—ways that resonate with more familiar terms and processes, and that speak to different audiences: faculty who have already embraced such work and those who have not, funders, trustees, policymakers, and students. And of course what makes sense in any of these circumstances may change over time as the work is integrated into and transforms academic culture.

2. Support a wide range of opportunities to cultivate the skills and habits of inquiry into teaching and learning. If the practices of the scholarship of teaching and learning are to be woven into institutional life and work, they must be cultivated in multiple sites and settings. Leaders can help introduce such practices into the wide range of campus initiatives on teaching and learning that offer opportunities for inquiry-based professional development today.

As noted in Chapter 3, a good number of campuses have created fellowship programs loosely modeled on the CASTL Scholars Program, inviting faculty to propose a scholarship of teaching and learning project, providing stipends and in some cases release time for those selected, and bringing them together over time to assist and learn from one another.[6] Such programs play a powerful role in creating a critical mass of expertise, idea champions, and energy and models for future work; we recommend that all campuses consider such opportunities as they create an overall strategy for incorporating the scholarship of teaching and learning into the institutional fabric.

But an integrative vision of the scholarship of teaching and learning means planting seeds for such work across the institution. And this is, in fact, not hard to do, as initiatives that focus on, inquire into, and seek to improve student learning become increasingly widespread. For instance, many campuses today are experimenting with student portfolios as a mechanism for documenting learning over time. But portfolios (as their most thoughtful proponents now recognize) can also be catalysts for helping students become more active, intentional agents in the trajectory of their own development, a goal that clearly invites the kind of inquiry that scholars of teaching and learning engage in: What role should the student play in developing his or her portfolio? What artifacts are most likely to stimulate deep self-reflection? What stages do learners go through as they develop the capacity to direct their own learning?

Similarly, many campuses today, motivated in part by higher retention goals, are redesigning the freshman year, creating learning communities, special seminars, and the like. Adding the scholarship of teaching and learning to the picture means being systematic about exploring, tracking, and making public the effects of these changes.

Efforts like these—and there are many others—are natural sites for cultivating the values and practices of the scholarship of teaching and learning, and for integrating them into the institution. To be clear, we are not suggesting that the language of the scholarship of teaching and learning be laid on top of every occasion or activity focused on the exploration and improvement of student learning, or that the scholarship of teaching and learning "take over." What we *are* suggesting is that leaders recognize, articulate, and encourage the inquiry practices invited by these initiatives and help them develop a sense of common cause with one another that can add up to larger changes in the campus culture.

To put the point differently (and to pick up on the argument of Chapter 3) its cycle of inquiry, evidence, and improvement makes the scholarship of teaching and learning a powerful form of professional growth and development, and a process closely aligned with the best current thinking and practice of those who provide leadership for faculty development—be it through centers for teaching or through any of the wide array of learning-focused initiatives that are increasingly finding homes on campuses today. In short, the scholarship of teaching and learning not only requires professional development (as faculty expand their repertoire of methods for making learning visible, for instance, and trade ideas with those who share their commitment to inquiry); it strengthens and supports development. Indeed, our integrative vision argues for fewer one-time, technique-oriented teaching workshops and for more sustained study by faculty across a wide range of fields, as they seek to understand their own students' journey from novice to expert learners. Such work is, we believe, the face of faculty development in the future.

3. Connect the scholarship of teaching and learning to larger, shared agendas for student learning and success. Bringing scholars of teaching and learning together around agendas that invite collaboration and cross-fertilization builds relationships among individuals with common interests in ways that can significantly advance institutional initiatives and goals.

Connections may be relatively loose; this is often the case with fellowship programs like those mentioned in the preceding recommendation: scholars are brought together periodically to share ideas, critique one another's study designs, and report on findings, but typically each person is pursuing her or his own project, often on very different topics. Forging tighter connections with larger, shared agendas is no great leap, however. In the final year of the CASTL fellowship program, for instance, we invited proposals from individuals interested in exploring integrative learning, and all participants thus shared an interest in approaches that would help students pull together the various aspects of their educational experience. Some campuses have employed similar collaborative models, bringing scholars of teaching and learning together around themes such as undergraduate research, the relationship of affective and cognitive development, and liberal learning. Organizing around a central theme, as, for example, Michigan State University has done through a series of topic-based faculty learning communities (see Cox, 2004), has enabled people to join with others who care about a particular pedagogical approach or learning issue and develop networks that are both supportive and informed.

Taking the point a step further, we think of campuses that have brought the scholarship of teaching and learning to bear on department-, program-, or institution-wide efforts, using its practices to help rethink the outcomes of the major, to redesign general education, or (as in the previous recommendation) to reconceptualize faculty development. This kind of connection comes with risks; the scholarship of teaching and learning can recede into the background or be seen as merely a tool. But leaders who encourage and support these kinds of connections send strong signals about the importance of this work and its critical role in ongoing improvement.

It is worth noting that this recommendation has implications for financial support. Funding special scholarship of teaching and learning projects, fellowship opportunities, and programs, even at modest levels, is one of the most powerful signals leaders can send about the work's value to the campus. On the other hand, funding can be a death knell when it is "special" and temporary, and when the work in question is therefore seen as marginal, unconnected to core operations. Leaders must look for ways to support and fund the scholarship of teaching and learning's connections with other, valued aspects of institutional mission and work, such as curriculum revision, professional development, or assessment.

4. Foster exchange between the campus scholarship of teaching and learning community and those with responsibility for institutional research and assessment. These two higher education movements can strengthen each other in important ways, building toward an integrated, multilayered system of evidence gathering and use for the ongoing improvement of student learning.

As noted in Chapter 4, the scholarship of teaching and learning and institutional assessment have different histories, champions, and cultures. But they also share some central values and practices—a sharp focus on learning, habits of gathering and using evidence for improvement, and a commitment to sharing results—and on some campuses the two communities are now beginning to interact, albeit gingerly. Campus leaders can encourage such exchange and help move it in productive directions.

The first step is simply to start the conversation: to bring leaders from the two communities together to explore common ground—and differences. A next step might entail selective data sharing or further inquiry around issues of common interest. On three CASTL campuses, for instance, assessment data from the National Survey of Student Engagement provided a platform for further, deeper work by a group of scholars of teaching and learning. The goal, as participants described it, was "to use the scholarship of teaching and learning to expand on, explain, or question the results," and to provide a richer picture of student learning, with (in this case) a special focus on students' first-year experience (Institutional Culture Group, 2009, p. 4).[7] At St. Olaf College (as reported in Chapter 4), a similar process was organized around the results of the Collegiate Learning Assessment. In the same spirit, a reader of a draft of this volume wondered whether the assessment office might commission groups of scholars of teaching and learning to explore specific learning outcomes—a good idea. Turning the tables, perhaps scholars of teaching and learning might ask leaders of assessment and institutional research to provide data that would provide a larger context for their own investigations. Ultimately, this kind of bridge building between assessment and the scholarship of teaching and learning can help establish an integrated, multilevel system of evidence gathering and use—a critical resource for both internal improvement and external reporting, especially through accreditation.

Campus leaders can help move the institution in these directions by seizing opportunities to show how the work of scholars of teaching and learning bears on larger, more cross-cutting questions about student learning, creating an openness to a wide range of evidence, and making a place for nuanced—albeit often small-scale—findings that point, in turn, to next questions for institutional and program-level assessment. Such connections do not happen by accident; leadership is critical.

5. Work purposefully to bring faculty roles and rewards into alignment with a view of teaching as scholarly work. Many campuses have revised institutional policies and language, but much remains to be done to craft guidelines for evaluation, documentation, and peer review that adequately recognize the scholarship of teaching and learning. Leaders must also push this work forward at the department and program level where policies are translated into practice.

Not surprisingly, promotion and tenure issues are often at the top of the list when scholars of teaching and learning are asked about what would help them do such work. As noted in Chapter 5, several national studies (Glassick, Huber, and Maeroff, 1997; O'Meara, 2000; O'Meara and Rice, 2005) indicate that significant, if uneven, progress has been made toward giving the intellectual work of teaching a more prominent, legitimate place in faculty roles and rewards. And many campuses have revised, or are working on, promotion and tenure guidelines toward this end, some with explicit language about the scholarship of teaching and learning, some with more sophisticated descriptions of what excellent teaching is all about. But writing evaluation criteria, guidelines for documentation, and protocols for peer review that better capture the intellectual work involved in teaching is clearly a continuing challenge. It will require upper-level leadership to stimulate honest debate, encourage new thinking, establish safe spaces to experiment, and develop the processes and tools to move new policies into action.

Further, as many campuses have told us, institutional guidelines are only (or perhaps not *even*) half the battle, because it's at the departmental level that the rubber meets the road. Not surprisingly, then, on campuses that have made significant progress toward recognizing new forms of scholarship (in teaching and otherwise), administrators have turned the question back to faculty for deliberation in their own programs. They understand that the transformation of roles and rewards is a long-term agenda that must be worked out not only in policy but also in practice, where issues of definition and standards will be tackled. The point, after all, is not simply to reward the scholarship of teaching and learning, but to reward *good* scholarship of teaching and learning.[8] Doing so takes leadership at all levels, and sustained commitment at the top.

6. Take advantage of and engage with the larger, increasingly international teaching commons. Campus leaders can make a place for the scholarship of teaching and learning *within* the institution by supporting it though words, actions, and funding. But signals from outside the institution matter as well, and there is much to be gained by connecting with the broader scholarship of teaching and learning community and the opportunities it affords.

The International Institute for SoTL Scholars and Mentors, sponsored by a group of campuses (originally as part of the Carnegie program, but now operating independently) and hosted by them on a rotating basis, offers mentoring to faculty looking for a friendly setting where they can push ahead with a scholarship of teaching and learning project. Western Carolina University has established a summer institute that brings together campus teams from places committed to "the Boyer Model," many with a special interest in the scholarship of teaching and learning. Georgia Southern University hosts an annual international conference on the scholarship of teaching and learning, and several institutions in London have taken turns hosting a similar event.

Disciplinary and professional societies offer opportunities as well, both here and abroad, and a number of organizations and institutions have contributed to the larger infrastructure of support by creating online resources, social networks, tools, and peer-review processes that scholars of teaching and learning can tap into. Finally—to mention just one more example—the International Society for the Scholarship of Teaching and Learning provides its members with an annual conference, special interest groups, a newsletter, and a sense of professional identity and affiliation.[9]

In all of these cases, and many not mentioned, what we have found is that opportunities to be part of the larger, increasingly international teaching commons are both a powerful motivation for scholars of teaching and learning *and* an important outcome. Joining and contributing to the larger "conversation" is, after all, something faculty expect—and something expected *of* them—in their work as scholars more generally. It's critical as well to the knowledge-building potential of the scholarship of teaching and learning. Rubbing shoulders (and ideas) with colleagues from other settings helps move what would otherwise be valuable but local work to a larger stage and wider use. Such exchange is especially powerful because research on learning and teaching has taken quite different directions in different countries, and a more cosmopolitan awareness of these varied traditions can strengthen work on all fronts.

Additionally, these kinds of experiences beyond the campus can move faculty toward *local* leadership roles—a development that administrators can encourage by creating campus platforms and visibility for their work, and new roles and responsibilities that invite them to lead others. We have seen the fruits of such opportunities over and over, as faculty who make a name for themselves as scholars of teaching and learning move into positions in teaching centers, formal administration, faculty governance, curricular reform, and more general advocacy for teaching and learning.

A footnote to this point: campuses that have seriously embraced and made a place for the scholarship of teaching and learning often have resources and lessons to share beyond the institution, be it with individual scholars looking for a place to pursue their work (for instance as a visiting fellow), or with campuses looking for a model to move them in similar directions. Stepping forward to provide leadership for others is not only a generous move, but one that brings increased visibility to the campus and provides further momentum for local work. We encourage leaders on "advanced" campuses to think about proposing a conference session, hosting a conference or workshop, or writing about their work so that others—in the spirit of the scholarship of teaching and learning—can learn from and build on it.

7. Develop a plan and time line for integrating the scholarship of teaching and learning into campus culture, and monitor progress. Developed collaboratively with others who have a stake and interest in the work, a good plan provides a shared sense of direction, purpose, and momentum, and reinforces connections to institutional goals and mission.

One of the most notable lessons from campus work on the scholarship of teaching and learning is the importance of a "sense of destination" (Institutional Culture Group, 2009, p. 10). Accordingly (and harkening back to our first recommendation), the most critical task for top-level administrators is to articulate the role and place of such work in the institution's future—and to work with others, at all levels, to devise a plan and strategy for moving ahead. What do we hope to accomplish? What are the major impediments? What resources will support the work, and where can allies be found? What milestones should be in view and on what time line? How will progress be measured, and by whom? And how will that progress be shared, and leveraged, with those outside the institution, including parents and prospective undergraduate students, graduate students who will soon be looking for academic positions, funders, and policymakers?

The notion of monitoring progress has been central to CASTL, and that experience is worth sharing here. As part of their commitment to the program, participating campuses were asked at several points along the way to document the impact of the scholarship of teaching and learning in their institutional setting along a number of dimensions.[10] And though it's probably fair to say that no campus was fully satisfied with its progress, there was a general sense that taking a candid look at impact was a healthy thing—one that increases motivation and guides next steps. Toward this end, we encourage campuses to adapt the 2009 CASTL Survey included in Appendix A, but also to invent their own templates and rubrics for monitoring progress, as some have done. But even less structured stocktaking can be valuable. For instance, much can be accomplished when leaders periodically meet with the scholarship of teaching and learning community on campus to ask about progress, to think together about next steps, and to discuss how to bring the work and its results to bear on issues of institutional concern. We recommend as well that leaders sometimes accompany faculty to national and international meetings, such as the International Society for the Scholarship of Teaching and Learning, to show support and to educate themselves more broadly about this consequential and growing movement.

8. Recognize that institutionalization is a long-term process. Integrating the scholarship of teaching and learning into the ongoing work and life of the campus will necessarily entail setbacks and slowdowns. Success will require sustained leadership, creativity, and flexibility on the part of everyone involved.

Making an institutional place for the scholarship of teaching and learning is a balancing act. As every savvy leader knows, there's a fine line between support and appropriation. The faculty we have worked with are clear in wanting support and advocacy from upper-level administrators. But many are also nervous about where such interest might lead. Will what begins as an invitation to engage in inquiry become a requirement, something all faculty *must* do? Will a focus on this new form of scholarship morph over time into a two-track faculty, those pursuing "regular" research and those who specialize in pedagogy? Will the institution's need to demonstrate educational effectiveness overtake the intellectual impulse that moves faculty toward such work, shifting the focus from knowledge building and improvement to accountability and proof? Will the scholarship of teaching and learning become a mere marketing ploy? As we heard over and over from CASTL survey respondents, the scholarship of teaching and learning can't be a mandated "top-down" program, "for that would kill it for sure."

Rather, leaders should think of themselves as teachers, working with others to transform their understandings, their commitments, their beliefs, and their skepticism. Certainly it is important to create opportunities for people new to the initiative to get involved, but finding ways to sustain the interest and engagement of those who are more experienced is critical as well. This means remaining open to—and indeed encouraging—new models, new programs and methods of support, and new opportunities to advance the larger, longer-term scholarship-of-teaching-and-learning vision. This is best done by keeping the goal of the work—improving student learning—clearly in view, and by asking all along the way the questions asked of Lee Shulman a decade ago: What should this work look like in 10 years? How will we know if we're "getting there"?

THE FUTURE OF THE PROFESSORIATE

The scholarship of teaching and learning movement has prospered in large part, we believe, because it has been invitational in tone, deliberately welcoming to any and all faculty (full-time and adjunct, senior and more junior, whatever the field or institutional type) who wish to put a toe in the water—or even to dive headfirst into the surf. This openness is consistent with the movement's language: this is *scholarly* work, not a bureaucratic requirement.

At the same time, as campus administrative leaders and faculty are well aware, it is hard not to be struck by the escalating demands in the academy today. Even as serious intellectual work on learning and teaching has begun to make a place for itself in campus culture, so have pressures in other directions: rising expectations, even in so-called "teaching institutions," for traditional research publications; urgings in the direction of more interdisciplinary scholarship; growing commitments to community engagement; new opportunities but also new challenges in the use of technology; high-profile imperatives around assessment, accountability, student recruitment, retention, and advising; and—most to the point here—an increasingly urgent public call to move much larger numbers of students toward more meaningful forms and levels of learning. This press to raise college success rates is, as one foundation put it, "the big goal," and it comes with high stakes for this country's future (Lumina Foundation, 2009).

We believe the stakes are high for the professoriate as well. For one thing, rising expectations for student learning have come at a time of diminishing resources for higher education, as both public funding and the value of endowments drop. Doing more with less, campuses are struggling and faculty are stretched thin just about everywhere we look. And, as is now well known, more than half of today's professoriate hold positions that are part-time or contingent, making it difficult to do sustained work on pressing institutional agendas for student learning—or anything else, for that matter (Schuster and Finkelstein, 2006). Not surprisingly, some have worried that the academic profession is becoming a less attractive proposition for the best and brightest—and indeed, less a profession than a kind of work for hire.

In the face of these realities, it is hard to imagine that faculty can find time, energy, or motivation to take on new work. And yet, that is just what many are now doing as they take up the mantle of the scholarship of teaching and learning and set their sights on finding the best roads to a better education for more students. And perhaps, after all, this is not surprising, for such work enacts the values of inquiry, evidence, and excellence that are at the heart of academic life and identity.

The scholarship of teaching and learning is not a panacea, but its practices and vision are already improving the educational experience for students, faculty, and institutions. If there is a scholarship of teaching and learning utopia, it is not a final destination but a "way of navigating" educational challenges today and tomorrow (Draeger and Price, 2009, p. 10).

The world of college and university teaching has come a long way since *Scholarship Reconsidered* introduced the idea of a "scholarship of teaching," not as a specialized area of endeavor but as an approach to teaching and scholarship available to all faculty. Since then, as we hope this new book exemplifies, the conversation has moved from definitional debates to questions of impact, and the focus has shifted from the design of individual projects to collaborative work that can influence institutional change. It is no longer necessary, or even desirable, for professors to teach as they had been taught: in pedagogical solitude. Faculty today (and tomorrow) can engage in inquiry and innovation with colleagues, drawing on and contributing to the larger teaching commons. And in that commons, they will find a literature that is far richer than the familiar staple of teaching tips and anecdotes, including systematic studies by faculty investigating teaching and student learning in college classrooms and programs. Across town and across the globe, these faculty are bringing their diverse contexts and perspectives to bear in ways that promise real benefits to students, who are themselves increasingly diverse in all the ways that matter in teaching and learning. One need not wait for Utopia U to see these shifts. They're happening now. And they hold great promise for the profession of teaching, for students, and for higher education.

Notes

1. This quotation is from "Inventing the Future" (Shulman, 2000).

2. These questions were raised at the final convening of CASTL campuses in October 2009, where participants discussed four "blue sky" scenarios of the future. The

scenarios, intended as conversation starters, are included in Appendix C, with thanks to Barbara Cambridge, who designed and facilitated the session. Cambridge was the inaugural director of the CASTL Campus Program.

3. The notion of a scholarship of teaching and learning utopia emerged from work in the CASTL theme group on institutional culture and policy, coordinated by Buffalo State College. Our thanks to John Draeger from that institution, and to Linda Price from the Open University (UK) for sharing their paper on the topic. Those looking for lighter fare on the same topic may enjoy Keith Trigwell's satirical account of a utopian future for the scholarship of teaching and learning in the United Kingdom, "where 20 years in the future, SoTL is so embedded in HE culture that we scarcely notice it; where there is a SoTL Thought for the Day on Radio 4's Today programme, and where the DNA of an extinct sub-species of humanity, labelled 'RAE [the UK's high-stakes Research Assessment Exercise] researcher', is stored in a flask in a museum" (as reported in Duncan and Maharg, 2005, p. 2).

4. In its much-circulated *Greater Expectations* report, the Association of American Colleges and Universities argues that higher education must help students become "intentional learners," able to connect and integrate the various elements of their undergraduate experience (2002).

5. See Chapter 2 in this volume for a discussion of an initiative to "decode the disciplines" at Indiana University (Pace and Middendorf, 2004).

6. Examples of this approach are mentioned in earlier chapters: the Center Scholars at the University of Wisconsin-Milwaukee, CILA Associates at St. Olaf College, and the "Decoding the Disciplines" learning community at Indiana University. But fellowship programs have become widespread. The following list is merely a sampling of such programs from within CASTL: Central European University, Creighton University, Kennesaw State University, Michigan State University, Southeast Missouri State, University College Cork, University of Colorado, University of British Columbia, and University of Waterloo.

7. Scholars of teaching and learning from Buffalo State College, Western Carolina University, and Rose-Hulman Institute of Technology used the Classroom Survey of Student Engagement (CLASSE) to drill down into institutional-level National Survey of Student Engagement results, focusing their efforts on freshman composition and first-year seminars.

8. Though there has been much discussion about "rigor," issues of quality (that is, standards) have not, thus far, been much in view in debates about the place of the scholarship of teaching and learning in promotion and tenure, perhaps because more basic definitional questions have taken precedence. Responding to our 2009 CASTL Survey, one international campus wrote, "Some staff believe they are engaged in a sustained and significant level of scholarship of teaching and learning enquiry, but are not.... We have in some ways been our own downfall in that senior staff in an effort to encourage scholarship of teaching and learning activity didn't discriminate or demarcate what was of an acceptable level."

9. This listing is necessarily illustrative, not exhaustive. And of course it may change, as those who have previously sponsored events or provided support pass

the torch to new people and places. Although there is no single comprehensive source of information about the current crop of professional development opportunities, the web site of the International Society for the Scholarship of Teaching and Learning, with its online newsletter, *The International Commons*, regularly includes announcements of upcoming events and opportunities (see http://www.issotl.org/).

10. In 2007, CASTL staff (Tony Ciccone, Barbara Cambridge, Mary Taylor Huber, and Pat Hutchings) took a stab at outlining 10 cross-cutting areas of impact, coming up with a list that was later refined with the help of coordinators from CASTL's Institutional Leadership and Affiliates Program. The list directed attention to contributions that the scholarship of teaching and learning is making to: important agendas and initiatives in higher education; changes in how teachers teach, and understanding how that change happens; how educators understand and talk about learning; direct and indirect effects on student learning and success; knowledge of conditions that affect the exchange and improvement of pedagogy; strengthening development programs for higher education professionals; informing change in institutional policies and practices; the culture of academic life; changes in the definition and evaluation of scholarship; and the growth and evolution of the larger movement (see Ciccone, 2008).

Exploring Impact

A Survey of Participants in the CASTL Institutional Leadership and Affiliates Program, 2009

Anthony Ciccone
Mary Taylor Huber
Pat Hutchings
Barbara Cambridge

*T*his document was prepared for and distributed at the final gathering of campuses participating in the Carnegie Academy for the Scholarship of Teaching and Learning, October 21, 2009, Bloomington, Indiana. It has been edited and reformatted for inclusion in this volume.

In the winter of 2009, after more than a decade of work, the Carnegie Academy for the Scholarship of Teaching and Learning (CASTL) invited institutions participating in the CASTL Institutional Leadership and Affiliates Program to respond to a survey focused on the work's impact. This document provides a summary and sampling of responses.

Designed collaboratively by The Carnegie Foundation for the Advancement of Teaching's leadership team and by CASTL Institutional Leadership and Affiliates coordinators from participating institutions, the survey instrument reflects the program's recent focus on *institutional impact*. Thus, whereas an earlier CASTL survey (see Huber and Hutchings's *The Advancement of Learning*, 2005) explored the impact of the scholarship of teaching and learning on the teaching practices, career paths, and scholarly engagement of individual faculty, this 2009 survey focuses on four broad areas of institutional practice and policy:

- How faculty approach teaching
- The character of the student learning experience
- The institutional culture in support of teaching

- The contribution of the scholarship of teaching and learning to other campus initiatives and agendas

As noted in the introduction to the survey instrument, there are difficulties inherent in any attempt to characterize the impact of the scholarship of teaching and learning on an entire institution. This is especially so with large and decentralized campuses, institutions with multiple campuses, and organizations that bring together diverse campuses and individuals.[1]

Attempting to mitigate those difficulties, the survey employed a seven-point scale designed to capture a wide range of patterns of impact, from "widespread" to "localized," from "deep" to "mixed," and finally to "no discernible impact." (The scale was adapted from *Riding the Waves of Change: Insights from Transforming Institutions*, a 2001 occasional paper from the American Council on Education Project on Leadership and Institutional Transformation and The Kellogg Forum on Higher Education Transformation.) The survey also included open-ended questions soliciting comments, examples, reflections, and uncertainties. Several questions focus explicitly on the future: lessons for a next stage of work, next steps for the institution, and critical issues for the future of the scholarship of teaching and learning movement.

The survey was distributed by e-mail on January 22, 2009, to representatives from 103 institutions; these included U.S. campuses from all major categories of the Basic Carnegie Classification of Institutions of Higher Education, 17 institutions from outside the United States, a number of educational associations or consortia, and one discipline-based organization. All were participants in the CASTL Institutional Leadership and Affiliates Program, which ran from 2006 through 2009. Typically the survey was completed by the individual serving as CASTL "point person" for the institution; the instrument invited respondents to complete the survey in consultation or collaboration with others in their setting, and about half reported doing so.

Following several reminder notices, a total of 59 surveys were returned by May 1, 2009, for a response rate of 57 percent.

This report of survey results aims to provide evidence and understanding of what the scholarship of teaching and learning movement has accomplished and how it can achieve a lasting place in the work of higher education institutions. Individual faculty may find it useful in thinking about how their work fits within and contributes to the larger interest in educational improvement; administrative leaders may discover useful ways to support pedagogical scholarship and maximize its benefits on their campuses; funders and educational associations may find promising new directions to advance and encourage. Although the formal CASTL program concluded at the end of 2009, the results of this survey strongly suggest that the scholarship of teaching and learning can and will continue to grow.

IMPACT ON FACULTY AS TEACHERS

How would you describe the impact of engagement with the scholarship of teaching and learning on the ways that faculty approach teaching on your campus?

Respondents from 58 institutions answered this question, with the majority reporting that the scholarship of teaching and learning made a significant difference for some faculty and a more modest one for others. Among the changes most often reported were shifts toward greater use of active learning strategies in the classroom, new ways of sharing pedagogical insights and practices with others, and more interest in and use of evidence about student learning.

A number of respondents reported that engagement with the scholarship of teaching and learning had led faculty members to embrace *new classroom approaches*. One campus, for instance, surveyed its own faculty and found that 90 percent say they are using more active learning strategies. Looking across institutional types, service learning and problem-based learning were among the approaches frequently mentioned. In some settings, larger groups of faculty and sometimes entire programs were engaged in new kinds of teaching, with the sciences most frequently mentioned. At a large research university, inquiry into the use of clickers by a faculty member in physics led to the adoption of that technology across the department and in several other large courses in science, technology, engineering, and mathematics.

With many educators trying out new approaches in their classrooms, the survey also suggested that faculty have new opportunities—and a new sense of *permission—to share ideas and learn from one another*. Often, these developments took the form of groups of faculty meeting together to share the results of their practice and inquiry. A public liberal arts college created an ongoing roundtable for this kind of exchange, reporting that 30 percent of faculty have now participated. A community college reported that "faculty not only discussed their teaching and their students' work on a weekly basis but also sent interdisciplinary teams into one another's classrooms to discuss student work." There were examples of new vehicles for exchange as well, including campus-sponsored journals at several institutions, and, on another, an online resource (run through the library) where faculty could document and share their scholarship of teaching and learning.

Also clear is that, as one respondent put it, a growing number of faculty *"hunger for more information about how their students are doing."* In some settings, engagement with the scholarship of teaching and learning led more faculty to read the research literature on learning. In others it prompted interest in new methods for uncovering what and how students are learning. Most notably, perhaps, survey results revealed an emergent intersection between the scholarship of teaching and learning and assessment, with many of the same individuals involved in these two activities, and with influences in both directions. In some settings, for instance, scholars of teaching and learning have enlarged their inquiry beyond their own classrooms and helped to shape program-level assessment work.

In general, it seems safe to say that faculty who become engaged in the scholarship of teaching and learning are also likely to be involved in other innovative and reform-oriented activities. The result is a mix of influences that strengthen one another in ways that are cumulatively significant.

IMPACT ON THE STUDENT LEARNING EXPERIENCE

How would you describe the impact of engagement with the scholarship of teaching and learning on the student learning experience on your campus?

The majority of 57 respondents identified ways—from modest to significant—that the scholarship of teaching and learning has had an impact on their students' experience. Respondents reported an increased involvement of students in the scholarship of teaching and learning, some positive changes in student attitudes toward learning, and a range of evidence about the impact of the scholarship of teaching and learning on the student experience.

Students are becoming more and *more involved in the scholarship of teaching and learning*, including engaging in internships to analyze undergraduate research practices, conducting focus groups that yielded data applicable to institutional needs, and serving on faculty and student teams doing such projects as a "study on factors that facilitate and inhibit the learning of under-represented students." Although one respondent indicated that "student involvement is minimal," another kind of answer was more frequent—for example, that "the redesign of entire courses, syllabi, and reconsideration of teaching methods have occurred in various departments as a result of the recognition of the importance of engaging students as partners in studying the learning process."

Students are developing *more positive attitudes toward and engagement with their learning*. Because research shows that engagement and learning are closely linked, inquiring into either or both can yield important insights. Engagement was emphasized in reports like these: "30 percent of our students participated in a research project with a faculty member outside of course or program requirements"; Lesson Study projects yielded "improvement in students' learning gains and responses to assignments"; and students involved with faculty in the scholarship of teaching and learning were "more willing to change their approaches to learning—both inside and outside the classroom." On other campuses, data from the National Survey of Student Engagement

(NSSE) confirmed findings from the scholarship of teaching and learning. One campus reported, "We have solid results on the Canadian comparatives for the five significant areas of NSSE questions."

Evidence to document the effect of the scholarship of teaching and learning on the student experience ranged from little to lots. Some campuses reported knowing "little about students during or after scholarship of teaching and learning projects," employing "no organized mechanism to assess changes in dimensions of student learning," and locating "few empirical indicators that learning is directly influenced by the scholarship of teaching and learning alone." Yet other campuses found convincing data about impact. They reported improved attitudes of students toward their teachers and themselves as learners, positive effects of particular pedagogies on student learning, and a growing emphasis on undergraduate research options, use of student research assistants, and community engagement. Many campuses reported new efforts to assess impact. For example, one said that "research within the University is currently under way to evaluate the student experience more fully." Evidence of impact is being increasingly sought and found.

IMPACT ON THE INSTITUTIONAL CULTURE OF TEACHING

How would you describe the impact of engagement with the scholarship of teaching and learning on the culture of teaching on your campus?

Of the 57 respondents to this question, nearly two-thirds (36) reported that the impact of engagement with the scholarship of teaching and learning at their institution was widespread. For seven of these respondents, the impact was also deep; for 20, it was mixed; and for nine it was generally not deep. The 20 who reported localized impact were evenly split on its level of penetration. Only one reported no discernible impact at all.

Comments focused on enhanced interest in teaching issues on campus, the development of a more collaborative teaching culture, growth in the numbers of faculty engaged in the scholarship of teaching and learning, and issues about the place of the scholarship of teaching and learning in systems of faculty roles and rewards.

A rise of *interest in teaching and learning* was widely reported, in some cases spurred by the move "toward curricular development and assessment in keeping with learning outcomes," as one community college leader said. Elsewhere, growing numbers of faculty have "become aware of the large literature that exists on teaching and learning, and from which they can draw for their own teaching." The level and extent of pedagogical conversation is also up: for instance, one campus leader said that dialogue on "what should be taught and whether our students are learning" has become "passionate."

Teaching has also become more *"collaborative, social, group-oriented,"* one respondent wrote, "something that is done, shared, talked about between faculty, students, staff." Several told stories about dramatic transformations: younger faculty raising the level of sophistication in departmental discussions by contributing material from books and articles encountered in faculty workshops; a science professor who had not given a writing assignment in 40 years listening to colleagues and starting to ask students to write research papers on aspects of the field they find interesting. As a result, one campus leader wrote, "the bar for assessment and excellence in teaching has been raised."

Engagement in more formal programs for the scholarship of teaching and learning, though often concentrated in "pockets," is also up. A respondent at one baccalaureate institution noted that thanks to local and system-wide teaching scholars programs, "the accumulation of campus scholarship of teaching and learning is growing."

However, comments indicated a continuing *lag in recognition and reward.* Although the scholarship of teaching and learning has contributed to "a change in the prevailing understanding of what is expected of professors as teachers," it is not necessarily valued in retention, tenure, and promotion. Some complained that official documents "mostly pay lip service to teaching," while others say that the scholarship of teaching and learning is still treated as "the 'poor cousin' to disciplinary research." A more nuanced perspective is reported at one baccalaureate college: "Scholarship of teaching and learning work is considered positively in hiring and promotion decisions, but it is not considered a substitute for scholarly work in one's field."

IMPACT ON DEPARTMENT OR PROGRAM INITIATIVES

How would you describe the impact of engagement with the scholarship of teaching and learning on the design or implementation of other department or program initiatives and agendas on your campus?

Respondents from 57 institutions answered this question. Approximately half reported a modest or significant impact on some departments and programs, while an additional 25 percent reported a modest or significant impact on many departments or programs.

When asked to choose from a list of 16 department or program initiatives that might have been affected, respondents most often mentioned *pedagogical innovation* (45), *faculty development* (45), *assessment* (39), and *curriculum revision* (38).

Examples seemed to point to three types of impact. Engagement with the scholarship of teaching and learning *improved the climate* for an initiative (for instance, assessment), provided *principles to guide the work* (for instance, faculty inquiry), or created *products* (for instance, directed studies) that significantly informed or improved the initiative.

Since scholarly work on teaching most often starts in an individual classroom, one would expect to find an impact on *pedagogical innovation*. Survey respondents noted that faculty who engage in such work "get the ball rolling" in their departments and serve as "role models" for other individuals, thus increasing the numbers of faculty who understand and value the work, and improving the climate for innovation. The central principles of the scholarship of teaching and learning were frequently cited as changing the way faculty think about pedagogical innovation—that is, "less as serendipity and more as a thoughtful practice." In the most advanced cases, scholarly projects and products were seen as leading to widespread and deep innovations, for example "highly innovative strategies and approaches" (to teaching writing), new technologies for tracking student understanding, and the creation of online course components. The scholarship of teaching and learning also connected individual classrooms to program innovation, for example (as reported by one campus), by enabling faculty to apply results from the National Survey of Student Engagement to their instruction in writing and first-year courses.

Several campuses reported that principles, practices, and products of the scholarship of teaching and learning have had a significant effect on *faculty development*, moving beyond a focus on generic tips and strategies to asking and beginning to answer consequential questions about student learning. Respondents noted that they use "concepts of the scholarship of teaching and learning in designing workshops and communicating with faculty." Speaking for many, one noted that a faculty development program in physics had "certainly been influenced by the scholarship of teaching and learning. People are now much more careful about specifying learning outcomes and thinking of ways to measure them." The scholarship of teaching and learning was often the method of choice for organizing development activities around campus themes, such as "professional dispositions and values," and, in at least one case, it has been used to reconceptualize faculty development itself as a process in three phases—reflective practice, scholarly teaching, and systematic inquiry into teaching and learning.

The scholarship of teaching and learning is often mentioned as having had an effect on *assessment*. Departments where faculty have been engaged in inquiry into the students' experience have a better understanding of learning outcomes because "they have assessed student learning in their classrooms," and are "noticeably less hostile to institutional assessment." Respondents also noted specific programs (the first-year experience, general education) and majors (biology) where scholarship of teaching and learning work has been woven into assessment approaches. One national organization cited its work in studying the effectiveness of education in its area as "an illustration of the scholarship of teaching and learning because it started with a question about student learning that led to data collection, analysis, and ultimately publication and dissemination of tested instructional materials."

Respondents also reported that scholarship of teaching and learning principles and products have made *curriculum revision* easier, citing the "synergy" that develops when curricular redesign is undertaken by faculty familiar with stating and studying learning outcomes. One psychology department used a scholarship of teaching and learning study of its capstone course to revise both the course and the major.

IMPACT ON SCHOOL/COLLEGE OR CAMPUSWIDE INITIATIVES

How would you describe the impact of engagement with the scholarship of teaching and learning on the design and/or implementation of other school/college or campuswide initiatives and agendas on your campus?

Respondents from 56 institutions answered this question. Approximately one-third reported a modest or significant impact on *many* school/college or campuswide initiatives, while an additional 25 percent reported a modest or significant impact on *some* school/college or campuswide initiatives.

When asked to choose from the list of 16 school/college or campuswide initiatives that might have been affected, respondents pointed to three areas that also emerged in the parallel question about department- and program-level activity—*faculty development* (38), *curriculum revision* (24), and *assessment* (21)—but a new area, *teaching, learning and technology* (24), was also frequently mentioned.

Specific examples were hard to come by, and respondents most often provided general statements of impact on campuswide practices—for instance, the evaluation of teaching, tenure and promotion processes, work with the institutional review board, and faculty development grants—rather than specific initiatives. One respondent noted that this was "perhaps the area of least impact," while another put it more positively: "The focus isn't on the scholarship of teaching and learning, but those values and principles are brought into the discussion as good practice," and noted that "culling out specific examples doesn't accurately reflect the underlying scholarship of teaching and learning influence."

Specific examples of significant impact, however, were mentioned, particularly in the areas of *faculty and graduate student development*; respondents noted that fellowship programs and courses on teaching were often created or restructured according to scholarship of teaching and learning principles or focused on certain campuswide initiatives, for instance e-portfolios, student research opportunities, applied learning programs, or first-year programs. Two campuses reported significant *impact on campuswide assessment initiatives* that involved the Collegiate Learning Assessment (CLA)—in one case, studying the CLA results to improve the use of e-portfolios; in the other, to connect the CLA results "to the design of assignments and assessment in individual classrooms."

In summary, the effect of engagement with the scholarship of teaching and learning on campuswide initiatives seems most likely to be found in the perspective and knowledge that individuals familiar with the scholarship of teaching and learning bring to the table.

IMPROVEMENTS IN STUDENT LEARNING

One of the questions many of us are often asked is whether engagement in the scholarship of teaching and learning leads to improvements in student learning. How do you or would you answer this question? What would you point to as evidence for this connection on your campus?

Fifty-two respondents answered this question, offering comments that ranged from positive assertions ("improvements can be attributed to the scholarship of teaching and learning on a case by case basis") to more nuanced evidence ("more faculty spend more time and effort on teaching which might improve learning"). Many expressed puzzlement ("we need help here"), and a few even questioned the premise ("I don't think there is a straight path from an intervention to improvement in student learning").

Some of the *positive statements* were stunningly precise ("73 percent of our faculty are reporting a slight increase in student learning in their assessment projects"). Others, noting rising scores on student exit exams or student ratings of instructors engaged in the work, were cautious about what caused the effect. One judicious responder pointed to surveys that show "greater numbers of faculty engaging in those practices we know are correlated with increased student learning."

Many nuanced comments pointed to *possible indirect effects* of faculty engagement with the scholarship of teaching and learning. One noted that many faculty had redesigned their online courses thanks to "campus studies on the effectiveness of online teaching." Others offered more general perspectives: "any time spent thinking through teaching and learning ... allows us to be aware of the need for a variety of approaches," for instance, or "a focus on scholarly teaching and elements of the scholarship of teaching and learning has helped ... maintain a strong focus on sustaining and enhancing student learning."

Clearly this question touched a nerve, spurring many to voice *puzzlement and frustration over the difficulties of documentation*, if not outright despair. Variations on "this is a real challenge" were common. Responses noted that it takes time to improve the student experience—and they had not yet had sufficient time; that most evidence at hand was "qualitative and anecdotal," and that "confounding factors, study design, measurement issues, and intervening variables make answering this question very difficult."

Many respondents mentioned the work of individual scholars, some of whom had done simple pre-post tests or used more ambitious comparative methodologies. But very few leaders had seen anything they considered "conclusive campuswide evidence." One commented that a meta-analysis of individual cases might help pull the many, disparate results of individual studies together.

Finally, there were respondents who just *don't think this question leads to a fruitful line of inquiry*: "Straightforward quantitative improvement of student learning [cannot] be pinpointed and traced over time, but [there is] evidence of changes in student behavior and ways of thinking.... If teachers and students report positive changes in student learning and back this up by discussions of specific examples of student work, then that is all the evidence we need."

USING TECHNOLOGY

Do you use technology to advance the knowledge and practice of the scholarship of teaching and learning on your campus? How? How have you used technology to share work and to learn from others?

Although 10 institutions had nothing to say about the uses of technology to advance the scholarship of teaching and learning, it is clear from those that did choose to comment that technology plays increasingly important and varied roles, ranging from the classroom to the much broader teaching commons.

At the classroom level, technological innovations presented *occasions for inquiry*. Clickers were among the examples most often cited; scholars of teaching and learning on a number of campuses have conducted systematic (and promising) studies of the impact of this new pedagogical tool. The use of electronic student portfolios was mentioned as well; studies of e-portfolios as prompts for reflection have attracted the attention of scholars of teaching and learning in a number of settings. In general, one might say that where new approaches appeared in the classroom, the scholarship of teaching and learning was often not far behind.

Technology also provides *new tools for data collection and analysis* for scholars of teaching and learning. Several campuses noted the use of online surveys to capture students' perceptions of teaching and learning. Scholars of teaching and learning at a large research university are employing "digital story telling" as a research tool. And a small liberal arts college has recently begun using a commercially available electronic data management system (TracDat) as a tool for assessing student learning—though "not yet understanding its full capacity."

A good number of respondents also reported that technology provides *tools for documenting and sharing the scholarship of teaching and learning*. The Carnegie Foundation's KEEP Toolkit[2] has been the tool of choice in a number of CASTL settings, allowing scholars of teaching and learning (even without sophisticated technological skills) to construct multimedia web sites that capture the richness of their projects. Somewhat in the same spirit, one research university has developed "a gallery of local course portfolios" which provide "learning objects" for faculty development, and a liberal arts college has videotaped "structured interviews with faculty who have done scholarship of teaching and learning projects," then edited them down to four or five minutes for easy access and sharing. Many campuses (typically through the agency of a teaching and learning center but occasionally through the library or some other entity) described the development of web sites with examples of and resources for the scholarship of teaching and learning.

Running through all of these themes is a key finding about the power of technology in building *the teaching commons*. Although some campuses (perhaps including those that skipped this question) felt that technology is "not really" a major element in their scholarship of teaching and learning work, or is "not well used," it is difficult not to be struck by the myriad new web sites, listservs, digital repositories, multimedia galleries, wikis, e-portfolios, and online journals that are popping up almost daily, and which for many in this movement play a major role in helping to expand and enrich the conversation about teaching and learning.

LESSONS USEFUL TO OTHERS

What are one or two lessons from your engagement with the scholarship of teaching and learning on your campus that would be useful to others?

Respondents from 56 institutions answered this question, offering lessons about community-building, the disciplines, keeping the effort faculty-led, administrative support, valuing the work, and the use of key terms (for instance, the "scholarship of teaching and learning"). Less frequent, but important to mention, were statements endorsing the value of engaging students in the work.

Many institutions emphasized the importance of *building communities* around the scholarship of teaching and learning or offered techniques for doing so. There's a need, one wrote, to develop a "critical mass" of people involved in the work, to "engage widespread and ongoing conversations." "Start with one small project," one leader advised, "like a reading circle or brown bag discussions." One recommended "faculty learning communities" as the way to go, while another suggested a curriculum grant program as a way to "get people involved in the systemic evaluation of their projects as a precursor to the scholarship of teaching and learning," and moving "people as a cohort through the execution of their grants to foster peer critique and learning." A number of respondents mentioned that it was important to involve scholars from *all the disciplines* in the work, using it to spark *cross-disciplinary conversations*.

Several colleagues underlined the importance of making (and keeping) the scholarship of teaching and learning a faculty-led, *grassroots* movement, while noting the value of having distinguished campus scholars as champions, and the added benefit of *support from highly placed administrators*. "Having the full support of the president, provost, as well as other campus leaders makes teaching and learning significant," an especially important signal, this person noted, at a research university.

Challenges in valuing and naming the work were noted frequently, with research and publication at the crux of the issue. One master's institution leader called "the scholarship of teaching and learning" a "cumbersome" term, preferring "teaching paper or teaching publication" which doesn't mark the work as something different from other forms of scholarship. However, this perspective can have the effect of separating the work from teaching itself. For instance, a doctoral university leader commented that his institution's tenure and promotion procedures allowed no space for the documentation of the scholarship of teaching and learning that was "not specifically defined as part of the research component."

These issues of recognition and reward also play a role in *explaining the work to faculty and drawing them in*. For instance, one community college respondent thought it important to "reframe 'classroom research' so that faculty would not be intimidated or turned off by the idea of engaging meaningful exploration of teaching and learning." And another doctoral university colleague suggested that the term "scholarship of teaching and learning" not be used: "engaging faculty in intellectual inquiry into what they care about in their student's understanding is a welcome invitation in ways that having added expectations in 'scholarship' is definitely not." Yet, elsewhere, the term can be a plus. As one international colleague noted, using "'the scholarship of teaching and learning' is much better than using the term 'pedagogy,' which is not very highly regarded."

SIGNS OF PROGRESS

What are one or two of the most promising signs of progress in teaching and learning that engagement with the scholarship of teaching and learning has contributed to on your campus?

Responses to this question fell most often into one of three categories: improvement in mood or attitude among faculty, changes in campus practices, and increasingly sophisticated language and conversation about teaching and learning.

Several respondents made a point to note that engagement with the scholarship of teaching and learning had improved faculty mood, noting *increased enthusiasm and excitement for teaching* and a greater belief in the possibility that *faculty could make a difference in student learning* by studying it in their classrooms. This enthusiasm manifested itself in greater numbers of applicants for grants, higher levels of proposal submissions to teaching conferences, and increased participation in campus initiatives related to teaching and learning.

Respondents also pointed to progress made in *changing key institutional practices*. For some (clearly this change is not yet widespread), this included recognition of the scholarship of teaching and learning in the reward structure (tenure and promotion) by departments and administrators. In some settings, such work has been accepted as a legitimate form of research; in others, it has led to a rethinking of the campus teaching evaluation or award systems, often in conjunction with teaching portfolios. Similar impact was noted in "higher expectations for program evaluation" and "more sophisticated discussion of assessment."

Many respondents chose to highlight *changes in the language and conversation about teaching and learning* due to engagement with the scholarship of teaching and learning. New interlocutors, including younger faculty and colleagues previously unlikely to attend teaching center events, seem to be joining the conversation. The former "discuss teaching with some of the same data-rich sophistication that they discuss their research," one respondent noted, while another noted that early adopters continue to be involved.

While two respondents attributed increased sophistication in discussions of teaching and learning to a shared concept of the scholarship of teaching and learning, others noted the more *general effects of engagement with inquiry.* "The term 'learning' is now used across campus in discussions of pedagogy," one respondent reported, while another noted increased questioning of the "conventional wisdom" about teaching and learning and more interest in evidence. This attention to evidence of student learning seems to build increased respect for teaching.

In sum, it is clear that many respondents believe that conversations about teaching and learning are growing more frequent and more sophisticated, whether in larger "communities of like-minded, dedicated faculty" or in new settings where a single scholar of teaching finds unexpected interest among colleagues in talking about learning.

ANTICIPATED NEXT STEPS

What are one or two initiatives around the scholarship of teaching and learning that you anticipate undertaking on your campus in the near future? Why?

Responses to this question fell most often into one of two categories: activities that increase participation in and visibility of the work, and connections to other initiatives.

Many respondents chose to emphasize activities that would increase *awareness of and participation in scholarly inquiry.* These might be structural, such as creating teaching centers "grounded in the scholarship of teaching and learning as a way to study many common questions," or programmatic, such as developing (online) seminars and tutorials for new and experienced scholars of teaching and learning, local and regional conferences, and internal grants and publications. Innovations in this area, such as the use of learning communities mentored by experienced faculty, support for collaborative work at the program, department, or school level, and plans for leadership institutes and consortia (regional or theme-based) testify to the maturity of the work at certain institutions.

Although one respondent suggested the need to "continue to promote the scholarship of teaching and learning as a program in its own right," most emphasized the value of *ongoing or expanded connections to specific initiatives.* Several chose to mention working with graduate students through learning communities or "modules on teaching and learning that encourage a scholarship of teaching and learning approach." Others noted that the scholarship of teaching and learning informs discussions of teaching evaluation, effectiveness, and excellence.

The relationship between the scholarship of teaching and learning and campus initiatives will clearly remain nuanced. The results of scholarly inquiry into teaching and learning will be used, some institutions told us, as a rationale to *create or expand curricular initiatives* in service learning and to support curricular changes that "privilege the broad questions of the discipline." The scholarship of teaching and learning will also serve as an organizing principle to develop or study initiatives in online programs, developing students as researchers, and "bridging the gap between liberal arts and professional education." Indeed, one institution plans to do *multi-institutional collaborative scholarship of teaching and learning* with its transfer partners "to identify barriers to learning for transfer students and facilitate their academic adjustment."

Finally, the current budget situation across higher education prompted several institutions to mention "staying in *maintenance* mode." Clearly, the need to be "more explicit about the connection of the scholarship of teaching and learning to larger campus initiatives" will be an important part of this strategy. As mentioned earlier, one of the most fruitful connections may be with *institutional assessment*.

ISSUES FOR THE MOVEMENT'S FUTURE

What are one or two of the most important issues that the scholarship of teaching and learning as a movement must address in the near future?

Perhaps because it came at the end of the survey, this question attracted only 36 respondents—but many raised multiple issues important to the future of the scholarship of teaching and learning as a movement. Not surprisingly, leaders are already wrestling with most of these issues in their own organizations.

A few specific pedagogical challenges (online learning, civic engagement) and institutional agendas (assessment) were mentioned as areas where the scholarship of teaching and learning could make important contributions. But several respondents cited the more general issue of translating theory into practice: "We need to generate an audience of committed readers for all this work," "do better at building on knowledge of the pedagogical literature," and "make the application of scholarship of teaching and learning work truly widespread." Exploring the link between engaged teaching and improved learning was a priority for some, and key to "showing why it is important to support faculty who are doing this work."

Many commented on the *relationship between rigor and reach* in the scholarship of teaching and learning. "We understand the importance of maintaining rigor," one colleague wrote, "but can there be some altering of perception whereby all faculty can perceive the scholarship of teaching and learning as approachable and accessible?" For some, accessibility is the bigger issue, especially for faculty in the humanities and fine arts, who are put off by the dominant "social science models." For others, struck by the "uneven quality" of conference presentations, rigor is the more urgent issue if the work is to gain respect. Still, people were wary about merging the scholarship of teaching and learning with traditional kinds of educational research: "What are appropriate models for doing the scholarship of teaching and learning well without professionalizing it as a field exclusive to a small number of specialists?"

However it is construed, the *scholarship of teaching and learning requires support* in the form of "resources, strategies, and venues in which to share, connect, and engage." Specific suggestions included work with institutional review boards to help them understand the nature of research done under the scholarship of teaching and learning banner; the education of administrators who have "good reasons to be supportive, but aren't simply because they don't know about the work"; and new publications to assist those who lead scholarship of teaching and learning efforts. Several mentioned the need to strengthen international networks, and colleagues in the United States worried about what would happen now that CASTL was concluding its work: "We still need a national organization to provide models and ideas, and to rally individual faculty and their institutions around the scholarship of teaching and learning banner."

How can the scholarship of teaching and learning fit into *the realities of professional life for the twenty-first-century professoriate*? Respondents mentioned the importance of getting the work onto doctoral students' radar screens, providing models for how to incorporate the scholarship of teaching and learning into one's regular teaching practice, and making this work accessible for part-time faculty. As one said: "We need to focus on how these persons are initiated into their teaching role so that they understand and adopt the philosophical underpinnings that are guiding our work with students. We need to figure out how to provide adjuncts with faculty development opportunities without burdening them further, as well as how to provide salaries that demonstrate that we value what they do."

Finally, respondents returned to the overarching problem of *recognition and reward*. For many, this means first and foremost changing guidelines so that the scholarship of teaching and learning counts in annual reviews, salary considerations, and promotion and tenure. Colleagues pointed out, however, that this also requires better strategies for assessing the quality of the work and for gaining peer acceptance, whether one is concerned with its development as teaching or as research. "How," one respondent asked, "do we continue to increase understanding of the scholarship of teaching and learning and its value in the reward system?"

SUMMARY OF QUANTITATIVE RESPONSES

Table A.1 Areas of Institutional Impact

How would you describe the impact on your campus of engagement with the scholarship of teaching and learning on:

	How faculty approach teaching (n = 58)	The student learning experience (n = 55)	The culture of teaching (n = 57)	Department or program initiatives (n = 57)	Campuswide initiatives (n = 56)
Widespread and deep	5	2	7	4	3
Widespread yet mixed	23	17	20	14	18
Widespread but not deep	2	1	9	3	2
Localized and deep	9	13	6	13	6
Localized yet mixed	14	18	8	16	14
Localized but not deep	4	3	6	5	6
No discernible impact	1	1	1	2	7

Table A.2 Importance of Affiliation with a National Initiative

How important has it been for your campus to be a part of the larger national scholarship of teaching and learning initiative?

Not At All	A Little	Somewhat	Very Much	A Great Deal
0	3	9	28	18
0%	5%	16%	48%	31%

Table A.3 Impact on Department/Program Initiatives

Department/Program Initiatives in:	No. of Campuses
Pedagogical innovation	45
Faculty development	45
Assessment	39
Curriculum revision	38
Teaching, learning, and technology	37
Evaluation of teaching	24
First-year experience	23
Undergraduate research	23
Accreditation	18
Graduate student professional development	17
Service learning	17
Civic engagement	15
General education reform	14
Electronic portfolios	12
Retention programs	12
Capstone courses	11

Table A.4 Impact on Campuswide Initiatives

Campuswide Initiatives in:	No. of Campuses
Faculty development	38
Curriculum revision	24
Teaching, learning, and technology	24
Assessment	21
First-year experience	20
General education reform	18
Pedagogical innovation	17
Evaluation of teaching	16
Undergraduate research	15
Accreditation	14
Service learning	12
Civic engagement	12
Retention programs	12
Capstone courses	8
Electronic portfolios	6
Graduate student professional development	5

EXPLORING IMPACT: THE SURVEY INSTRUMENT

This survey instrument was designed for research on the institutional impact of the scholarship of teaching and learning. Please feel free to use or adapt it for use at your own institution or association, and identify it as based on a questionnaire designed by the leadership of the Carnegie Academy for the Scholarship of Teaching and Learning (CASTL) Institutional Leadership and Affiliates Program.

Section One: How Faculty Approach Teaching

This section asks about the impact of engagement with the scholarship of teaching and learning on *how faculty approach teaching* on your campus.

For instance, are there indications that more faculty are consulting resources from research and practice on teaching and learning? Participating in workshops or other professional development opportunities on teaching and learning? Sharing course materials or discussing the goals, methods, and effectiveness of instruction with colleagues? Studying and writing about their students' learning? Documenting their teaching and their students' learning in ways that others can learn from? Collaboratively designing inquiry into teaching and learning with other colleagues?

1. How would you describe the impact of engagement with the scholarship of teaching and learning on how faculty approach teaching on your campus? Choose the description that best applies.
   - ☐ *Widespread and deep*, that is, on many individuals or programs, in significant ways
   - ☐ *Widespread yet mixed*, that is, on many individuals or programs, some in modest ways, some in significant ways
   - ☐ *Widespread but not deep*, that is, on many individuals or programs across campus, but in modest ways
   - ☐ *Localized and deep*, that is, on some individuals and programs, in significant ways
   - ☐ *Localized yet mixed*, that is, on some individuals and programs, some in modest ways, some in significant ways
   - ☐ *Localized but not deep*, that is, on some individuals and programs, in modest ways
   - ☐ There has been no discernible impact
2. What examples or stories support this description of the impact of engagement with scholarship of teaching and learning on how faculty approach teaching on your campus?

Section Two: The Student Learning Experience

This section asks about the impact of engagement with the scholarship of teaching and learning on the *student learning experience* on your campus.

For instance, is there greater use of classroom assessment techniques? Are undergraduates more involved in conversations about teaching and learning? More sophisticated in their feedback to faculty? More capable of reflecting on and assessing their own learning? Are undergraduate students involved as co-inquirers in faculty projects on teaching and learning? Have faculty scholarship of teaching and learning projects described and documented changes in student learning?

1. How would you describe the impact of engagement with the scholarship of teaching and learning on the student learning experience on your campus? Choose the description that best applies.
   - ☐ *Widespread and deep*, that is, on many individuals or programs, in significant ways
   - ☐ *Widespread yet mixed*, that is, on many individuals or programs, some in modest ways, some in significant ways
   - ☐ *Widespread but not deep*, that is, on many individuals or programs across campus, but in modest ways
   - ☐ *Localized and deep*, that is, on some individuals and programs, in significant ways
   - ☐ *Localized yet mixed*, that is, on some individuals and programs, some in modest ways, some in significant ways
   - ☐ *Localized but not deep*, that is, on some individuals and programs, in modest ways
   - ☐ There has been no discernible impact

2. What examples or stories support this description of the impact of engagement with the scholarship of teaching and learning on the student learning experience on your campus?

Section Three: How the Culture of Teaching Has Changed

This section asks about the impact of engagement with the scholarship of teaching and learning on the *culture of teaching* on your campus.

For instance, have there been changes in the ways teaching and learning are talked about? Do departments or programs hold regular discussions among faculty about improving curricula, pedagogy, advising, and/or assessment? Have top-level academic leaders and faculty in leadership positions taken significant steps to support the scholarship of teaching and learning? Is work in the scholarship of teaching and learning considered positively in hiring, promotion, or award decisions? Are there new or enhanced opportunities for internal and external funding for scholarship of teaching and learning work? Have there been changes in the way teaching is evaluated on campus?

1. How would you describe the impact of engagement with the scholarship of teaching and learning on the culture of teaching on your campus? Choose the description that best applies.
   □ *Widespread and deep*, that is, on many individuals or programs, in significant ways
   □ *Widespread yet mixed*, that is, on many individuals or programs, some in modest ways, some in significant ways
   □ *Widespread but not deep*, that is, on many individuals or programs across campus, but in modest ways
   □ *Localized and deep*, that is, on some individuals and programs, in significant ways
   □ *Localized yet mixed*, that is, on some individuals and programs, some in modest ways, some in significant ways
   □ *Localized but not deep*, that is, on some individuals and programs, in modest ways
   □ There has been no discernible impact

2. What examples or stories support this description of the impact of engagement with the scholarship of teaching and learning on the culture of teaching on your campus?

Section Four: How Initiatives Are Advanced

This section has two parts. It asks about the impact of engagement with the scholarship of teaching and learning on (a) department or program initiatives and agendas, and (b) on school/college or campuswide initiatives and agendas.

1. How would you describe the impact of engagement with the scholarship of teaching and learning on the design and/or implementation of other *department or program* initiatives and agendas on your campus? Choose the description that best applies.
   □ *Widespread and deep*, that is, on many other department or program initiatives and agendas, in significant ways
   □ *Widespread yet mixed*, that is, on many other department or program initiatives and agendas, some in modest ways, some in significant ways
   □ *Widespread but not deep*, that is, on many other department or program initiatives and agendas, but in modest ways
   □ *Localized and deep*, that is, on some other department or program initiatives and agendas, in significant ways

    □ *Localized yet mixed,* that is, on some other department or program initiatives and agendas, some in modest ways, some in significant ways

    □ *Localized but not deep,* that is, on some other department or program initiatives and agendas, in modest ways

    □ There has been no discernible impact

2. Which of the following department or program initiatives have benefited from engagement in the scholarship of teaching and learning? Check all that apply.

    □ Curriculum revision

    □ Pedagogical innovation

    □ Assessment

    □ Accreditation

    □ General education reform

    □ Retention programs

    □ First-year experience

    □ Service learning

    □ Undergraduate research

    □ Teaching, learning, and technology

    □ Civic engagement

    □ Electronic portfolios

    □ Capstone courses

    □ Faculty development

    □ Evaluation of teaching

    □ Graduate student professional development

3. Please provide examples for some of the initiatives you selected where the scholarship of teaching and learning impact has been significant. Has scholarship of teaching and learning work been used to advance other *department or program* initiatives not mentioned here?

4. How would you describe the impact of engagement with the scholarship of teaching and learning on the design and/or implementation of other *school/college or campuswide* initiatives and agendas on your campus? Choose the description that best applies.

    □ *Widespread and deep,* that is, on many other school/college or campuswide initiatives and agendas, in significant ways

    □ *Widespread yet mixed,* that is, on many other school/college or campuswide initiatives and agendas, some in modest ways, some in significant ways

    □ *Widespread but not deep,* that is, on many other school/college or campuswide initiatives and agendas, across campus, but in modest ways

☐ *Localized and deep*, that is, on some other school/college or campuswide initiatives and agendas, in significant ways

☐ *Localized yet mixed*, that is, on some other school/college or campuswide initiatives and agendas, some in modest ways, some in significant ways

☐ *Localized but not deep*, that is, on some other school/college or campuswide initiatives and agendas, in modest ways

☐ There has been no discernible impact.

5. Which of the following *school/college or campuswide* initiatives have benefited from campus engagement in the scholarship of teaching and learning? Check all that apply.

☐ Curriculum revision
☐ Pedagogical innovation
☐ Assessment
☐ Accreditation
☐ General education reform
☐ Retention programs
☐ First-year experience
☐ Service learning
☐ Undergraduate research
☐ Teaching, learning, and technology
☐ Civic engagement
☐ Electronic portfolios
☐ Capstone courses
☐ Faculty development
☐ Evaluation of teaching
☐ Graduate student professional development

6. Please provide examples for some of the initiatives you selected where the scholarship of teaching and learning impact has been significant. Has scholarship of teaching and learning work been used to advance other school/college or campuswide initiatives not mentioned here?

Section Five

1. One of the questions many of us are often asked is whether engagement in the scholarship of teaching and learning leads to improvements in student learning. How do/would you answer this question? What would you point to as evidence for this connection on your campus? In your broader experience?

2. Do you use technology to advance the knowledge and practice of the scholarship of teaching and learning on your campus? How? How have you used technology to share work and to learn from others?

3. What are one or two lessons from your engagement with the scholarship of teaching and learning on your campus that would be useful to others?

4. What are one or two of the most promising signs of progress in teaching and learning that engagement with the scholarship of teaching and learning has contributed to on your campus?

5. What are one or two initiatives around the scholarship of teaching and learning that you anticipate undertaking on your campus in the near future? Why these particular initiatives?

6. What are one or two of the most important issues that the scholarship of teaching and learning as a movement must address in the near future?

7. On the 0–4 scale below, how important has it been for your campus to be a part of the larger national scholarship of teaching and learning initiative?

    0 = Not at all

    1 = A little

    2 = Somewhat

    3 = Very much

    4 = A great deal

8. Other comments?

Demographic/context questions

1. Institution

2. Institutional demographics

    Number of undergraduate students

    Number of faculty

3. CASTL participation (Check all that apply)
   - ☐ Phase I Campus Program: 1998–2001
   - ☐ Phase II Campus Cluster Program: 2002–2005
   - ☐ Phase III Institutional Leadership Program: 2006–2009

4. Campus contact person for Institutional Leadership and Affiliates Program

    Name and e-mail

5. Person who took the lead in completing this form

    Name and e-mail

6. Would you be willing to talk with us further (phone, e-mail)?

7. Were others (e.g., faculty, students, administrators) consulted in the process of completing this questionnaire? Please describe your process.

Notes

1. Most questions ask about developments "on your campus." But some respondents represented more than one campus (in the case of multicampus institutions, or organizations whose members come from a wide range of settings). It appears that they typically answered on behalf of multiple sites, but that was sometimes difficult to do; thus, in some instances respondents made it clear they were answering with their own campus in mind. Final tallies reported in the summaries that follow do not distinguish these two types of response: all responses are reported as if they were from a single campus unit.

2. The KEEP Toolkit can now be found through MERLOT http://about.merlot.org/KEEP.html.

The Carnegie Academy for the Scholarship of Teaching and Learning

An Overview of the Program

The Carnegie Academy for the Scholarship of Teaching and Learning (CASTL) was a major, long-term initiative of The Carnegie Foundation for the Advancement of Teaching. Established in 1998 under the leadership of Lee S. Shulman, the Foundation's president from 1997 to 2008, and partially supported in its first five years by The Pew Charitable Trusts, CASTL built on a conception of teaching as scholarly work proposed in the 1990 report, *Scholarship Reconsidered: Priorities of the Professoriate,* by former Carnegie Foundation president Ernest Boyer. The aim of the program was to support the development of a scholarship of teaching and learning that would (1) foster significant, long-lasting learning for all students; (2) enhance the practice and profession of teaching; and (3) bring to faculty members' work as teachers the recognition and reward afforded to other forms of scholarly work. CASTL came to a formal close in 2009. The program had three main components, working with individual faculty, scholarly and professional societies, and campuses.

CASTL Scholars

The program for CASTL Scholars (originally referred to as Pew Scholars, and later as Carnegie Scholars) focused on building a critical mass of scholars of teaching and learning whose work would show what was possible, illustrate the diverse shapes and forms the scholarship of teaching and learning could take, and serve as models for work by others.

CASTL Scholars were selected through a highly competitive, proposal-based process, with Foundation scholars and staff serving as reviewers of the approximately 200 applications received for each round of the competition. Between 1998 and 2006 (when this component of CASTL ended), 158 individuals in six cohorts served as CASTL Scholars, representing the full range of institutional types and disciplines and including both senior and junior faculty; several were from outside the United States.

Though details of the program evolved over time, each CASTL Scholar cohort participated in two summer residencies of approximately 10 days in length. The first was aimed at helping participants refine their plans for the scholarship of teaching and learning project described in their proposal; a parallel residency, the following summer, provided an opportunity for Scholars to present the results of their work and to think together about implications, how to build on the work, and outlets and opportunities for engaging others. Each cohort also met for a briefer time in January, to report on progress and to strategize about issues arising in the work. With one exception, residencies were held at or near the Carnegie Foundation, in the San Francisco Bay area.

CASTL Scholars received a modest stipend from the Carnegie Foundation, and all on-site costs were covered as well. Campuses (that is, the office of the provost or the equivalent) were required to provide support for Scholars' travel to and from the Foundation, to make appropriate scheduling arrangements (for example, release time from a course or committee work), and to create opportunities for sharing the work on campus. Most Scholars also presented and published their work in contexts beyond the campus.

The Scholarly and Professional Societies Program

Because the scholarship of teaching and learning places a strong emphasis on disciplinary context, scholarly and professional societies were seen as critical partners in CASTL's work. Beginning in 1999, these groups were invited to a series of convenings, where they traded ideas and strategies for bringing greater attention to teaching and learning and creating opportunities for members to engage in scholarly work on pedagogy.

Representatives from participating organizations attended one or more such convenings, typically held in Washington, D.C. These groups were at different stages in their engagement with the scholarship of teaching and learning, some with a longer history of serious work on pedagogy, some just beginning to think about support for teaching. Some were active leaders throughout CASTL's work, whereas others were just beginning to explore the scholarship of teaching and learning. Over the years, many of them established new outlets, venues, structures, and policies to support a more scholarly view of teaching and learning. These efforts were often shaped by CASTL Scholars who assumed leadership roles in bringing their field more fully into the scholarship of teaching and learning movement.

The Campus Program

The CASTL Campus Program, originally coordinated in partnership with the American Association for Higher Education (AAHE), organized institutions of all types to cultivate the conditions necessary to support the scholarship of teaching and learning and to pursue such work in ways that would make a difference in the local setting. Campus engagement unfolded in three phases.

The Carnegie Teaching Academy Campus Program ran from 1998 through 2001, under the direction of Barbara Cambridge, vice president for programs at AAHE. Participation grew over time, with 70 campuses enrolled by the end of 1998, and 190 by 2001. Three commitments were required for participation. Institutions were asked to create a "campus conversation" to familiarize people with the concept of the scholarship of teaching and learning and to formulate a definition tailored to the local academic culture; to generate and pursue a "study and action plan," identifying a local issue or opportunity to which the scholarship of teaching and learning could contribute; and to report on their progress over time. A final "Mapping Progress" exercise documented the effects of their efforts on various aspects of institutional practice and policy.

The CASTL Institutional Leadership Clusters ran from 2002 through 2005. Campuses that had demonstrated appropriate progress in their Mapping Progress Report were invited to apply for leadership roles in a next stage of CASTL work, organized around agendas for building the scholarship of teaching and learning as a field—for instance, creating networks, establishing venues and outlets for the work, and providing training for those new to it. Subsequently, a total of 98 institutions were grouped in 12 "clusters." These clusters worked under the CASTL umbrella, but the design of this stage of work (and the next) was deliberately aimed at more distributed leadership, with each cluster setting its own goals and timelines, and organizing its own activities.

The final phase of work with campuses, the **CASTL Institutional Leadership and Affiliates Program**, ran from 2006 through 2009. Whereas earlier phases of campus work were organized primarily to develop the idea and practices of the scholarship of teaching and learning itself, this third phase was aimed as well at bringing such work more fully into the mainstream of institutional life.

Approximately 150 institutions were organized in 12 theme-based groups, and in a thirteenth—the CASTL Affiliates—which had no specific theme and which remained open to new campuses throughout the program. These groups convened for the first time in conjunction with the 2006 meeting of the International Society for the Scholarship of Teaching and Learning in Washington, D.C., and for a final time at the same meeting in 2009, in Bloomington, Indiana. In between, each group was expected to arrange and participate in two meetings on its own. The leaders of these groups also met annually at the Carnegie Foundation to take stock of their respective and collective progress and to plan for next steps. Groups (as described by participants themselves early in their work) and their member institutions were as follows:

1. **Building Scholarship of Teaching and Learning Communities (abbreviated title used in this volume: Communities Group)**
   Working collaboratively to develop local multidisciplinary communities, integrated with others worldwide, these institutions are building awareness, understanding, support, and practice of the scholarship of teaching and learning within and beyond local communities. Goals include: influencing academic culture to recognize a continuum of scholarship of teaching and learning activities; establishing common and rigorous outcome measures with personal, professional, and programmatic implications; and disseminating successful scholarship of teaching and learning initiatives.

   Coordinating Institution: The Ohio State University

   Dartmouth College; Kwantlen Polytechnic University (formerly Kwantlen University College); Queen's University; Ryerson University; Southeast Missouri State University; University of Glasgow

2. **Building Scholarship of Teaching and Learning Systemwide (System Group)**
   The five systems involved in this initiative work together to share and develop models for building scholarship of teaching and learning systemwide. Each system brings unique ideas and talents to the table, and by combining strengths they create new and usable models. They collaborate across and within systems to create infrastructures, processes, communication systems, and scholarship of teaching and learning projects that can be used by each system as well as by other institutional leaders.

   Coordinating Institution: The University of Wisconsin System

   [UWC-Baraboo/Sauk County; UWC-Barron County; UW-Eau Claire; UW Extension Offices; UWC-Fond du Lac; UWC-Fox Valley; UW-Green Bay; UW-La Crosse; UW-Madison; UWC-Manitowoc;

UWC-Marathon County; UWC-Marinette; UWC-Marshfield/Wood County; UW-Milwaukee; UW-Oshkosh; UW-Parkside; UW-Platteville; UWC-Richland; UW-River Falls; UWC-Rock County; UWC-Sheboygan; UW-Stevens Point; UW-Stout; UW-Superior; UWC-Washington County; UWC-Waukesha; and UW-Whitewater]

City University of New York [Kingsborough Community College; Baruch College; John Jay College of Criminal Justice; Borough of Manhattan Community College; Bronx Community College; LaGuardia Community College; Brooklyn College; City College; Lehman College; Hostos Community College; The Graduate Center; The CUNY School of Professional Studies; City University School of Law; Queens College; New York City College of Technology; Medgar Evers College; Hunter College; Queensborough Community College; The College of Staten Island; and York College]

Miami Dade College [Homestead Campus; InterAmerican Campus; Hialeah Campus; Kendall Campus; Medical Center Campus; North Campus; West Campus; and Wolfson Campus]

University of Colorado System [Boulder; Colorado Springs; Denver; and Health Sciences Center]

University of North Carolina System [Appalachian State University; East Carolina University; Elizabeth City State University; Fayetteville State University; North Carolina Agricultural and Technical State University; North Carolina Central University; North Carolina School of the Arts; North Carolina State University; University of North Carolina at Asheville; University of North Carolina at Chapel Hill; University of North Carolina at Charlotte; University of North Carolina at Greensboro; University of North Carolina at Pembroke; University of North Carolina at Wilmington; Western Carolina University; and Winston Salem State University]

3. **Cognitive Affective Learning and the Scholarship of Teaching and Learning (Cognitive Affective Group)**

These institutions share a commitment to understanding the connections between the cognitive and affective in teaching and learning. They value and support the development of holistic educational theories and practice that promote deep and enduring learning and ethical and civic engagement.

Coordinating Institution: Oxford College of Emory University

Creighton University; Kennesaw State University; St. Martin's University; University of Massachusetts Dartmouth; University of Portland; University of the Pacific

4. **Communities of Practice Pooling Educational Resources to Support Scholarship of Teaching and Learning (COPPER Group)**

   The group focuses on processes for supporting effective communities of practice, centering on collaboration at and across institutions, the practice of scholarship of teaching and learning at individual, campus, and group levels, and ways to share resources.

   Coordinating Institution: Middlesex Community College

   Glendale Community College; Minnesota State University; Northern Essex Community College; Pine Manor College; Salem State University

5. **Cross-Cutting Themes in the Scholarship of Teaching and Learning (Cross-Cutting Themes Group)**

   These institutions are concerned with how to grow a scholarship of teaching and learning program, how to link disparate and ongoing related programs, how to integrate levels of interest within an institution (classroom, program, and campuswide assessment), how to support faculty, and how to involve students in understanding the point of our efforts and how to assess.

   Co-coordinating Institutions: Carleton College and Douglas College

   Center of Inquiry in the Liberal Arts at Wabash College; City College of San Francisco; Eastern Michigan University; San Jose State University; University of Charleston

6. **Expanding the Scholarship of Teaching and Learning Commons (Commons Group)**

   This diverse group of institutions of higher education acknowledges the many dimensions of work that communities and individuals contribute to the scholarship of teaching and learning. A common interest lies in how individuals and institutions enter into this area of scholarship and how they engage with it progressively and developmentally. The projects under way by each of our CASTL partners enrich and broaden the scholarship of teaching and learning within and beyond our institutional borders. Our collaboration will extend this work by developing a new electronic repository to serve the international scholarship of teaching and learning community.

   Coordinating Institution: Indiana University

   Clark Atlanta University; Georgetown University; Houston Community College; MERLOT Cooperative; University of British Columbia; University of Kansas; University of Michigan; University of Nebraska-Lincoln

7. **Graduate Education: The Integration of Research, Teaching, and Learning (Graduate Education Group)**

These institutions are involved in mapping the landscape of scholarship of teaching and learning in graduate education. Key issues in this process include the education of graduates and faculty as agents of change, as leaders, as citizens, and as lifelong learners. One overarching question is "What does it mean to be an engaged scholar?"

Coordinating Institution: University College Cork

Association of American Geographers; Central European University; the Center for the Integration of Research, Teaching, and Learning [includes Howard University; Michigan State University; The Pennsylvania State University; University of Colorado at Boulder; and University of Wisconsin-Madison]; Rutgers, The State University of New Jersey

8. **Integrating the Scholarship of Teaching and Learning into Institutional Culture: Philosophy, Policy, and Infrastructure (Institutional Culture Group)**

This group of institutions is collaborating to foster inquiry and leadership for the improvement of student learning and teaching, develop and synthesize knowledge about teaching and learning, and promote institutional change in support of teaching and learning. Projects include: assessing the impact of scholarship of teaching and learning; fostering and sustaining scholarship of teaching and learning communities of practice; identifying and sharing best practices for peer evaluation/review of teaching; integrating rewards for scholarship of teaching and learning into salary, tenure, promotion, and other forms of recognition; exploring ways to use existing data as a basis for evidence-based inquiry into student learning.

Coordinating Institution: Buffalo State College

Centre for Excellence in Media Practice at Bournemouth University; The Open University; Rose-Hulman Institute of Technology; University of New South Wales; University of Victoria; Western Carolina University

9. **Liberal Education: Core Curriculum (Liberal Education Group)**

This group begins with the definition of liberal learning offered by the Association of American Colleges and Universities as education that is "characterized by challenging encounters with important issues, and more a way of studying than a specific course or field of study" ("Resources On: Liberal Education"). The group will investigate the uses of the scholarship of teaching and learning to develop, advance, and sustain liberal learning in different institutional contexts and with different goals.

Coordinating Institution: St. Olaf College

College of San Mateo; Eastern Washington University; Liverpool Hope University; Massachusetts College of Liberal Arts; North Carolina Agricultural and Technical State University; St. Jerome's University; University of Cincinnati; University of Wisconsin-Whitewater

10. **Mentoring Scholars of Teaching and Learning (Mentoring Group)**
These institutions are focused on planning, delivering, and assessing the annual CASTL Institute for Developing Scholars of Teaching and Learning. The Institute is designed for three primary audiences: faculty members who are new to the work and are interested in beginning projects; faculty members who have a work-in-progress and want to move it forward through mentoring by CASTL Scholars; and administrators who are supporting and championing the work.

Coordinating Institution: Rockhurst University

Columbia College Chicago; Creighton University; Morehead State University; Truman State University; University of Houston-Clear Lake

11. **Student Voices in the Scholarship of Teaching and Learning (Student Voices Group)**
This group of institutions is committed to engaging students as collaborative partners in improving teaching and learning: creating models that reconceptualize learning spaces and roles, while investigating, expanding, sharing, and reflecting upon experiences of learning founded on participation, reciprocity, and trust toward the development of student voices in the scholarship of teaching and learning.

Coordinating Institution: Western Washington University

California State University, Long Beach; Elon University; Illinois State University; North Seattle Community College; University of Nevada, Las Vegas

12. **Undergraduate Research and the Scholarship of Teaching and Learning (Undergraduate Research Group)**
This group focuses on the intersection of undergraduate research and the scholarship of teaching and learning. "Beginning with the end in mind," the group addresses five questions: What is undergraduate

research (inquiry, discovery, investigation) and how can responses to this question be contextualized by institutional nature and values while striving for "common ground"; Why should we integrate undergraduate research; What is the nature of the impact of undergraduate research with students, faculty, institutions; How do we gather evidence of student undergraduate research learning, faculty learning, institutional learning; How do we build on the best of what is known, share our learning, and contribute to the larger conversations about undergraduate research?

Coordinating Institution: Vancouver Island University (formerly Malaspina University-College)

Centre for Active Learning at University of Gloucestershire; Council on Undergraduate Research; University of Akron; University of Alberta; University of Central Florida; University of Illinois Urbana-Champaign; University of Maryland, Baltimore County; University of Notre Dame; University of Waterloo

13. **CASTL Affiliates (Affiliates Group)**

CASTL Institutional Leadership Program Affiliates are campuses, disciplinary societies, and higher education organizations making a commitment to the scholarship of teaching and learning by exploring the place of such work in their settings, and by undertaking activities that provide support and recognition for ongoing inquiry into evidence-based improvement of student learning.

Coordinating Institution: Loyola Marymount University

Dominican University; Hampshire College; Holyoke Community College; Indian River Community College; Indiana University-Purdue University Fort Wayne; Indiana University-Purdue University Indianapolis; Maryville University; National Center for Science and Civic Engagement; Northern Alberta Institute of Technology; Park University; Southern Connecticut State University; Thompson Rivers University; University of Central Missouri; University of Manitoba; University of Rochester; Viterbo University

Looking Back from 2030

*T*his document was prepared for the final convening of the CASTL Institutional Leadership and Affiliates Program meeting, October 21, 2009, in
Bloomington, Indiana. Barbara Cambridge wrote the four scenarios not as
utopias, but as possible futures for higher education, and she led the discussion
of them at that event. Readers should feel free to copy and use this document
(with appropriate attribution) as a prompt for discussion of the future of the
scholarship of teaching and learning.

At today's event, we have celebrated the outcomes of practice and research
undertaken by CASTL individuals, teams, groups, and institutions. The progress
of the scholarship of teaching and learning movement is far reaching, yet
not complete.

In this session we look to the future—2030, to be exact. Looking at each
scenario below describing the teaching and learning environment 20 years
from now, consider how we got there. What did we do to get from now to
then? How did we maintain and increase the momentum of the scholarship of
teaching and learning? What actions enabled the conditions in the scenario?

SCENARIO ONE

It is hard to believe that in 2009 few students and faculty members studied
the science of learning as part of their undergraduate and graduate degrees.

Because they knew so little about the neurological, psychological, and social aspects of learning, they defined disciplines and professions only by the content of the subject areas and professions. Fortunately, the scholarship of teaching and learning movement revealed the importance of knowing how novices and experts enter into and flourish in disciplines and professions. Now, in 2030, every undergraduate student takes a required course about learning as part of general education, and a required course about learning in his or her discipline as part of the major; graduate students, no matter for what profession they are preparing, take a required course in learning so that they know how to be lifelong learners.

These courses are hybrid: online, in the classroom, and in the field. They are taught by interdisciplinary faculty teams from colleges and universities around the world and in business, government, and other settings. Students apply learning from these courses in other classes through assignments that encourage reflection and analysis. Because information changes so rapidly, knowing about learning is a prized asset as people adjust to more and more information applied in new contexts throughout their lifetimes. Learning about learning is a core purpose of higher education.

SCENARIO TWO

Believe it or not, teaching in 2009 was sometimes regarded as less important than research. Part of the reason was that funding for research centered on what was considered at that time the content of disciplines and professions. In fact, colleges and universities felt that their authority and status were established most firmly by the dollars brought in for research.

Dollars are still important today, but in 2030, government, foundations, and colleges and universities themselves know that learning is a research topic of urgent and continuing importance—one that benefits not only from traditional research models but also from practitioner inquiry. The scholarship of teaching and learning movement that had in 2009 begun to yield powerful new insights about how students learn has now spurred funders to support practitioners who do scholarly inquiry into teaching and learning. Departments within the federal government, including Education and Labor; foundations, both large and small; and all types of colleges and universities provide significant funding for research that centers on knowledge generation and application about teaching and learning.

In turn, faculty careers can be reliably based on the scholarship of teaching and learning, and most faculty members engage in it in at least modest ways as part of their regular classroom and program responsibilities. Institutions are eager to be known for the depth and breadth of scholarly inquiry into teaching and learning that characterize their campuses. Public support for inquiry into teaching and learning—and for the pedagogical and curricular innovation it informs—is high and sustained. In short, current conditions are highly conducive to systematic inquiry into teaching and learning that adds to the research base, informs pedagogical practice, and advances student learning.

SCENARIO THREE

Because digital literacy has become more and more central to the way that people make meaning, learning online is now an expected part of the educational experience of all citizens. Multimedia authoring, evidence of learning from multiple venues integrated through technology, and representation of self and learning online have revolutionized the paltry assessment measures of 2009. Every undergraduate student begins his or her postsecondary career with an electronic portfolio from previous schooling, which is now a hybrid of in-school, out-of-school, and online learning. These e-portfolios accentuate the ways in which individual students learn, their developmental stages of learning in different fields, and the abilities on which college instruction builds.

The first week of every college and university course is spent in mutual analysis of e-portfolios. Students are taught how to study draft syllabi in faculty members' e-portfolios and how to map the goals of the course onto their current stage of learning in the subject area. Students set goals for themselves for the course and study classmates' e-portfolios to understand what the class community will need to do to support one another. Faculty members study students' e-portfolios to determine pedagogies for the course. Students and faculty members adjust course content and pacing to fit the needs of the particular course community.

Because learning is a social activity, faculty members and students provide feedback to one another within e-portfolios throughout the course. The faculty member's e-portfolio includes rationales for course content, videos of classroom instruction, explanation of ongoing research relating to the course, and a blog for discussing the progress of the course. The students' e-portfolios include individual goals with periodic reflection about progress toward those goals; evidence of learning through social networking entries, papers, tests, photographs, videos, and reports; feedback from fellow students; and blogs. These practices demonstrate the significant change from 2009 in faculty and student assessment perspectives and practices.

SCENARIO FOUR

In 2030 higher education no longer occurs primarily in traditional institutions. Colleges divide up specialties to avoid the expense of duplication of offerings and share instructional responsibilities with other organizations, including businesses; grades 11–14 often exist in the same space—physical and virtual; and learners can continue to earn lifelong learning credits from various sources throughout their lifetimes, credits honored by employers and necessary for individuals keeping up with rapid changes in culture and the workplace. For faculty and students engaged in the scholarship of teaching and learning, these changes provide new sites and practices to study. Rapid development of new technologies facilitates new methods of inquiry in this scholarly work. Technologically facilitated ways of documenting learning, easy-to-use analytic software, semantic mapping, and ease of interactions across databases are just some examples of these technologies.

Although in 2009 the context for learning was not highly regarded as an area for study (in fact, the research paradigm at that time valued findings that were widely generalizable and context-free), in 2030 new contexts for learning are so significantly different from former ones that faculty in all disciplines are ethically bound to investigate their effects. Because most people are involved in higher education throughout their lifetimes, the scholarship of teaching and learning includes a focus on ever-changing educational contexts.

REFERENCES

Adelman, C. (2008). *Learning Accountability from Bologna: A Higher Education Policy Primer*. Washington, D.C.: Institute for Higher Education Policy.

Adelman, C. (2009). *The Spaces Between Numbers: Getting International Data on Higher Education Straight*. Washington, D.C.: Institute for Higher Education Policy. http://www.ihep.org/research/GlobalPerformance.cfm.

Albers, C. (2004). Foreword to *The Scholarship of Teaching and Learning: Strengthening Education Through Research and Collaboration*. Buffalo: Buffalo State College of the State University of New York.

American Association of State Colleges and Universities. "Programs: American Democracy Project." Accessed June 2010. http://www.aascu.org/programs/adp/about.htm.

American Association of University Professors. (1994). "The Work of Faculty: Expectations, Priorities, and Rewards." *Academe*, *80*(1), 35–48.

Angelo, T. A. (1998). *Classroom Assessment and Research: An Update on Uses, Approaches, and Research Findings*. New Directions for Teaching and Learning, Number 75. San Francisco: Jossey-Bass.

Angelo, T. A. (2001). "Doing Faculty Development as If We Value Learning Most: Transformative Guidelines from Research and Practice." *To Improve the Academy*, *19*, 97–112.

Angelo, T. A., and Cross, K. P. (1993). *Classroom Assessment Techniques: A Handbook for College Teachers*. Second edition. San Francisco: Jossey-Bass.

166

Arreola, R. A. (2000). *Developing a Comprehensive Faculty Evaluation System.* Second edition. San Francisco: Jossey-Bass/Anker.

Arreola, R. A., Theall, M., and Aleamoni, L. M. (2003). "Beyond Scholarship: Recognizing the Multiple Roles of the Professoriate." Paper presented at the American Educational Research Association Convention, Chicago, Apr. 2003. http://www.cedanet.com/meta/#chronologyofdevelopment.

Association of American Colleges and Universities. (2002). *Greater Expectations: A New Vision for Learning as a Nation Goes to College.* Washington, D.C.: Association of American Colleges and Universities.

Association of American Colleges and Universities. (2007). *College Learning for the New Global Century: A Report from the National Leadership Council for Liberal Education and America's Promise.* Washington, D.C.: Association of American Colleges and Universities.

Association of American Colleges and Universities. (2008). *Our Students' Best Work: A Framework for Accountability Worthy of Our Mission.* Statement from the Board of Directors. Second edition. Washington, D.C.: Association of American Colleges and Universities.

Association of American Colleges and Universities. (2009). *Learning and Assessment: Trends in Undergraduate Education: A Survey Among Members of the Association of American Colleges and Universities.* Washington, D.C.: Association of American Colleges and Universities.

Association of American Colleges and Universities. Home page. Accessed Dec. 18, 2010. http://www.aacu.org/.

Baldwin, R. G. (1990). "Faculty Careers: Stages and Implications." In J. H. Schuster and D. W. Wheeler (eds.), *Enhancing Faculty Careers: Strategies for Renewal.* San Francisco: Jossey-Bass.

Banta, T. W., Griffin, M., Flateby, T. L., and Kahn, S. (2009). *Three Promising Alternatives for Assessing College Students' Knowledge and Skills.* National Institute for Learning Outcomes Assessment Occasional Paper, Number 2. Urbana, Ill.: National Institute for Learning Outcomes Assessment.

Barr, R. B., and Tagg, J. (1995). "From Teaching to Learning: A New Paradigm in Undergraduate Education." *Change, 27*(6), 13–25.

Bass, R. (1999). "The Scholarship of Teaching: What's the Problem?" *Inventio: Creative Thinking About Learning and Teaching, 1*(1). http://doit.gmu.edu//archives/feb98/randybass.htm.

Bass, R. Telephone interview by Anthony Ciccone. Nov. 24, 2009.

Bass, R., and Bernstein, D. (2005). "The Scholarship of Teaching and Learning." *Academe, 91*(4), 37–43.

Bass, R., and Eynon, B. (eds.). (2009). "The Difference That Inquiry Makes: A Collaborative Case Study of Technology and Learning, from the Visible Knowledge Project." *Academic Commons,* Jan. 2009. http://www.academiccommons.org/issue/January-2009.

Beckman, M., and Hensel, N. (2009). "Making Explicit the Implicit: Defining Undergraduate Research." *CUR Quarterly, 29*(4), 40–44.

Bernstein, D. (2008a). Foreword to J. Eddy (ed.), *Reflections from the Classroom: 2007–2008*, Vol. 10. Lawrence: University of Kansas Center for Teaching Excellence.

Bernstein, D. (2008b). "Peer Review and Evaluation of the Intellectual Work of Teaching." *Change, 40*(2), 48–51.

Bernstein, D. (2010). "Case 4: University of Kansas: A Multi-faceted Approach to Incorporating Inquiry into Learning and Teaching." In J. M. Robinson, P. Savory, G. Poole, T. Carey, and D. Bernstein, *Peer Review of Teaching Project—CASTL: Expanding the SOTL Commons Cluster Final Report.* Report to the Carnegie Academy for the Scholarship of Teaching and Learning Institutional Leadership Program, Feb. 2010. Lincoln: Digital Commons@University of Nebraska-Lincoln. http://digitalcommons.unl.edu/imsereports/5/.

Bernstein, D. "Greetings and Your Advice." Private e-mail message to Pat Hutchings. July 5, 2010.

Bernstein, D., Addison, W., Altman, C., Hollister, D., Komarraju, M., Prieto, L. R., Rocheleau, C. A., and Shore, C. (2009). "Toward a Scientist-Educator Model of Teaching Psychology." In D. F. Halpern (ed.), *Undergraduate Education in Psychology: A Blueprint for the Future of the Discipline.* Washington, D.C.: American Psychological Association.

Bernstein, D., Bunnell, S., and Collins, C. (2008). "The Academic Program as a Unit of Analysis for Scholarship of Teaching and Learning." Presentation at the International Society for the Scholarship of Teaching and Learning Annual Meeting, Edmonton, Alberta, Canada, Oct. 2008.

Bernstein, D., Burnett, A. N., Goodburn, A., and Savory, P. (2006). *Making Teaching and Learning Visible: Course Portfolios and the Peer Review of Teaching.* San Francisco: Jossey-Bass/Anker.

Bernstein, D., and Huber, M. T. (2006). "What Is Good Teaching? Raising the Bar Through *Scholarship Assessed.*" Presentation at the International Society for the Scholarship of Teaching and Learning Annual Meeting, Washington, D.C., Nov. 2006.

Bierman, S., Ciner, E., Lauer-Glebov, J., Rutz, C., and Savina, M. (2005). "Integrative Learning: Coherence out of Chaos." *Peer Review, 7*(1), 18–20.

Blaich, C. Telephone interview by Pat Hutchings and Mary Huber. Nov. 4, 2010.

Blaich, C., and Wise, K. (2010). "Wabash National Study Workshop: Conversations with Students." Meeting Agenda, Nov. 11–13, 2010. Crawfordsville, Ind.: Center of Inquiry in the Liberal Arts, Wabash College.

Bok, D. C. (2006). *Our Underachieving Colleges: A Candid Look at How Much Students Learn and Why They Should Be Learning More.* Princeton, N.J.: Princeton University Press.

Bollier, D. (2001). *Public Assets, Private Profits: Reclaiming the American Commons in an Age of Market Enclosure.* Washington, D.C.: New America Foundation.

Bollier, D. (2003). *Preserving the Academic Commons.* Keynote presentation at the Eighty-Ninth Annual Meeting of the American Association of University Professors, June 2003. Los Angeles: The Norman Lear Center, USC Annenberg School for Communication and Journalism.

Bond, L. (2009). *Toward Informative Assessment and a Culture of Evidence.* Stanford, Calif.: The Carnegie Foundation for the Advancement of Teaching.

Borgman, C. (2007). *Scholarship in the Digital Age: Information, Infrastructure, and the Internet.* Cambridge, Mass.: MIT Press.

Boyer, E. L. (1990). *Scholarship Reconsidered: Priorities of the Professoriate.* Princeton, N.J.: The Carnegie Foundation for the Advancement of Teaching.

Brancaccio-Taras, L. (2010). "The Journey in SoTL." Presentation at the Second Annual Provosts' Conference on Teaching and Learning, LaGuardia Community College, Long Island City, N.Y., Mar. 2010.

Brancaccio-Taras, L. No subject. Private e-mail message to Pat Hutchings. May 24, 2010.

Braskamp, L. A., and Ory, J. C. (1994). *Assessing Faculty Work: Enhancing Individual and Institutional Performance.* San Francisco: Jossey-Bass.

Braxton, J., Luckey, W., and Helland, P. (2002). *Institutionalizing a Broader View of Scholarship Through Boyer's Four Domains.* ASHE-ERIC Higher Education Report, Vol. 29, Number 2. San Francisco: Jossey-Bass.

Brown, J. S., and Duguid, P. (2000). *The Social Life of Information.* Boston: Harvard Business School Press.

Bryk, A. S., and Gomez, L. (2008). "Ruminations on Reinventing an R&D Capacity for Educational Improvement." Prepared for the American Enterprise Institute Conference on the Supply Side of School Reform and the Future of Educational Entrepreneurship, Oct. 2007. Revised Jan. 2008. http://www.carnegiefoundation .org/elibrary/ruminations-reinventing-rd-capacity-educational-improvement.

Calder, L. (2006). "Uncoverage: Toward a Signature Pedagogy for the History Survey." *Journal of American History*, *92*(4), 1358–1371.

Calder, L. "Re: You're Retiring?" Private e-mail message to Mary Huber. Oct. 28, 2009.

Cambridge, B. (ed.). (2004a). *Campus Progress: Supporting the Scholarship of Teaching and Learning.* Washington, D.C.: American Association for Higher Education.

Cambridge, B. (2004b). "Transforming Campus Cultures Through the Scholarship of Teaching and Learning." In B. Cambridge (ed.), *Campus Progress: Supporting the Scholarship of Teaching and Learning.* Washington, D.C.: American Association for Higher Education.

Cambridge, D. (2010). *CTCH 604: The Scholarship of Teaching and Learning.* Syllabus. Washington, D.C.: George Mason University. http://ctch604.onmason.com/.

Campus Compact. "About Us." Accessed June 2010. http://www.compact.org/about/ history-mission-vision/.

Carey, M. (2010). "Engaging Departments Initiative." *The International Commons*, 5(3), 13. http://www.issotl.org/newsletter.html.

Carey, M., Gale, R., Manarin, K., and Rathburn, M. (2010). "Critically Reading the Word and the World." Presentation at the Centennial Symposium on Scholarship of Teaching and Learning, Banff, Alberta, Canada, Nov. 2010.

Carnegie Foundation for the Advancement of Teaching. (1999). *Fostering a Scholarship of Teaching and Learning.* Video. Menlo Park, Calif.: The Carnegie Foundation for the Advancement of Teaching and West Peak Media.

Carnegie Foundation for the Advancement of Teaching. (2008). *Basic Skills for Complex Lives: Designs for Learning in the Community College*. Stanford, Calif.: The Carnegie Foundation for the Advancement of Teaching.

Carnegie Foundation for the Advancement of Teaching. "Gallery of Teaching and Learning." Accessed Dec. 2010. http://gallery.carnegiefoundation.org/.

Cashin, W. E. (1988). *Student Ratings of Teaching: A Summary of the Research.* Idea Paper Number 20. Manhattan: Center for Faculty Evaluation and Development, Kansas State University. http://www.theideacenter.org/category/helpful-resources/knowledge-base/idea-papers.

Cashin, W. E. (1996). *Developing an Effective Faculty Evaluation System.* Idea Paper Number 33, Manhattan: Center For Faculty Evaluation and Development, Kansas State University. http://www.theideacenter.org/category/helpful-resources/knowledge-base/idea-papers.

Centra, J. A. (1993). *Reflective Faculty Evaluation: Enhancing Teaching and Determining Faculty Effectiveness*. San Francisco: Jossey-Bass.

Cerbin, W. (1996). "Inventing a New Genre: The Course Portfolio at the University of Wisconsin-LaCrosse." In P. Hutchings (ed.), *Making Teaching Community Property: A Menu for Peer Collaboration and Peer Review*. Washington, D.C.: American Association for Higher Education.

Chism, N. (2008). "The Scholarship of Teaching and Learning: Implications for Professional Development." Keynote presentation at the Thai Professional and Organizational Development (POD) Network Workshop, Bangkok, Apr. 2008. http://www.thailandpod.net/resources.html.

Chism, N., and Sanders, D. (1986). "The Place of Practice-Centered Inquiry in Faculty Development." In M. Svinicki (ed.), *To Improve the Academy*, 6, 56–64.

Cho, J., and Davis, A. (2008). "How Jay Got His Groove Back and Made Math Meaningful." Multimedia Websites by participants in Strengthening Pre-collegiate Education in Community Colleges. Stanford, Calif.: The Carnegie Foundation for the Advancement of Teaching. http://www.cfkeep.org/html/stitch.php?s = 13143081975303&id = 87553800444634.

Ciccone, A. (2004). "Furthering the Scholarship of Teaching and Learning the Wisconsin Way." In B. Cambridge (ed.), *Campus Progress: Supporting the Scholarship of Teaching and Learning*. Washington, D.C.: American Association for Higher Education.

Ciccone, A. (2008). "Examining the Impact of SoTL." *The International Commons*, *3*(1), 12–13.

Ciccone, A., Huber, M. T., Hutchings, P., and Cambridge, B. (2009). *Exploring Impact: A Survey of Participants in the CASTL Institutional Leadership and Affiliates Program*. Stanford, Calif.: The Carnegie Foundation for the Advancement of Teaching.

Ciccone, A., Meyers, R. A., and Waldmann, S. (2008). "What's So Funny? Moving Students Toward Complex Thinking in a Course on Comedy and Laughter." *Arts and Humanities in Higher Education*, *7*(3), 308–322.

Cognitive Affective Group (CASTL Institutional Leadership Group on Cognitive Affective Learning and the Scholarship of Teaching and Learning). (2009). *CAL Leadership Program: Final Report*. Final Report to the Carnegie Academy for the Scholarship of Teaching and Learning. Stanford, Calif.: The Carnegie Foundation for the Advancement of Teaching.

Colbeck, C. (2002). Editor's Notes to C. Colbeck (ed.), *Evaluating Faculty Performance.* New Directions for Institutional Research, Number 114. San Francisco: Jossey-Bass.

Colby, A., Ehrlich, T., Beaumont, E., and Stephens, J. (2003). *Educating Citizens: Preparing America's Undergraduates for Lives of Moral and Civic Responsibility*. San Francisco: Jossey-Bass.

Cook, C. E. (2004). Introduction to Section I in B. Cambridge (ed.), *Campus Progress: Supporting the Scholarship of Teaching and Learning*. Washington, D.C.: American Association for Higher Education.

Coppola, B. P., and Jacobs, D. C. (2002). "Is the Scholarship of Teaching and Learning New to Chemistry?" In M. T. Huber and S. P. Morreale (eds.), *Disciplinary Styles in the Scholarship of Teaching and Learning: Exploring Common Ground*. Washington, D.C.: American Association for Higher Education.

Cox, M. D. (2004). "Introduction to Faculty Learning Communities." In M. D. Cox and L. Richlin (eds.), *Building Faculty Learning Communities*. New Directions for Teaching and Learning, Number 97. San Francisco: Jossey-Bass.

Cox, R., Huber, M. T., and Hutchings, P. (2005). *Survey of CASTL Scholars*. Appendix to M. T. Huber and P. Hutchings, *The Advancement of Learning: Building the Teaching Commons*. Stanford, Calif.: The Carnegie Foundation for the Advancement of Teaching.

Craft, R. G. (2000). "Teaching Excellence and the Inner Life of Faculty." *Change*, *32*(3), 48–52.

Cross, K. P. (1986). "A Proposal to Improve Teaching: Or, What 'Taking Teaching Seriously' Should Mean." *AAHE Bulletin*, *39*(1), 9–14.

Cross, K. P., and Steadman, M. H. (1996). *Classroom Research: Implementing the Scholarship of Teaching*. San Francisco: Jossey-Bass.

Cruz, L., Ellern, J., Ford, G., Moss, H., and White, B. J. (2009). Recognition and Reward: SOTL and the Tenure Process at a Regional Comprehensive University.

MountainRise, the International Journal of the Scholarship of Teaching and Learning, 5(3). http://mountainrise.wcu.edu/index.php/MtnRise/issue/view/15.

Curry, B. K. (1991). "Institutionalization: The Final Phase of the Organizational Change Process." *Administrator's Notebook, 35*(1), 1–5.

Delpish, A., Darby, A., Holmes, A., Knight-McKenna, M., Mihans, R., King, C., and Felten, P. (2010). "Equalizing Voices: Student-Faculty Partnership in Course Design." In C. Werder and M. Otis (eds.), *Engaging Student Voices in the Study of Teaching and Learning*. Sterling, Va.: Stylus.

Dewar, J., and Bennett, C. (2010). "Situating SoTL Within the Disciplines: Mathematics in the United States as a Case Study." *International Journal of the Scholarship of Teaching and Learning, 4*(1). http://academics.georgiasouthern .edu/ijsotl/v4n1/essays_about_sotl/_DewarBennett/index.html.

Dewar, J., and Cohn, M. (2010). "A Synthesis of the Challenges Facing SoTL at Carnegie Affiliates Institutions." *Transformative Dialogues: Teaching and Learning eJournal, 3*(4). http://kwantlen.ca/TD/TD.4.1/.

Dewar, J., Dailey-Hebert, A., and Moore, T. (2010). "The Attraction, Value and Future of SoTL: Carnegie Affiliates' Perspective." *Transformative Dialogues: Teaching and Learning eJournal, 3*(4). http://kwantlen.ca/TD/TD.4.1/.

Diamond, R. M., and Adam, B. E. (eds.). (1995). *The Disciplines Speak: Rewarding the Scholarly, Professional, and Creative Work of Faculty*. Washington, D.C.: American Association for Higher Education.

Diamond, R. M., and Adam, B. E. (eds.). (2000). *The Disciplines Speak II: More Statements on Rewarding the Scholarly, Professional, and Creative Work of Faculty*. Sterling, Va.: Stylus.

Diaz, A., Middendorf, J., Pace, D., and Shopkow, L. (2008). "The History Learning Project: A Department 'Decodes' Its Students." *Journal of American History, 94*, 1211–1224.

Draeger, J., and Price, L. (2009). "Which Way to SoTL Utopia?" Paper presented at the International Society for the Scholarship of Teaching and Learning Annual Meeting, Bloomington, Ind., Oct. 2009.

Driscoll, A., and Lynton, E. (1999). *Making Outreach Visible: A Guide to Documenting Professional Service and Outreach*. Washington, D.C.: American Association for Higher Education.

Drummond, T., and Owens, K. S. (2010). "Capturing Student Learning." In C. Werder and M. M. Otis (eds.), *Engaging Student Voices in the Study of Teaching and Learning*. Sterling, Va.: Stylus.

Duffy, D. "CASTL." Private e-mail message to Pat Hutchings. Feb. 6, 2009.

Duncan, N., and Maharg, P. (2005). "Scholarship of Teaching and Learning Conference." Review of City University Scholarship of Teaching & Learning Conference. http://zeugma.typepad.com/zeugma/2005/05/paul_maharg .html#more.

Eckel, P., Green, M., and Hill, B. (2001). *Riding the Waves of Change: Insights from Transforming Institutions.* "On Change V," Occasional Paper Series of the ACE Project on Leadership and Institutional Transformation and The Kellogg Forum on Higher Education Transformation. Washington, D.C.: American Council on Education.

Eder, D. "Comment on Meritorious Teaching Agreement at SIUE." Post to POD ListServ, POD@Listserv.nd.edu. July 21, 2010.

Edgerton, R. (2005). Foreword to K. O'Meara and R. E. Rice (eds.), *Faculty Priorities Reconsidered: Rewarding Multiple Forms of Scholarship.* First edition. San Francisco: Jossey-Bass.

Edgerton, R., Hutchings, P., and Quinlan, K. (1991). *The Teaching Portfolio: Capturing the Scholarship in Teaching.* Washington, D.C.: American Association for Higher Education.

Ellison, J., and Eatman, T. K. (2008). *Scholarship in Public: Knowledge Creation and Tenure Policy in the Engaged University; A Resource on Promotion and Tenure in the Arts, Humanities, and Design.* Imagining America Tenure Team Initiative on Public Scholarship. Syracuse, N.Y.: Imagining America.

Elton, L. (2000). "Danger of Doing the Wrong Thing Righter." In *Evaluate and Improve: Teaching in the Arts and Humanities,* Humanities and Arts Higher Education Network (HAN) Oct. 1999 conference proceedings. Milton Keynes, U.K.: Institute of Educational Technology, Open University.

Ewell, P. T. (2002). *Across the Grain: Learning from Reform Initiatives in Undergraduate Education.* Washington, D.C.: American Association of Higher Education. http://www.teaglefoundation.org/learning/resources.aspx.

Ewell, P. T. (2009). *Assessment, Accountability, and Improvement: Revisiting the Tension.* National Institute for Learning Outcomes Assessment Occasional Paper, Number 1. Urbana, Ill.: National Institute for Learning Outcomes Assessment. http://www.learningoutcomeassessment.org/occasionalpaperone.htm.

Faculty Development Group (CASTL Institutional Leadership Group on Cross-cutting Themes in the Scholarship of Teaching and Learning). (2009). "Integrative Structures for Faculty Development Programs and Services." PowerPoint presentation at the annual meeting of the International Society for the Scholarship of Teaching and Learning, Bloomington, Ind., Oct. 2009.

Faculty Survey of Student Engagement (FSSE). "Topical Findings." Bloomington: Indiana University Center for Postsecondary Research. Last modified 2009. http://fsse.iub.edu/_/?cid = 345.

Feito, J. A. (2007). "Allowing Not-Knowing in a Dialogic Discussion." *International Journal for the Scholarship of Teaching and Learning, 1*(1). http://academics .georgiasouthern.edu/ijsotl/v1n1/feito/ij_feito.htm.

Feito, J. A., and Donahue, P. (2008). "Minding the Gap: Annotation as Preparation for Discussion." *Arts and Humanities in Higher Education, 7*(3), 295–307.

Felten, P. Telephone interview by Anthony Ciccone. Nov. 23, 2009.

Felten, P., Kalish, A., Pingree, A., and Plank, K. M. (2007). "Toward a Scholarship of Teaching and Learning in Educational Development." In D. R. Robertson and L. B. Nilson (eds.), *To Improve the Academy*, Vol. 25. San Francisco: Jossey-Bass.

Ferrett, T. A., and Geelan, D. R. (eds.). (Forthcoming). *Connected Science: Strategies for Integrative Learning in College.* Bloomington: Indiana University Press.

Gaff, J., and Simpson, R. (1994). "Faculty Development in the United States." *Innovative Higher Education, 18*(3), 167–176.

Gale, R. A. (2008). "Points Without Limits: Individual Inquiry, Collaborative Investigation, and Collective Scholarship." In D. R. Robertson and L. Nilson (eds.), *To Improve the Academy*, Vol. 26. San Francisco: Jossey-Bass.

Gappa, J. M., Austin, A. E., and Trice, A. G. (2007). *Rethinking Faculty Work: Higher Education's Strategic Imperative.* San Francisco: Jossey-Bass.

Gawande, A. (2007). *Better: A Surgeon's Notes on Performance.* New York: Picador.

Gawande, A. (2009). "Testing, Testing." *The New Yorker*, Dec. 14, 2009. http://www.newyorker.com/reporting/2009/12/14/091214fa_fact_gawande.

Georgia Southern University. "Faculty Learning Communities Program, 2009–2010." http://academics.georgiasouthern.edu/cet/programs/flc.htm.

Gladwell, M. (2002). *The Tipping Point: How Little Things Can Make a Big Difference.* New York: Little, Brown.

Glassick, C. E., Huber, M. T., and Maeroff, G. I. (1997). *Scholarship Assessed: Evaluation of the Professoriate.* San Francisco: Jossey-Bass.

Glenn, D. (2009). "Wary of Budget Knife, Teaching Centers Seek to Sharpen Their Role." *Chronicle of Higher Education*, Aug. 18, 2009. Subscription required. http://jobs.chronicle.com/article/Wary-of-Budget-Knife-Teaching/48049/.

Glenn, D. (2010). "Rating Your Professors: Scholars Test Improved Course Evaluations." *Chronicle of Higher Education*, Apr. 25, 2010. Subscription required. http://chronicle.com/article/Evaluations-That-Make-the/65226/.

Gomez, L. (2010). "Networked Improvement Communities: The Time Is Right for the Ties That Bind." *Carnegie Perspectives*, Apr. 2010. http://www.carnegiefoundation.org/perspectives/networked-improvement-communities-the-time-right-the-ties-bind.

Gordon, G., D'Andrea, V., Gosling, D., and Stefani, L. (2003). *Building Capacity for Change in Higher Education: Research on the Scholarship of Teaching.* Bristol: Higher Education Funding Council for England.

Graduate Education Group (CASTL Institutional Leadership Group on Graduate Education: The Integration of Research, Teaching, and Learning). (2009). *Final Report of University College Cork.* Final Report to the Carnegie Academy for the Scholarship of Teaching and Learning. Stanford, Calif.: The Carnegie Foundation for the Advancement of Teaching.

Grossman, P. L., Wilson, S. M., and Shulman, L. S. (1989). "Teachers of Substance: Subject Matter Knowledge for Teaching." In M. C. Reynolds (ed.), *Knowledge Base for the Beginning Teacher*. New York: Pergamon.

Gurung, R., Chick, N. L., and Haynie, A. (2008). *Exploring Signature Pedagogies: Approaches to Teaching Disciplinary Habits of Mind*. Sterling, Va.: Stylus.

Harvard Magazine. (2006). "Taking Teaching Seriously." *102*(2), 60–65.

Healey, M. (2000). "Developing the Scholarship of Teaching in Higher Education: A Discipline-Based Approach." *Higher Education Research and Development*, *19*(2), 169–189.

Hess, C., and Ostrom, E. (eds.). (2007). *Understanding Knowledge as a Commons: From Theory to Practice*. Cambridge, Mass.: MIT Press.

HistorySOTL. "The International Society for the Teaching and Learning in History." Accessed Dec. 2010. http://www.indiana.edu/~histsotl/blog/.

Howard, J. (2010). "Hot Type: No Reviews of Digital Scholarship = No Respect." *Chronicle of Higher Education*, May 23, 2010. Subscription required. http://chronicle.com/article/Hot-Type-No-Reviews-of/65644/.

Huber, M. T. (1998). *Community College Faculty: Attitudes and Trends, 1997*. Menlo Park, Calif.: The Carnegie Foundation for the Advancement of Teaching.

Huber, M. T. (1999). "Disciplinary Styles in the Scholarship of Teaching and Learning." Paper presented at the Seventh International Improving Student Learning Symposium, University of York, U.K., Sept. 1999.

Huber, M. T. (2004). *Balancing Acts: The Scholarship of Teaching and Learning in Academic Careers*. Washington, D.C.: American Association for Higher Education.

Huber, M. T. (2005). "The Movement to Recognize and Reward Different Kinds of Scholarly Work." *Anthropology in Action*, *12*(1), 48–56.

Huber, M. T. (2006). "Disciplines, Pedagogy, and Inquiry-Based Learning About Teaching." In C. Kreber (ed.), *Exploring Research-Based Teaching*. New Directions for Teaching and Learning, Number 107. San Francisco: Jossey-Bass.

Huber, M. T. (2008a). "Books Worth Reading: Review of *The Courage to Teach: Exploring the Inner Landscape of a Teacher's Life (10th Anniversary Edition)*, by Parker J. Palmer, and *Enhancing Learning through the Scholarship of Teaching and Learning: The Challenges and Joys of Juggling*, by Kathleen McKinney." *Change*, *40*(3), 53–56.

Huber, M. T. (2008b). *The Promise of Faculty Inquiry for Teaching and Learning Basic Skills*. Stanford, Calif.: The Carnegie Foundation for the Advancement of Teaching.

Huber, M. T. (2009). "Teaching Travels: Reflections on the Social Life of Classroom Inquiry and Innovation." *International Journal for the Scholarship of Teaching and Learning*, *3*(2). http://academics.georgiasouthern.edu/ijsotl/v3n2/invited_essays/_Huber/index.htm.

Huber, M. T. (2010a). "CASTL Has Concluded: Long Live the Scholarship of Teaching and Learning." *Arts and Humanities in Higher Education*, *9*(1), 5–7.

Huber, M. T. (2010b). "Rigor and Research in the Scholarship of Teaching and Learning: Broadening the Range of Methodologies Brought by the Disciplines."

Paper presented at the London Scholarship of Teaching and Learning (SoTL) 8th International Conference, U.K., May 2010.

Huber, M. T., and Hutchings, P. (2005). *The Advancement of Learning: Building the Teaching Commons*. San Francisco: Jossey-Bass.

Huber, M. T., Hutchings, P., and Shulman, L. S. (2005). "The Scholarship of Teaching and Learning Today." In K. A. O'Meara and R. E. Rice (eds.), *Faculty Priorities Reconsidered: Rewarding Multiple Forms of Scholarship*. San Francisco: Jossey-Bass.

Huber, M. T., and Morreale, S. P. (2002). "Situating the Scholarship of Teaching and Learning: A Cross-Disciplinary Conversation." Introduction to M. T. Huber and S. P. Morreale (eds.), *Disciplinary Styles in the Scholarship of Teaching and Learning: Exploring Common Ground*. Washington, D.C.: American Association for Higher Education and The Carnegie Foundation for the Advancement of Teaching.

Hutchings, P. (1996). *Making Teaching Community Property: A Menu for Peer Collaboration and Peer Review*. Washington, D.C.: American Association for Higher Education.

Hutchings, P. (ed.). (1998). *The Course Portfolio: How Faculty Can Examine Their Teaching to Advance Practice and Improve Student Learning*. Washington, D.C.: American Association for Higher Education.

Hutchings, P. (ed.). (2000). *Opening Lines: Approaches to the Scholarship of Teaching and Learning*. Menlo Park, Calif.: The Carnegie Foundation for the Advancement of Teaching.

Hutchings, P. (2007). "Theory: The Elephant in the Scholarship of Teaching and Learning Room." *International Journal for the Scholarship of Teaching and Learning*, *1*(1). http://academics.georgiasouthern.edu/ijsotl/v1n1/essays/hutchings/index.htm.

Hutchings, P. (2010). *Opening Doors to Faculty Involvement in Assessment*. National Institute for Learning Outcomes Assessment Occasional Paper, Number 4. Urbana, Ill.: National Institute for Learning Outcomes Assessment.

Hutchings, P., Bjork, C., and Babb, M. (2002). *The Scholarship of Teaching and Learning in Higher Education: An Annotated Bibliography*. Menlo Park, Calif.: The Carnegie Foundation for the Advancement of Teaching. http://carnegiefoundation.org/scholarship-teaching-learning/resources.

Hutchings, P., and Huber, M. T. (2008). "Placing Theory in the Scholarship of Teaching and Learning." *Arts and Humanities in Higher Education*, *7*(3), 229–244.

Hutchings, P., and Shulman, L. S. (1999). "The Scholarship of Teaching: New Elaborations, New Developments." *Change*, *31*(5), 10–15.

Indiana University Bloomington. "Scholarship of Teaching & Learning at Indiana University Bloomington." Accessed July 2010. http://www.indiana.edu/~sotl/index.shtml.

Indiana University College of Arts and Sciences Policy Committee. (2006). *Policy on College Criteria for Promotion to Full Professor (1999–2000; Reviewed 2006)*. Bloomington: Indiana University College of Arts and Sciences. http://college.indiana.edu/faculty/policy/collegepolicies/fullprofessor.shtml.

Institutional Culture Group (CASTL Institutional Leadership Group on Integrating the Scholarship of Teaching and Learning into Institutional Culture: Philosophy, Policy and Infrastructure). (2009). Final Report to the Carnegie Academy for the Scholarship of Teaching and Learning. Stanford, Calif.: The Carnegie Foundation for the Advancement of Teaching.

International Society for the Scholarship of Teaching and Learning. (2009). *ISSOTL09: Shared Futures, Emerging Knowledge, Solid Foundations*. Bloomington, Ind., Annual Conference Proceedings, Oct. 2009. http://www.issotl.org/conferences.html.

International Society for the Scholarship of Teaching and Learning. "SOTL Resources." Accessed Dec. 2010. http://www.issotl.org/SOTL.html.

Jacobs, D. (2000). "A Chemical Mixture of Methods." In P. Hutchings (ed.), *Opening Lines: Approaches to the Scholarship of Teaching and Learning*. Menlo Park, Calif.: The Carnegie Foundation for the Advancement of Teaching.

Jacobs, D. (2004). "An Alternative Approach to General Chemistry: Addressing the Needs of At-Risk Students with Cooperative Learning Strategies." http://gallery .carnegiefoundation.org/collections/castl_he/djacobs/index2.htm.

Kalish, A., and Stockley, D. (2009). "Building Scholarly Communities: Supporting the Scholarship of Teaching & Learning with Learning Communities." *Transformative Dialogues: Teaching and Learning eJournal, 3*(1). http://kwantlen.ca/TD/TD.3.1/.

Karoff, R., Martin, R., Kornetsky, L., and Huber, M. T. (2008). "Liberal Education and the Scholarship of Teaching and Learning: An Integrated-System Approach." Abstract for Conference Program of the Annual Meeting of the Association of American Colleges and Universities, Jan. 2008. http://www.aacu.org/meetings/ annualmeeting/AM08/concurrentsessions.cfm.

Kreber, C. (2006). "Research-Based Teaching in Relation to Academic Practice: Some Insights Resulting from Previous Chapters." In C. Kreber (ed.), *Exploring Research-Based Teaching*. New Directions for Teaching and Learning, Number 107. San Francisco: Jossey-Bass.

Kreber, C. (2007). "What's It Really All About? The Scholarship of Teaching and Learning as an Authentic Practice." *International Journal for the Scholarship of Teaching and Learning, 1*(1). http://academics.georgiasouthern.edu/ijsotl/v1n1/ essays/kreber/index.htm.

Kuh, G. (2008). *High-Impact Educational Practices: What They Are, Who Has Access to Them, and Why They Matter*. Washington, D.C.: Association of American Colleges and Universities.

Kuh, G., and Ikenberry, S. (2009). *More Than You Think, Less Than We Need: Learning Outcomes Assessment in American Higher Education*. Abridged version. Urbana, Ill.: National Institute for Learning Outcomes Assessment.

Lambert, L. (1993). Foreword to L. Lambert and S. L. Tice (eds.), *Preparing Graduate Students to Teach: A Guide to Programs That Improve Undergraduate Education and Develop Tomorrow's Faculty*. Sterling, Va.: Stylus.

Lamont, M. (2009). *How Professors Think: Inside the Curious World of Academic Judgment*. Cambridge, Mass.: Harvard University Press.

Larson, A. (2010). "Higher Education's Big Lie." *Inside Higher Education*, June 3, 2010. http://www.insidehighered.com/views/2010/06/03/larson.

Lederman, D. (2010). "The Completion Cacophony." *Inside Higher Education*, Mar. 3, 2010. http://www.insidehighered.com/news/2010/03/03/complete.

Lee, A. (2009). *From Teaching to Learning: Leading Change at a Large Research-Intensive University; A Personal Reflection.* Sydney, Aus. http://www.guidelinesonlearning.com/.

Leger, A., Van Melle, E. E., Mighty, J., and Stockley, D. (2009). "Creating a Foundation for SoTL and Academic Advancement at Queen's University." *Transformative Dialogues: Teaching and Learning eJournal*, *3*(1). http://kwantlen.ca/TD/TD.3.1/.

Linkon, S., and Bass, R. (2008). "On the Evidence of Theory: Close Reading as a Disciplinary Model for Writing About Teaching and Learning." *Arts and Humanities in Higher Education*, *7*(3), 245–61.

Lochbaum, J. "Question About SOTL and Accreditation." Private e-mail message to Pat Hutchings. Aug. 25, 2009.

Lumina Foundation for Education. (2009). *A Stronger Nation Through Higher Education: How and Why Americans Must Meet a "Big Goal" of College Attainment.* Indianapolis: Lumina Foundation for Education.

Lynton, E. A. (1995). *Making the Case for Professional Service.* Washington, D.C.: American Association for Higher Education.

Maricopa Center for Learning and Instruction. "Maricopa Institute of Learning." Last modified July 2007. http://www.mcli.dist.maricopa.edu/mil.

Mathieu, R. "Question About CIRTL." Private e-mail message to Pat Hutchings. June 22, 2010.

McKinney, K. (2007a). *Enhancing Learning Through the Scholarship of Teaching and Learning: The Challenges and Joys of Juggling.* San Francisco: Jossey-Bass.

McKinney, K. (2007b). "The Student Voice: Sociology Majors Tell Us About Learning Sociology." *Teaching Sociology*, *35*, 112–124.

McKinney, K. "Faculty Evaluation Policies." Private e-mail message to Mary Huber. June 21, 2010.

McKinney, K., Jarvis, P., Creasey, G., and Herrmann, D. (2010). "A Range of Voices in the Scholarship of Teaching and Learning." In C. Werder and M. M. Otis (eds.), *Engaging Student Voices in the Study of Teaching and Learning.* Sterling, Va.: Stylus.

MERLOT (Multimedia Educational Resource for Learning and Online Teaching). "About Us." Accessed Dec. 2010. http://taste.merlot.org/.

Merton, R. K. (1968). *Social Theory and Social Structure.* Revised edition (orig. 1949). New York: Free Press.

Michael, R., Case, K. A., Danielson, M. A., Hill, L., Lochbaum, J., McEnery, L., and Perkins, K. (2010). "Mentoring New Scholars of Teaching and Learning: The

National CASTL Institute Model." *Transformative Dialogues: Teaching and Learning eJournal*, 3(3), 1–15. http://kwantlen.ca/TD/TD.3.3/.

Michigan State University College of Education. "Center for the Scholarship of Teaching and Learning." Accessed Dec. 2010. http://www.educ.msu.edu/cst/.

Miller, R., and Morgaine, W. (2009). "The Benefits of E-Portfolios for Students and Faculty in Their Own Words." *Peer Review*, 11(1), 8–12.

Mills, D., and Huber, M. T. (2005). "Anthropology and the Educational 'Trading Zone': Disciplinarity, Pedagogy and Professionalism." *Arts and Humanities in Higher Education*, 4(1), 5–28.

Modern Language Association. (2007). "Report of the MLA Task Force on Evaluating Scholarship for Tenure and Promotion." *Profession*, 9–71.

National Commission on Excellence in Education. (1983). *A Nation at Risk: The Imperative for Educational Reform*. Washington, D.C.: GPO.

National Commission on the Future of Higher Education. (2006). *A Test of Leadership: Charting the Future of U.S. Higher Education*. Washington, D.C.: GPO.

National Governors Association. (1986). *Time for Results: The Governors' 1991 Report on Education*. Washington, D.C.: National Governors Association.

National Survey of Student Engagement. (2009). *Assessment for Improvement: Tracking Student Engagement Over Time—Annual Results*. Bloomington: Indiana University Center for Postsecondary Research.

Nelson, C. E. (2003). "Doing It: Selected Examples of Several of the Different Genres of the Scholarship of Teaching and Learning." *The Journal on Excellence in College Teaching*, 14(2–3), 85–94.

New Leadership Alliance for Student Learning and Accountability. "About Us: Who We Are." Accessed Dec. 14, 2010. http://www.newleadershipalliance.org/who_we_are/about_us/.

North Carolina Agricultural and Technical State University Academy for Teaching and Learning. "The Wabash-Provost Scholars Program at NC A&T." Accessed Nov. 2010. http://www.ncat.edu/~atl/Wabash-national-study/wpscholars.html.

Nummedal, S. G. (1996). "Classroom Assessment as a Context for Faculty Conversation and Collaboration at California State University-Long Beach." In P. Hutchings (ed.) *Making Teaching Community Property: A Menu for Peer Collaboration and Peer Review*. Washington, D.C.: American Association for Higher Education.

Obama, B. (2009). "Address to Joint Session of Congress." Washington, D.C., Feb. 24, 2009. http://www.whitehouse.gov/the_press_office/remarks-of-president-barack-obama-address-to-joint-session-of-congress/.

O'Brien, M., Goos, M., and members of Teaching and Educational Development Institute (TEDI)/Higher Education Research and Scholarship (HERS) Team. (2008). "Creating Excellence in the Scholarship of Teaching and Learning at UQ." Initiative overview. Brisbane, Aus.: University of Queensland. http://www.uq.edu.au/teaching-learning/docs/CESoTL_Overview.doc.

O'Meara, K. (2000). "Climbing the Academic Ladder: Promotion in Rank." In C. A. Trower (ed.), *Policies on Faculty Appointment: Standard Practices and Unusual Arrangements*. San Francisco: Jossey-Bass/Anker.

O'Meara, K. (2005). "Effects of Encouraging Multiple Forms of Scholarship in Policy and Practice." In K. O'Meara and R. E. Rice (eds.), *Faculty Priorities Reconsidered: Rewarding Multiple Forms of Scholarship*. San Francisco: Jossey-Bass.

O'Meara, K., and Rice, R. E. (eds.). (2005). *Faculty Priorities Reconsidered: Rewarding Multiple Forms of Scholarship*. San Francisco: Jossey-Bass.

O'Meara, K., Terosky, A. L., and Neumann, A. (2008). "Faculty Careers and Work Lives: A Professional Growth Perspective." *ASHE Higher Education Report*, *34*(3), 1–221.

Ostrom, E. (1990). *Governing the Commons: The Evolution of Institutions for Collective Action*. New York: Cambridge University Press.

Ostrom, E. (2005). *Understanding Institutional Diversity*. Princeton, N.J.: Princeton University Press.

Pace, D. (2004). "The Amateur in the Operating Room: History and the Scholarship of Teaching and Learning." *American Historical Review*, *109*(4), 1171–1192.

Pace, D., and Middendorf, J. (eds.). (2004). *Decoding the Disciplines: Helping Students Learn Disciplinary Ways of Thinking*. New Directions for Teaching and Learning, Number 98. San Francisco: Jossey-Bass.

Palmer, P. (2007). *The Courage to Teach: Exploring the Inner Landscape of a Teacher's Life*. Tenth Anniversary edition. San Francisco: Jossey-Bass.

Palumbo, A., and Scott, A. (2005). "Bureaucracy, Open Access, and Social Pluralism: Returning the Common to the Goose." In P. du Gay (ed.), *The Values of Bureaucracy*. Oxford, U.K.: Oxford University Press.

Paulsen, M. B. (2002). "Evaluating Teaching Performance." In C. Colbeck (ed.), *Evaluating Faculty Performance*. New Directions for Institutional Research, Number 114. San Francisco: Jossey-Bass.

Phipps, A., and Barnett, R. (2007). "Academic Hospitality." *Arts and Humanities in Higher Education*, *6*(3), 237–254.

Poole, G. "Question About Faculty Evaluation Policy." Private e-mail message to Mary Huber. June 21, 2010.

Prosser, M. (2008). "The Scholarship of Teaching and Learning: What Is It? A Personal View." *International Journal for the Scholarship of Teaching and Learning*, *3*(2). http://academics.georgiasouthern.edu/ijsotl/v2n2/invited_essays/_Prosser/index.htm.

Rehrey, G. No subject. Private e-mail message to Pat Hutchings. June 29, 2010.

Richlin, L. (2001). "Scholarly Teaching and the Scholarship of Teaching." In C. Kreber (ed.), *Scholarship Revisited: Perspectives on the Scholarship of Teaching*, New Directions for Teaching and Learning, Number 86. San Francisco: Jossey-Bass.

Riordan, T. (2008). "Disciplinary Expertise Revisited: The Scholarship of Teaching and Learning Philosophy." *Arts and Humanities in Higher Education, 7*(3), 262–275.

Robinson, P., Gingras, J., Cooper, L., Waddell, J., and Davidge, E. (2009). "SoTL's Watershed Moment: A Critical Turning Point for SoTL at Ryerson University." *Transformative Dialogues: Teaching and Learning eJournal, 3*(1). http://kwantlen .ca/TD/TD.3.1/.

Robinson, J. M., Savory, P., Poole, G., Carey, T., and Bernstein, D. (2010). *CASTL: Expanding the SOTL Commons Cluster; Final Report, February 2010.* Lincoln: DigitalCommons@University of Nebraska-Lincoln. Final Report to the Carnegie Academy for the Scholarship of Teaching and Learning. http://digitalcommons. unl.edu/imsereports/5/.

Sandefur, J. (2007). "Problem Solving: What I Have Learned from My Students." In K. H. Ko and D. Arganbright (eds.), *Enhancing University Mathematics: Proceedings of the First KAIST International Symposium on Teaching.* CBMS Issues in Mathematics Education, Vol. 14. Washington, D.C.: American Mathematical Society.

Savina, M. "Initiatives." Private e-mail message to Anthony Ciccone. Mar. 1, 2010.

Schneider, C. G., and Shoenberg, R. (1999). "Habits Hard to Break: How Persistent Features of Campus Life Frustrate Curricular Reform." *Change, 31*(2), 30–35.

Schodt, D. Telephone interview by Pat Hutchings. Aug. 17, 2009.

Schroeder, C. (ed.). (2007). *From Speculation to Evidence: Examining Student Learning and Perceptions in General Education Courses.* Collection of Projects in the Scholarship of Teaching and Learning by Center Scholars. Milwaukee: Center for Instructional Improvement and Development, University of Wisconsin-Milwaukee.

Schroeder, C. M., and Associates. (2010). *Coming in from the Margins: Faculty Development's Organizational Development Role in Institutional Change.* Sterling, Va.: Stylus.

Schroeder, C., Brooke, C., and Freeman, S. (2006). "Maturation of Campus-based Scholarship of Teaching and Learning Programs: Defining Features for Thriving with Momentum." Panel presentation at the CASTL Colloquium on the Scholarship of Teaching and Learning, Madison, Wis., Apr. 2006.

Schuster, J. H., and Finkelstein, M. J. (2006). *The American Faculty: The Restructuring of Academic Work and Careers.* Baltimore, Md.: Johns Hopkins University Press.

Seldin, P. (1997). *The Teaching Portfolio: A Practical Guide to Improved Performance and Promotion/Tenure Decisions.* San Francisco: Jossey-Bass/Anker.

Seymour, E. (2001). "Tracking the Processes of Change in U.S. Undergraduate Education in Science, Mathematics, Engineering, and Technology." *Science Education, 86,* 79–105.

Seymour, E., Wiese, D., Hunter, A., and Daffinrud, S. M. (2000). "Creating a Better Mousetrap: On-line Student Assessment of Their Learning Gains." Paper presented to the National Meetings of the American Chemical Society Symposium on "Using

Real-World Questions to Promote Active Learning," San Francisco, Mar. 2000. http://www.salgsite.org/about.

Shavelson, R. J. (2010). *Measuring College Learning Responsibly: Accountability in a New Era.* Stanford, Calif.: Stanford University Press.

Shea, M. "Faculty Evaluation and Teaching Positions." Private e-mail message to Mary Huber. June 24, 2010.

Sheppard, S. D., Macatangay, K., Colby, A., and Sullivan, W. M. (2009). *Educating Engineers: Designing for the Future of the Field.* San Francisco: Jossey-Bass.

Shulman, L. S. (1987). "Knowledge and Teaching: Foundations of the New Reform." *Harvard Educational Review, 57*(1), 1–22.

Shulman, L. S. (1993). "Teaching as Community Property: Putting an End to Pedagogical Solitude." *Change, 25*(6), 6–7.

Shulman, L. S. (1998). "Course Anatomy: The Dissection and Analysis of Knowledge through Teaching." In P. Hutchings (ed.), *The Course Portfolio: How Faculty Can Examine Their Teaching to Advance Practice and Improve Student Learning.* Washington, D.C.: American Association for Higher Education.

Shulman, L. S. (2000). "Inventing the Future." Conclusion to P. Hutchings (ed.), *Opening Lines: Approaches to the Scholarship of Teaching and Learning.* Menlo Park, Calif.: The Carnegie Foundation for the Advancement of Teaching.

Shulman, L. S. (2004). "Visions of the Possible: Models for Campus Support of the Scholarship of Teaching and Learning." In L. S. Shulman, *Teaching as Community Property: Essays on Higher Education.* San Francisco: Jossey-Bass.

Smith, M. B. (2010). "Local Environmental History and the Journey to Ecological Citizenship." In M. B. Smith, R. S. Nowacek, and J. L. Bernstein (eds.), *Citizenship Across the Curriculum.* Bloomington: Indiana University Press.

Smith, M., Nowacek, R. S., and Bernstein, J. L. (eds.). (2010). *Citizenship Across the Curriculum.* Bloomington: Indiana University Press.

Sorcinelli, M. D., Austin, A. E., Eddy, P. L., and Beach, A. L. (2005). *Creating the Future of Faculty Development: Learning from the Past, Understanding the Present.* San Francisco: Jossey-Bass/Anker.

Spencer Foundation. "Research." Accessed Dec. 2010. http://www.spencer.org/content.cfm/research.

Stanny, C. "UWF T&P Guidelines." Post to POD Listserv POD@Listserv.nd.edu. Feb. 5, 2010.

Stigler, J. W., Givvin, K. B., and Thompson, B. J. (2009). *What Community College Developmental Mathematics Students Understand About Mathematics.* The Carnegie Foundation for the Advancement of Teaching Problem Solution Exploration Papers. Stanford, Calif.: The Carnegie Foundation for the Advancement of Teaching.

System Group (CASTL Institutional Leadership Group on Building Scholarship of Teaching and Learning Systemwide). (2009). *Leadership Group: Building SoTL System Wide.* Final Report to the Carnegie Academy for the Scholarship of Teaching and Learning. Stanford, Calif.: The Carnegie Foundation for the Advancement of Teaching.

Task Force on Teaching and Career Development to the Faculty of Arts and Sciences. (2007). *A Compact to Enhance Teaching and Learning at Harvard.* Cambridge, Mass.: Harvard University.

Teagle Foundation. "Grantmaking." Accessed Dec. 14, 2010. http://www. teaglefoundation.org/grantmaking/education.aspx.

Tinto, V. (1997)."Classrooms as Communities: Exploring the Educational Character of Student Persistence." *Journal of Higher Education, 68*(6), 599–623.

U.S. General Accounting Office. (2003). *College Completion: Additional Efforts Could Help Education with Its Completion Goals.* GAO-03–568, Report to the Ranking Minority Members, Committee on Health, Education, Labor, and Pensions, U.S. Senate, and Committee on Education and the Workforce, House of Representatives. Washington, D.C.: GPO.

University of British Columbia. (2006). *Agreement on the Conditions of Appointment for Faculty.* Vancouver, Can.: University of British Columbia. http://www.hr.ubc .ca/faculty-relations/collective-agreements/appointment-faculty.

University of Notre Dame. (2007). *Evaluating a T&R Faculty Member's Teaching: Guidelines for Preparing a Case for Renewal/Tenure/Promotion.* Advisory Committee to the Provost on the Evaluation of Teaching. https://www3.nd.edu/~provost/ academic-resources-and-information/AcademicResourcesandInformationOfficeofthe ProvostGuidelinesforPreparingaCaseforRenewa.shtml.

Vancouver Island University. "VIU Teaching & Learning Centre." Accessed Dec. 2010. http://viu.ca/teaching/.

Walker, G. E., Golde, C. M., Jones, L., Bueschel, A. C., and Hutchings, P. (2008). *The Formation of Scholars: Rethinking Doctoral Education for the Twenty-first Century.* San Francisco: Jossey-Bass.

Washington Center for Improving the Quality of Undergraduate Education. "Learning Communities National Resource Center." Accessed Dec. 2010. http://www. evergreen.edu/washcenter/project.asp?pid = 73.

Weimer, M. E. (2006). *Enhancing Scholarly Work on Teaching and Learning: Professional Literature That Makes a Difference.* San Francisco: Jossey-Bass.

Welsh-Huggins, A. (2010). "OSU's President Gordon Gee Challenging Faculty Tenure at Nation's Biggest Campus." *The Associated Press,* Feb. 4, 2010. http://www. cleveland.com/nation/index.ssf/2010/02/osus_president_gordon_gee_chal.html.

Wenger, E. (1998). *Communities of Practice: Learning, Meaning, and Identity.* Cambridge, U.K.: Cambridge University Press.

Werder, C., and Otis, M. M. (eds.). (2010). *Engaging Student Voices in the Study of Teaching and Learning.* Sterling, Va.: Stylus.

Werder, C., Ware, L., Thomas, C., and Skogsberg, E. (2010). "Students in Parlor Talk on Teaching and Learning: Conversational Scholarship." In C. Werder and M. M.

Otis (eds.), *Engaging Student Voices in the Study of Teaching and Learning.* Sterling, Va.: Stylus.

Wieman, C., Perkins, K., and Gilbert, S. (2010). "Transforming Science Education at Large Research Universities: A Case Study in Progress." *Change, 42*(2), 7–14.

Wildavsky, B. (2010). *The Great Brain Race: How Global Universities Are Reshaping the World.* Princeton, N.J.: Princeton University Press.

Wineburg, S. (2001). *Historical Thinking and Other Unnatural Acts: Charting the Future of Teaching the Past.* Philadelphia: Temple University Press.

NAME INDEX

SUBJECT INDEX